spring 2022

Mission

The *Community Literacy Journal* is an interdisciplinary journal that publishes both scholarly work that contributes to theories, methodologies, and research agendas and work by literacy workers, practitioners, and community literacy program staff. We are especially committed to presenting work done in collaboration between academics and community members, organizers, activists, teachers, and artists.

We understand "community literacy" as including multiple domains for literacy work extending beyond mainstream educational and work institutions. It can be found in programs devoted to adult education, early childhood education, reading initiatives, or work with marginalized populations. It can also be found in more informal, ad hoc projects, including creative writing, graffiti art, protest songwriting, and social media campaigns.

For us, literacy is defined as the realm where attention is paid not just to content or to knowledge but to the symbolic means by which it is represented and used. Thus, literacy refers not just to letters and to text but to other multimodal, technological, and embodied representations, as well. Community literacy is interdisciplinary and intersectional in nature, drawing from rhetoric and composition, communication, literacy studies, English studies, gender studies, race and ethnic studies, environmental studies, disability studies, critical theory, linguistics, cultural studies, education, and more.

Subscriptions

Donations to the *CLJ* in any amount can be made with a check made out to "FIU English Department," with *Community Literacy Journal* in the memo line.

Send to:

> Paul Feigenbaum
> Department of English
> Florida International University
> DM462D
> 11200 SW 8th St.
> Miami, FL 33199

Donors at the $40 level or above will receive a courtesy print subscription of the academic year's issues.

Cover Artist and Art

This painting was created by artists at Life Pieces to Masterpieces using their signature sewn-canvas style.

At LPTM, our artistic process is "Connect, Create, Contribute, Celebrate!" This is the symbol for "Connect."

We must first connect with ourselves to connect with others. We develop an atmosphere for reflection and introspection and share our experiences and knowledge with others.

Submissions

Submissions for the Articles section of the journal should clearly demonstrate engagement with community literacy scholarship, particularly scholarship previously published in the *Community Literacy Journal*. The editors seek work that pushes the field forward in exciting and perhaps unexpected ways. Case studies, qualitative and/or quantitative research, conceptual articles, etc., ranging from 25-30 manuscript pages, are welcome. If deemed appropriate, we will send the manuscript out to readers for blind review. You can expect a report in approximately 10-12 weeks.

Community Literacy Journal is committed to inclusive citation practices and encourages authors to cite and acknowledge ideas of BIPOC scholars, activists, and organizers in community literacy.

The *Community Literacy Journal* also welcomes shorter manuscripts (10-15 pages) for three sections reviewed in-house:

Community Literacy Project and Program Profiles will discuss innovative and impactful community-based projects and programs that are grounded in best practices. We encourage community-based practitioners and non-profit staff to submit for this section. Profiles should draw on community literacy scholarship, but they are not expected to have the extended lit reviews that are customary in the articles section of the journal. If you are a community member wanting to submit, and it is your first time writing for an academic journal, we are happy to offer mentorship and answer questions. Pieces co-authored by multiple stakeholders in a project are also welcome.

Please submit using our online submission system. Contact the Project and Program Profiles Editor, Vincent Portillo, with questions at portilvi@bc.edu.

Issues in Community Literacy will offer targeted analysis, reflection, and/or complication of ongoing challenges associated with the work of community literacy. Potential subjects for this section include (but are not limited to): building/sustaining infrastructure, navigating institutional constraints, pursuing community literacy in graduate school, working with vulnerable populations, building ethical relationships, realizing reciprocity, and negotiating conflicts among partners. We imagine this as a space for practitioners to raise critical issues or offer a response to an issue raised in a previous volume of the CLJ.

We encourage community-based practitioners and non-profit staff to submit for this section. If you are a community member wanting to submit, and it is your first time writing for an academic journal, we are happy to offer mentorship and answer questions. Pieces co-authored by multiple stakeholders in a project are also welcome.

Please submit using our online submission system. Contact the Issues in Community Literacy Editor, Cayce Wicks, with questions at cwick003@fiu.edu.

Coda: Community Writing and Creative Work welcomes submissions of poetry, creative nonfiction, short stories, and multigenre work on any topics that have ensued from community writing projects. This may be work about community writing projects, and this may be expressed in ways we have yet to imagine. We ask authors to include a personal reflection about the submission itself—information about your community writing group (if you belong to one); your personal journey as a writer; what inspired you to write your piece; and anything else you'd care to share about your life—as an invitation for the author and Coda's readers to consider writing and activism as intertwined.

Contact Coda editors with questions at Coda.Editors@gmail.com.

Authors interested in contributing to the Book and New Media Review section should contact Jessica Shumake at jshumake@nd.edu.

Advertising

Community Literacy Journal welcomes advertising. The journal is published twice annually, in the Fall and Spring (November and May). Deadlines for advertising are two months prior to publication (September and March).

Ad Sizes and Pricing

Half page (trim size 5.5 x 4.25): $200
Full page (trim size 5.5 x 8.5): $350
Inside back cover (trim size 5.5 x 8.5): $500
Inside front cover (trim size 5.5 x 8.5): $600

Format

We accept .PDF, .JPG, .TIF or .EPS. All advertising images should be camera-ready and have a resolution of 300 dpi. For more information, please contact Veronica House (housev@colorado.edu) and Paul Feigenbaum (pfeigenb@fiu.edu).

Copyright © 2022 *Community Literacy Journal*
ISSN 1555-9734

Community Literacy Journal is a member of the Council of Editors of Learned Journals.

Production and distribution managed by Parlor Press.

Publication of the *Community Literacy Journal* is made possible through the generous support of the English Department and the Writing and Rhetoric Program at Florida International University. The *CLJ* is a journal of the Coalition for Community Writing. Current issues and archives are available open access at https://digitalcommons.fiu.edu/communityliteracy/

Editorial Board

Jonathan Alexander, *University of California Irvine*
Steven Alvarez, *St. John's University*
April Baker Bell, *Michigan State University*
Kirk Branch, *Montana State University*
Stephanie Briggs, *Be.Still.Move.*
Laurie Cella, *Shippensburg University*
David Coogan, *Virginia Commonwealth University*
Ellen Cushman, *Northeastern University*
Lisa Dush, *DePaul University*
Jenn Fishman, *Marquette University*
Linda Flower, *Carnegie Mellon University*
Beth Godbee, *Heart-Head-Hands.com*
Eli Goldblatt, *Temple University, Emeritus*
Laurie Grobman, *Pennsylvania State University Berks*
Shirley Brice Heath, *Stanford University*
Glenn Hutchinson, *Florida International University*
Tobi Jacobi, *Colorado State University*
Ben Kuebrich, *West Chester University*
Carmen Kynard, *Texas Christian University*
Paula Mathieu, *Boston College*
Seán Ronan McCarthy, *James Madison University*
Michael Moore, *DePaul University*
Beverly Moss, *The Ohio State University*
Steve Parks, *The University of Virginia*
Jessica Pauszek, *Boston College*
Eric Darnell Pritchard, *University of Arkansas Fayetteville*
Jessica Restaino, *Montclair State University*
Elaine Richardson, *The Ohio State University*
Lauren Rosenberg, *University of Texas at El Paso*
Tiffany Rousculp, *Salt Lake Community College*
Iris Ruiz, *University of California Merced*
Donnie Sackey, *University of Texas at Austin*
Rachael W. Shah, *University of Nebraska-Lincoln*
Erec Smith, *York College of Pennsylvania*
Stephanie Wade, *Searsport District High School, Maine*
Christopher Wilkey, *Northern Kentucky University*

COMMUNITY LITERACY *Journal*

Editors	Paul Feigenbaum, *Florida International University* Veronica House, *University of Denver*
Senior Assistant Editor and Issues in Community Literacy Editor	Cayce Wicks, *Florida International University*
Journal Manager	Erin Daugherty, *University of Arkansas at Fayetteville*
Book and New Media Review Editor	Jessica Shumake, *University of Notre Dame*
Consulting Editor and Project Profiles Editor	Vincent Portillo, *Boston College*
Coda: Community Writing and Creative Work Editorial Collective	Kefaya Diab, *Loyola University Maryland* Leah Falk, *Rutgers University, Camden* Chad Seader, *William Penn University* Alison Turner, *Independent Scholar, Denver* Kate Vieira, *University of Wisconsin, Madison* Stephanie Wade, *Searsport District High School, Maine*
Senior Copyeditor	Elvira Carrizal-Dukes, *University of Texas at El Paso*
Copyeditors	Adam Hubrig, *Sam Houston State University* Charisse Iglesias, *Community-Campus Partnerships for Health* Walter Lucken IV, *Wayne State University* Christine Martorana, *Florida International University* Keshia Mcclantoc, *University of Nebraska-Lincoln*

COMMUNITY LITERACY *journal*

Spring 2022
Volume 16, Issue 2

1 *Editors' Introduction*
   Veronica House and Paul Feigenbaum, with Vincent Portillo and Cayce Wicks

2021 Conference on Community Writing Plenary Address, Adapted

4 *Journeying To Purpose*
   Mary Brown and Phyllis Ryder

2021 Conference on Community Writing Keynote Address

14 *Liberating Powers: Community Building in Word, in Deed*
   Brigette Rouson

Articles

22 *Innovaciones y Historias: A Home- and Community-Based Approach to Workplace Literacy*
   Guadalupe Remigio Ortega, Alfonso Guzman Gomez, and Calley Marotta

47 *The Rules of the Road: Negotiating Literacies in a Community Driving Curriculum*
   Rebecca Lorimer Leonard and Danielle Pappo

63 *Crash Encounters: Negotiating Science Literacy and Its Sponsorship in a Cross-Disciplinary, Cross-Generational MOOC*
   Stephanie West-Puckett

spring 2022

Interview

89 *Democracy, Pedagogy, and Advocacy 2022*
Steve Parks and Srdja Popovic

Project and Program Profiles

107 *Stories from the Flood: Promoting Healing and Fostering Policy Change Through Storytelling, Community Literacy, and Community-based Learning*
Caroline Gottschalk Druschke, Tamara Dean, Margot Higgins, Marissa Beaty, Lisa Henner, Robin Hosemann, Julia Meyer, Ben Sellers, Sydney Widell, and Tenzin Woser

121 *Write Your Roots Disrupted: Community Writing in Performance in the Time of COVID*
Sarah Moon

132 *Bilingual Comics on the Border as Graphic Medicine: Journaling and Doodling for Dementia Caregiving during the COVID-19 Pandemic*
Elvira Carrizal-Dukes, Maria Isela Maier, Sarah Y. Jimenez, Jacob Martinez, David Hernandez, and Ronnie Dukes

Book and New Media Reviews

144 *From the Book and New Media Review Editor's Desk*
Jessica Shumake, Editor

145 *Linguistic Justice: Black Language, Literacy, Identity, and Pedagogy* by April Baker-Bell
Reviewed by Michael J. Benjamin

150 *On Teacher Neutrality: Politics, Praxis, and Performativity* edited by Daniel P. Richards
Reviewed by Jennifer Smith Daniel

158 *Mobility Work in Composition* edited by Bruce Horner, Megan Faver Hartline, Ashanka Kumari, and Laura Sceniak Matravers
Reviewed by Meng-Hsien (Neal) Liu

163 *Mapping Racial Literacies: College Students Write About Race and Segregation* by Sophie Bell
Reviewed by Angela F. Jacobs

167 *Turn This World Inside Out: The Emergence of Nurturance Culture*
   by Nora Samaran
   Reviewed by Erin Schaefer

Coda

177 *Editors' Introduction*
   Kefaya Diab, Leah Falk, Chad Seader, Alison Turner,
   Kate Vieira, and Stephanie Wade

179 *Bad Habits*
   Gustavo Guerra

180 *Frozen Margaritas*
   Gustavo Guerra

181 *Free Pride Hugs*
   Don Unger

187 *Finding the Buddha: Seeking Solace in Prison*
   Ryan Moser

192 *From The Missing Briefcase, Chapter 1*
   Devin O'Keefe and Justin Slavinski

197 *I Remember*
   Frank Morse

299 *Solía ser...*
   Vivian Lorena Carmona

201 *Soy quien soy ahora, cada uno es quien es por todo lo que ha sucedido,*
   Fresban Alexis Bueno

203 *Drought*
   H.L. Smith

205 *Notes*
   Parisa Mosavi (Pavie)

Editors' Introduction

Veronica House and Paul Feigenbaum, with Vincent Portillo and Cayce Wicks

This issue of *Community Literacy Journal* offers multiple responses to the question of how we, as Washington D.C. activists Mary Brown and Phyllis Ryder ask, "keep going forward when the world is on fire." In **"Journeying To Purpose,"** an adaptation of Brown's 2021 Conference on Community Writing Plenary Address, they write "about holding onto the transformational power of expression and relationship. We see building connections and finding your unique point of agency as essential for creating systemic change." They share the story and vision of the non-profit Life Pieces to Masterpieces, the first arts-based organization in the nation focused solely on meeting the needs of African American males from early childhood to adulthood through art. Through their stories and guidance, Brown and Ryder invite us to discover our gifts, get in touch with our pain, and "journey to purpose."

Following a similar line of thought, 2021 Conference on Community Writing Keynote Presenter Brigette Rouson reminds us that "Community is the site and shaper of liberation. Its sinews are substance–creating a muscular experience of being held on a collective journey. Community is source and it is system." Drawing on ancestral and embodied knowledges, Rouson's keynote address, **"Liberating Powers: Community Building in Word, in Deed,"** offers examples of, and invites us to join in, collective work toward liberation. Like Brown and Ryder, Rouson urges us to "say 'yes' to this awesome endeavor" of the long haul toward justice.

In our opening article, **"Innovaciones y Historias: A Home- and Community-Based Approach to Workplace Literacy,"** authors Guadalupe Remigio Ortega, Alfonso Guzman Gomez, and Calley Marotta engage with the literacy experiences of men employed as university custodial staff in order to propose a home- and community-based approach to workplace literacy. For individuals who are often denied the opportunity to showcase their literacy repertoires and desires within the context of their formal workplaces, this approach takes an assets-based approach to recognizing the participants' professional and vocational literacies across contexts. As Remigio Ortega, Guzman Gomez, and Marotta explain in their article, "We also draw from Latinx and Chincanx theories in education, writing studies, and transnational literacy studies to assert the value of understanding workplace literacies in relation to people's broader literate lives."

In the next article, **"The Rules of the Road: Negotiating Literacies in a Community Driving Curriculum,"** Rebecca Lorimer Leonard and Danielle Pappo share an ethnographic case study, borne from their partnership with a community language school, whose immigrant students asked for literacy support in earning driver's licenses. The article shows how cultural norms, unspoken rules, and embodied literacies infuse the experiences of immigrants with what the authors call "'rules of the road'—the unspoken social and literate rules that regulate literacies in the car and on the streets."

Stephanie West-Puckett asks us to imagine a cross-disciplinary and multi-partner project involving scientists, poets, and faculty teaching youth about science and the "crash encounters" that occur when different conceptions of literacy and knowledge-making meet. **"Crash Encounters: Negotiating Science Literacy and Its Sponsorship in a Cross-Disciplinary, Cross-Generational MOOC"** describes the youths' participation in a two-year Massive Open Online Collaboration (MOOC) funded by the National Science Foundation. Through this case study and associated theorizing, West-Puckett describes the "learners' unconventional and interdisciplinary writing and the cultural and disciplinary conflicts that emerged around it." In a reframing of science literacy as a series of crash encounters, West-Puckett prompts literacy practitioners to anticipate these "crashes" and offers suggestions for how to design and participate in interdisciplinary networks to create more dynamic and vibrant approaches to science literacy.

This issue's Interview section offers a conversation, **"Democracy, Pedagogy, and Activism: 2022,"** between long-time community literacy practitioner Steve Parks and Srdja Popovic, Visiting Researcher at the University of Virginia and founding member of the Otpor! ("Resistance!") movement, which helped instigate the fall of Slobodan Milošević's dictatorship in Serbia. This discussion emerged from ongoing collaborations that have included co-teaching a writing course on democratic advocacy and establishing the Democratic Futures Working Group. Popovic and Parks's wide-ranging conversation addresses the precarious state of democracy both nationally and globally, focusing particular attention on the advantages and limitations of contemporary narratives and practices of community organizing and activism as they compare to earlier models. The discussion then turns to the inadequacies of higher education to meet the moment of democratic advocacy in an era of increasingly illiberal authoritarianism both in the U.S. and abroad. In looking for productive ways forward, the discussants envision more inclusive frameworks for credentialing people to teach and produce knowledge about democracy and advocacy in and beyond university spaces.

This issue also includes three Project and Program Profiles. In **"Stories from the Flood: Promoting Healing and Fostering Policy Change Through Storytelling, Community Literacy, and Community-based Learning,"** authors Caroline Gottschalk Druschke, Tamara Dean, Margot Higgins, Marissa Beaty, Lisa Henner, Robin Hosemann, Julia Meyer, Ben Sellers, Sydney Widell, and Tenzin Woser share the work of co-creating a community literacy project, Stories from the Flood, as well as undergraduate community-based learning courses with the aim of working toward community healing, student learning, and structural change. As a partnership between university faculty members, former students, and the Driftless Writing Center, the goal of Stories from the Flood is to help community members in and around Wisconsin's Kickapoo River Watershed record, preserve, and share their flood experiences, with the aim of supporting community healing and serving as a resource for future conversations about flood recovery and resilience. Given the complexity of the Stories from the Flood, the authors argue that the success of such a project has everything to do with "dynamic reciprocity," whereby project participants build community by slowing down, working repeatedly and flexibly over time. In these ways, "Stories from the Flood" adds to a body of scholarship that speaks to ethical university-community intervention during our era of climate change.

In "**Write Your Roots Disrupted: Community Writing in Performance in the Time of COVID**," Sarah Moon describes the difficulties and disruptions that took place while developing and staging a food-themed public storytelling project during a pandemic. The article focuses on Write Your Roots (WYR), a community project that invites community members to write and stage a performance of a monologue about a personal food history. Moon builds upon the scholarship of Michel de Certeau, theorizing the importance of our private homes in relation to space, story, and activity. Finally, Moon's profile adds to a growing body of scholarship that speaks to the need of community writing projects as both lifeline and near impossibility during such difficult times.

In "**Bilingual Comics on the Border as Graphic Medicine: Journaling and Doodling for Dementia Caregiving during the COVID-19 Pandemic**," Elvira Carrizal-Dukes, Maria Isela Maier, Sarah Y. Jimenez, Jacob Martinez, Dave Hernandez, and Ronnie Dukes reflect on their collaborative project intended to use "graphic medicine" to provide culturally relevant educational materials for caregivers of Alzheimer's patients. Through live-streamed Zoom sessions for members of the El Paso community, these collaborators sought to provide a space for caregivers to not only become more informed about care for Alzheimer's patients through bilingual comics, but also to provide a space for participants to use the tools of journaling and doodling to improve stress management in the caregiving process.

Our Book and New Media Review section, edited by Jessica Shumake, includes several timely reviews from recent scholarship in community literacy. We thank Jessica and the various scholars who contributed reviews for this issue. We hope readers will also enjoy the second installment of "Coda: Community Writing and Creative Work," as edited by Kefaya Diab, Leah Falk, Chad Seader, Alison Turner, Kate Vieira, and Stephanie Wade.

2021 Conference on Community Writing Plenary Address, Adapted

Journeying To Purpose

Mary Brown and Phyllis Ryder

We write today about a journey to purpose. We write about how to keep going forward when the world is on fire. We write about holding onto the transformational power of expression and relationship. We see building connections and finding your unique point of agency as essential for creating systemic change.

The injustices from Treyvon Martin to George Floyd are all-too-frequent reminders that living in a Black body in the United States is precarious. The persistence and deadly consequences of racism can be almost overwhelming. Now we are in a geopolitical nightmare with the war in Ukraine. We saw the hatred and fear scaling the walls of the Capitol, plundering democracy. We see the right to vote more and more constrained. We see grandmothers and aunts, fathers and brothers taken by COVID. How do we keep going forward?

This is an essay about holding onto hope.

We strive to build a world of equity and shared humanity. Progressive scholars, community activists, and public intellectuals identify the barriers to equity and shared humanity as lying within white supremacist, capitalist, patriarchal structures—historical legal and cultural forces that justify and maintain systems of power. When the goal of justice and shared humanity is framed as ending "systemic racism," many assume that organizations who focus on inner reflection and personal connection are too naïve to make a difference. This is an essay about finding the power to dismantle oppression by beginning with the personal. Systemic structures are real but starting there takes you away from looking at you.

This is an essay about the process of sustainable social justice work: find your passion, pay attention to your pain, journey into your purpose.

1. Life Pieces to Masterpieces, an Introduction

The two of us are brought together through our love of Life Pieces to Masterpieces (LPTM), a DC nonprofit which Sister Mary co-founded and where she now serves as the Executive Director; Sister Phyllis serves as the Secretary of the Board. (At Life Pieces, we refer to each other with familial titles; so, for example. Mary Brown is Sister Mary; Phyllis Ryder is Sister Phyllis; and the boys and young men are given the title Brother. We carry that practice into this article.)

Life Pieces to Masterpieces is the first arts-based organization in the nation focused solely on meeting the needs of African American males from early childhood to adulthood. LPTM has helped shape the lives of more than 1,500 young men from some of DC's most underserved neighborhoods. People living in the census track around the Charles Drew Elementary School where LPTM is headquartered have a life expectancy over seven years lower than the DC average, and fifteen years lower than the nearby counties in Maryland and Virginia where Phyllis and Mary live (Robert Wood Johnson Foundation). Disparities in food access, school resources, and opportunities for employment and more create generational barriers to equity. Though local and national parks and streams wind throughout these DC wards east of the Anacostia River, few venture into green spaces for fear of rising gun violence.

The challenges of living in under-resourced neighborhoods are real; they bring trauma and sometimes despair. What is happening in Wards 7 & 8 is a confluence of -isms whose impact is devastating, but the message of Life Pieces is not only for young Black men and boys or those struggling under systems of oppression. We understand that *everyone* confronts pain and suffering that can tear them up, and that if we don't examine that trauma, if we don't have a way to reflect, we all continue to suffer and lose our sense of connection and hope. So, the message of Life Pieces is a message about shared humanity; we offer tools that we all can use, a way to move through a world of isolation and suffering without losing track of who you are and who you can be.

At Life Pieces, we believe that "We all enter life as a blank canvas. With love, security, and expression, we can each become a masterpiece." This approach is explained more comprehensively in the LPTM's mission: to use "artistic expression to develop character and leadership, unlock potential, and prepare African American boys and young men to transform their lives and communities." LPTM programs and events are suffused with songs, painting, speeches, performances, and other forms of expression. (The painting, "Connect," on the cover of this journal is an example of LPTM's signature sewn-canvas painting style.)

The program works. In communities where just over 50% of youth graduate from high school, 100% of the boys who participate in LPTM through their senior year graduate successfully. Nearly all enroll in college or other post-secondary career training.

This year, two graduating seniors have received university Presidential scholarships from Virginia State University and Delaware State University. This year, one of our seniors was invited to address members of the White House, Congress, and Senate for Black History Month. He was introduced by the Vice President of the United States, shared remarks, and then introduced the President of the United States. A week later, LPTM received international recognition with the Citizen Diplomat Award from Global Ties US.

Our Apprentices (as we call the young men and boys who join LPTM) have grown into young men who cofacilitate justice, equity, and inclusion workshops in the form of our Color Me Community sessions. In just one year, LPTM Apprentices, supported by staff, shared Color Me Community with fifteen other organizations in the DC-Metro area, as well as groups of activists, artists, and educators representing thirty-five countries (LPTM, "Color Me Community").

Much of LPTM's everyday programming is wrapped in a philosophy called the Human Development System, "a concrete set of beliefs and strategies that addresses the challenges that our young people and their families face through artistic expression, increased self-awareness, and positive decision-making. It is a proven system that enables our Apprentices to build a positive sense of identity and to develop the tools needed to navigate through challenging circumstances, prepare for their own futures, and give back to their communities" (LPTM, "Human Development System").

In this essay, we focus especially on one phrase that infuses LPTM programming. It derives from Buddhist philosophy: "Your thoughts, your words, and your actions determine your destiny."

When Sister Phyllis first began partnering with LPTM, she viewed these words with some skepticism. They seemed to reinforce an individualist approach to social change, one that ignored the broader structures that affect the destiny of Black lives in the US. What does it mean to "determine your destiny" when so many policies, laws, and cultural systems have built a structure that maintains white supremacy?

It took years of observing and listening to understand that this focus on personal choice is not about ignoring the -isms and other structures of inequity. Rather, it is about finding a way to claim your agency *despite* that system, *because* of that system. It's about acting and not only reacting. It's about taking the long view and finding a path forward that is fulfilling and sustainable. From that starting point, you have a much better chance of building coalitions and creating change. To show how this all works, we offer a process for finding a sense of purpose, which we illustrate by telling Sister Mary's story.

2. Using the Life Pieces to Masterpieces Human Development System to find Purpose

> *"When we are awakened to a sense of purpose, our power is limitless"*
>
> Buddhist philosopher, Daisaku Ikeda

The human process of becoming aware of why you are here on this planet is a shared one—a process for all humanity, regardless of anyone's race or identity.

Sister Mary has found her purpose with LPTM: "If you gave me a billion dollars, I would not be doing anything else," she says. "It gives me joy to see these three-year-olds who grow to talk about world peace and equity." Sister Mary's purpose is to create space for other people to find their purpose.

Your purpose lies somewhere in your gifts and your pain. First, you find your uniqueness, your innate creative ability. Then you pay attention to the source of your own personal pain. Finally, you ask: How can I use this thing that I do so well to address this pain? It's a long journey. But in the end, you arrive at a purpose. It gives you a toolkit for how to start the next thing.

We don't discover our gifts alone, and we didn't arrive at this understanding of the process to purpose alone. Sister Mary has been developing this approach since the start of LPTM 26 years ago, and the philosophy has incubated in this creative space. In particular, Shawn Hardnett (Brother Shawn), Founder and CEO of Statesman College Preparatory Academy for Boys, and William Pitts (Elder Bill), LPTM's Family Engagement Consultant, offered key insights and connections over the years.

2a. Discovering Gifts

Finding your innate creative ability is the first step on your journey to purpose. What is that thing you do so well that you know it? This is a gift that no one can question you about. This is a gift that everyone knows you have.

Sister Mary discovered one of her innate creative abilities early in life. At her graduation from daycare in New Orleans, she performed MLK's "I Have a Dream" speech. From then on, she knew she had a strength in public speaking. By freshman year at Xavier Prep, her teacher Sister Eileen saw her talent and coached her. Xavier was a top-rated debate school, and Mary excelled. She won tournaments hand over fist. There were trophies everywhere in her house. She competed in English and in French and was often the only Black girl in the competition. In 1980, Sister Eileen brought Mary to Boston for the National Catholic Forensic League tournament, and Mary won in three categories: Oratory, Duo Interpretation and Dramatic Interpretation. She was extraordinarily good.

The second gift Mary discovered was bringing people together. In Elementary School at St. Raphael, Mary was confident and connected with her classmates.

> I was one of very few Black kids in my 6th grade class. There was someone from Cuba. I was the darkest one. In photos, I'm usually standing near the nun because I was the teacher's pet. The nuns called me Little Mary Sunshine because of my personality. Even though my parents made me aware of my history and struggle, I was the butterfly. I always saw the glass half full.

Mary took it upon herself to organize her classmates. She wrote the scripts and planned the sets for Christmas Plays and told her classmates what to do—"You should say that line a little louder." She saw people's potential, even back then. This continued in high school, where she followed her sister's footsteps and joined choir and theater. She was on the Student Council. These positive experiences in school allowed her to grow her innate, creative ability of seeing possibilities.

> My gift lies in seeing the unseen. I can see the potential in people. I can see the potential of folks coming together. I have a vision for seeing what can happen if this person does this and that person does that.

You have to dig deep to discover your gift. Do the hard work: what do you do well?

How do you know when you've discovered your gift? It feels right. It's not very scientific, but you know it because you don't feel depleted. You don't feel overworked. It's something that fits how you identify yourself. You don't go around trying to fit into something that is not you. When you've found your gift, the work gives you joy. Even if you see a painful situation, it gives you joy that you have something to do to begin to address that situation. Your gift shows you the way into the new challenges.

2b. The Pain

The second step in finding purpose is to get in touch with your pain. As we talked about this step in Mary' process toward purpose, she at first emphasized how idyllic her childhood was: a beloved youngest child in a family of three brothers and three sisters, feeling confident and safe. Even when she described a rough transition from the predominantly white St. Raphael to a predominantly Black elementary school, Sister Mary felt strong in who she was. The experience, while unpleasant, didn't rattle her:

> I would get in fights because people would call me an Oreo—you are white on the inside and burned on the outside. Or fights with lighter skinned Blacks. I was not a happy camper. I stayed there one year. I didn't feel like I needed to adjust. I knew I was smart. I always had to defend myself. I was OK with me.

At first, as she thought back, the pain she described seemed a little distant, abstract.

> I was Catholic, with a white Jesus above my bed. At night, I would fall on my knees and pray for world peace and for everyone to get along and love one another no matter their color.
>
> I hate seeing people in pain. I had an innocence. I heard my parents talk about injustice. I didn't like fighting. I wanted everyone to be at peace.

But then she remembered the moment that undid her, the central pain that she has channeled into her purpose: the story of the ride in the green and white Plymouth.

> I was in the 5th grade. Maybe I had volleyball practice, so we were leaving the playground after dark. My dad was driving me home in a green and white Plymouth. White top, green sides. This was Daddy's car. We passed a 7-11 on the corner. Driving.
>
> A young, white police officer stopped us. My father turns to me and cautions "Do not say a word, Mary Edith." Because my strength is speaking out and he knows I would want to.
>
> My father spoke Italian, German, French; he highly valued standard English. He had been a medic in World War 2. He was a New Orleans Public School teacher. He taught physics and chemistry at Xavier Prep. He had a master's degree. He really believed in shared humanity.
>
> We are stopped by a young, White police officer who looked younger than my brothers.
>
> "This is a nice car you have."
>
> When the White man knocks on the window, Daddy's demeanor changes. I thought, "Did an alien just possess my dad?" My father always taught us to look people in the eye, be clear in your communication. But now he rolls the window down, hands on the wheel, chin to his chest. He does not make eye contact.

I'm looking at my dad and at the police officer, who is looking at my dad and at me. I'm sure the police officer sees my Black skin.

"This is a nice car you have."

My dad said, "yes Suh."

This is my single horrific experience that helped to shape the woman I am today. My dad was my hero.

"Yes, Suh."

"Where are you going?"

"Home, Suh."

"Do you have your license?"

"Yes, Suh."

"Can I see it?"

"I have to go in my wallet that's behind me, in my pants."

"Well get it out, boy."

"I'm going into my pants." He very slowly puts his hand behind him, pulls out his wallet.

"All right Daniel T. Brown Sr. Okay." The police officer goes away and comes back.

"All right, boy. Keep following the speed limit."

The school wasn't that far from my house. We were in a lower middle class Black neighborhood. All I saw was the streetlight or the moonlight shining on my dad's skin, dark almost purple. His jaw clenched. A single tear drop. He pulled his handkerchief from his pocket and dabbed his eye.

"Mary Edith, get your books. We're going inside."

We never talked about it for a long time.

Then my senior year, we were driving home in the dark again. I asked, "That thing that happened Daddy, I never forgot that."

He said in so many words: "Sometimes in life, Mary Edith, when you know that something you love is in immediate danger, it is more important to put your pride—to put everything to the side to protect what you love. It's not easy to do that. During that time, had I chosen to be belligerent, that could have cost me my life, and you your innocence and your life. It could have left your mother without a husband, your brothers & sister without a father and a little sister. I had to momentarily choose to put everything else aside.

"I saw where the power was. Even though the officer thought he was strong, he was choosing to act violently because he was weak. He needed to justify to himself and his reason to exist by seeking to demean me in front of my child.

"I, being the stronger of the two, the elder of the two, I realize weakness when I see it. I took my power of choice to put my artillery to the side to safeguard what I love."

He broke down what he loved about being a father. He talked about protecting my innocence. He didn't say it, but a little Black girl being raped at that time wouldn't be investigated. Or two bodies being missing wouldn't be found.

I never mentioned the tear.

I see that it took courage in that moment. He was prepared. I watched my father as a Black man having to negotiate a situation that could have meant his life and the innocence and life of his daughter. He was a World War II veteran. He and my mom had taught me about racism, and we knew about it – and I read *Invisible Man* in elementary school, and I listened to my parents sitting with White clergy from Xavier when they were talking about voting – but this was the first time I experienced it.

Sister Mary was a senior when she revisited that conversation with her dad. But the entire time since fifth grade, it had stayed with her. Now she understands this as the singular defining event in her life that shaped her:

That's where I got my power of choice. Thinking through things and pausing before acting. I saw that one false step could irrevocably cause pain to yourself others. You have to be mindful of how to choose your battle.

The combination of her gifts – speaking, connecting, seeing people's potential – plus the pain of this ride in the green and white Plymouth, came together to give Sister Mary her life's purpose. As a co-founder of LPTM, she infuses what she learned from this moment into her interactions. "It gives me joy to see boys who understand the power of choice like my dad had."

2c. The Purpose

At LPTM we understand that we are all an amalgamation of what we've been taught, what we've experienced, and what we've been exposed to. This is wisdom we have learned from Elder Bill. We understand the power of thinking through things and pausing before acting. We have tremendous agency by paying close attention to our thoughts, our words, our actions. Through all the mediums of expression, as we tell ourselves and others about our lives and experiences, we have to pay attention to how we tell the story, how we place ourselves in our stories.

At LPTM, we recognize the tremendous inequality that manifests in an under-resourced neighborhood, with all the structural deficits that reinforce that inequality. And to move forward with conviction and power, we need to claim our own agency despite these systems. We need to be able to name the oppressors and see the weakness of their frame; we need to be able to reject the distorted justifications that oppressors use to maintain their power.

At LPTM, though the Human Development System curriculum, we extend this analysis to provide tools for the young apprentices to analyze situations and understand the inherent potential behind any moment. For example, we model (drawing from Buddhist teachings) how to turn anger into courage (as Mary's father did). We model how to turn greed into compassion, how to turn ignorance into wisdom.

3. Finding Purpose as a Tool for Sustainable Social Justice Action

Those who have committed their lives to social justice work find a purpose in addressing human suffering. To make that work sustainable, we have to identify honestly and fully how the work connects to our own, personal pain. We have to look at the amalgamation of what we've been taught, what we've experienced, and what we've been exposed to, and we need to have the courage to go inside the good, the bad, the ugly of your life's journey from the time you were a child to today.

The Latin root for the word *passion* is *pati*, to suffer. What are you struggling to release yourself from, and where are you struggling to go? Look inward to see your gifts. Look inward to identify your true self, the part of who you are that you don't readily show to the world. What do you know about yourself?

Then put these together: Take what you do really, really well and look at the thing that attacked you and that you detest, what causes pain – use your thoughts words and actions to make a difference.

We know this is not easy. We have to re-learn it every day. It is a process. It takes courage to think through in your brain when you are afraid. Pausing to acknowledge your pain and to take note of where the power really is – that is a profound strength. It has to be cultivated. Discovering both your gifts and your self-awareness are on-going, constant processes.

This work is not only an intellectual approach; it has to constantly remain three dimensional. It is how you move through the world—who you physically are, dealing with all the -isms that would contain you. Pay attention to how you show up on the planet. People will react immediately to your physicality.

This philosophy is not an ephemeral tool, lofty in its idealism. It is a tool for confronting oppression day to day. These days, Life Pieces leans into this approach as we confront an existential crisis of gun violence. As pandemic restrictions have lifted, gun violence has spiked in the areas of DC where LPTM is located. In 2021 alone, according to the DC Police Department, 241 assaults with guns occurred in Ward 7. From November 2021 to March 2022, Drew Elementary School has been placed on lockdown a total of eight times. LPTM staff and management rushed the young boys off the Drew playground to shelter in place, while gunshots blasted; sometimes police helicopters thundered overhead to search for shooters.

Our children fear the gun violence around their homes. One LPTM thirteen-year-old noted that "I hear around 8 to over 25 gunshots per night." They have shared how they follow safety procedures in their own homes: sometimes the boys are responsible for making sure their younger siblings have scrambled under the bed or are fully hidden in the closet; they rush to close curtains and hope a bullet doesn't come through the window as they do. Just last month, a mother was killed by a stray bullet as she sat in a car only a few feet from Riverside Center, where our high school youth gather for Saturday programs. We continue to look for meeting spaces outside of Ward 7; we have been warned that the already intolerable levels of violence will be even worse this summer.

LPTM has implemented safety precautions within our signature after-school programming. We rush the boys off the playground, we hide in classrooms. This is happening in what we had promised would be a place of love and security.

In these moments, Sister Mary reminds the family at LPTM that violence is a symptom of the weak. Those causing violence seek to justify their power through control and domination. They are trying to kill and destroy something that they don't see in themselves—or something they hate in themselves, so they want to destroy it.

> People will think power is in a gun, money, kicking you in the gut until you taste blood.
>
> No, power is knowing that you have the choice to control your thoughts, words and actions. Power is thoughts words and actions to change anger into courage, greed into compassion, ignorance into knowledge.

Holding onto this approach in the midst of constant violence is a challenge. It takes courage to think through in your brain when you are afraid. It takes courage to love. It is tempting to point fingers and lay blame. There are many actors and stakeholders who have some responsibility for this rise in violence; there are many actors involved who would use this moment to garner fleeting attention without really committing to getting things done. And it is exhausting to try to make room in our own scared and tired hearts to see the soul-bags of the shooters, to remember the suffering and pain that causes a young man to pick up a gun. To get to hard-care solutions, you have to let go of the sensationalism and build on a network of honest connections, with other people who are doing the internal work to bring their real gifts and their real purposes to this issue. In this work, we lean into our partnerships where everyone has their own innate, creative abilities to bring to the table. We are not in this alone. This is a work in progress.

When we are awakened to a sense of purpose, our power is limitless.

The world needs answers and solutions to many social issues. The sustainable solution is through collectives who are rooted in self-awareness and can speak to the depth of their purpose. Who can come together and say, "This is who we are." When different individuals do their own things, reacting to a moment, they aren't rooted, so they are fleeting. They will come and go. But when people come together who have found purpose, they can effect systemic change that is longer lasting.

Finding purpose is a journey. We hope that we have offered you some tools to begin.

Works Cited

Life Pieces to Masterpieces. "Color Me Community." lifepieces.org/our-programs/color-me-community/.

Life Pieces to Masterpieces. "Human Development System." lifepieces.org/what-we-do/human-development-system/.

Robert Wood Johnson Foundation. "Life Expectancy: Could Where You Live Influence How Long You Live?" www.rwjf.org/en/library/interactives/whereyouliveaffectshowlongyoulive.html.

Author Bios

Mary Brown is the co-founder and Executive Director of Life Pieces to Masterpieces, a nonprofit in Washington, DC.

Phyllis Ryder is the Secretary of the Board for Life Pieces to Masterpieces and an Associate Professor of Writing at the George Washington University, where she teaches community-engaged writing classes.

This essay is written collaboratively, through shared conversations. The experience and wisdom are grounded in the LPTM Human Development System, an approach Mary Brown developed for the program in her role as co-founder, and which is "the heart of all our work at Life Pieces" (LPTM "What We Do"). Phyllis Ryder provided structure and framing. Together we asked questions of each other, probed for deeper understandings, compared our discoveries.

2021 Conference on Community Writing Keynote Address

Liberating Powers: Community Building in Word, in Deed

Brigette Rouson

Julian Clement Chase Award Ceremony
October 21, 2021, 7:00pm Eastern
Edited for Publication (Jan. 2022)

Giving thanks to the Creator, the conference organizers, especially Phyllis and Veronica, Cassandra for her generous intro. Special thanks to the family of Julian Clement Chase, and all who join in this emergent and urgent imagining of ourselves in community.

This keynote offers ways to make meaning of who we are and how we be, from our inner selves to collective formations. My intention is to offer principles and practice to build together for liberation and affirm the importance of communicating as we say "yes" to this awesome endeavor.

1. Who/where/when I enter . . .

I speak as a daughter of Vivian and Ervin, dedicating this keynote to Black parents who nurtured five Black children in a South of honey-baked racism, yet found recipes for progress. My parents served as educators, active in community leadership, who purposed every structure (neighborhood, church, sorority, fraternity, media) to make Black lives matter and create the Beloved Community—even before we used those terms.

I speak as a self-identified fugitive from university life, who left the ivory tower—part choice, part "constructive eviction"—to earn a living, co-parent, and follow new paths as resource organizer and "capacity builder." At the outset, I guided grantmaking for girls and young women leading change.

I speak as an East coast native beholding the beauty of every people and place in "Turtle Island" and beyond, supporting rematriation of indigenous land (Sogorea Te' Land Trust).

I speak seeking to walk in the world as abolitionist, since attending that first Critical Resistance Conference at UC-Berkeley in 1998. I speak as a feminist (and womanist) for as long as I can remember, trauma survivor, activist, one who revels in movement, music lover (including my son's jazz), reader of Afro-futurism and historical accounts of liberation (Kelly's *Freedom Dreams*, Ortiz), and always an unapologetic "race woman" for our times. In the words of trailblazer Anna Julia Cooper,

"Only the Black Woman can say 'when and where I enter, in the quiet, undisputed dignity of my womanhood, ... then and there the whole [Negro] race enters with me."—Anna Julia Cooper (Chimbanga).

Finally, I speak as a microcosm and ever-present possibility of the communal, inspired by the **concept of Ubuntu—I am because we are, and because we are, I am.** Community.

2. Community Is Liberation

With the wisdom of the ancestors and many countless people living embodied now, I define liberation as the assurance that everyone's needs and human rights are honored—and, more, we all lead mutually fulfilling lives in solidarity and joy.

Community is the site and shaper of liberation. Its sinews are substance—creating a muscular experience of being held on a collective journey. Community is source and it is system.

It's my amazing good fortune to work supporting social justice organizations to internalize racial justice with an intersectional lens. t the core is a call to give care on multiple levels of system—the inner/individual, the interpersonal, the institutional and societal. These are levels of who we are and how we roll, reflected in structures, practices, policies, group dynamics and organizational culture. It is this work from which I offer insights and invitations for you today.

In my work, a major commitment is to center relationships, and center Blackness—rooting out white supremacy, patriarchy, ageism, homophobia, transphobia, ableism—and practicing language justice. We reimagine what community can be without relentless homage to racial capitalism that insinuates itself into our bones, into our ways of being, and breaks us even as it pretends to sustain us.

For me and my colleagues, now is a time when we support groups to "walk the talk" by aligning internal culture and structures with what they advocate in the world. At best, it's about being the change—inspired by writers such as adrienne maree brown (*Emergent Strategy*) and Frederic Laloux (Reinventing Organizations). It requires devoting huge time and resources, being vulnerable, experimenting and benefiting from lessons of failure *and* success. It can be painful work, yet it yields treasure beyond measure.

We use the Sankofa principle of looking back to move forward. We invite the emergent, the exquisite collective care that makes healing paramount, the extravagance of wild ideas that re-create the commons—one space, one moment at a time—much like the phenomenon that is Sunday drumming in Malcolm X Park, poetically portrayed in this year's prize-winning monograph. Fortunately, we'll hear from author Chase Kleber and learn more of this work later in today's session.

3. Community-Building Is Reclaiming Our Authentic Selves—Our Common Humanity and Divinity

As a midwife of organizational and community change, I embrace core principles from the earliest points of human existence.

1st, returning to Ubuntu—I am because we are, and because we are, I am.
One scholar, Ogude, speaks of Ubuntu as "rooted in ... a relational form of personhood" "believing the common bonds within a group are more important than any individual arguments and divisions." In practice, it is "building a consensus around what affects the community. And ... [having] understood what is best for the community," embracing and working for it together. Ubuntu "extends to our relationships with the non-human world of rivers, plants and animals" (Ogude). This practice means being intentional about what and how we communicate. For to communicate is to relate, to create bonds with burdens and benefits.

We also learn to express community from the seven principles of Ma'at, the ancient Kemetic (or Egyptian) society's system of laws, named for the goddess who symbolizes highest morality. Major principles of Ma'at are Truth, Justice, Harmony, Balance, Order, Reciprocity and Propriety (Lee). In these principles we find the essence of aspirations and boundaries to form, advance, and express community. DC is at once local, regional, national and international; a sense of community can be elusive. Still, we rise by lifting up what makes life vibrant in this place—knowing it to be the Douglass Commonwealth, the 51st state—as we seek to decolonize our nation's capital.

By finding our voices and giving voice to harmony, balance, and order, we can be complete. In these times, I invite our attention to sages (such as Malidoma Patrice Some and Sonbonfu Some), who've opened our eyes to the essential task of mourning together. The endless pattern of violence against Black, Brown and other global majority people is ongoing "shock and awe" that tries to rob us of the power of community. Most recently in DC we have yet to hear prominent voices in the establishment express concern about a Black man, **An'Twan Gilmore,** being executed by police while sleeping in his car. News coverage was so fleeting that it slipped from consciousness within weeks, at best becoming a name between commas on a list far too long. When we do not fully process our loss, we have little room to understand how every principle of a moral society is being undermined. When we are in denial and disbelief about such deep violation of what binds us together, we cannot be present to life and the business of living.

To be our truest, highest, and best—we must heal collectively; while seeking truth, justice, propriety and reciprocity. May the spirit of Ma'at guide us.

4. Community-Building Is Learning, Decolonizing, Power-shifting

Transformation engages us fully—whole hearts, mind-body-spirit—in decolonizing ourselves and the formations in our lives. We refuse all ideas and actions that attempt to dehumanize, sprouting from concepts such as "manifest destiny"—the notion that by divine intent whiteness should dominate places, people, culture, economy, all life.

Transformation is grounded in intersectionality, inspired by the Combahee River Collective, Barbara Smith, Angela Davis, Barbara Ransby, Kimberlé Crenshaw and more. It is alive in Cara Page, the Kindred Healing Justice Collective, and many bold spirits rooted in Black feminist / Southern Black radical traditions of the US and global south; in offerings such as Emotional Emancipation Circles (a model from the Association of Black Psychologists and Community Healing Network) including those led in DC by Erika Totten; and works in progress by Aaron Goggans, Sandra Kim and others with the formation of Wild Seed Society. Through these models we know what it means to express and build community in the 21st century and for seven generations.

Transforming as community means we never banish ourselves to spectator roles, rather we keep cultivating change at every level of system (from inner/individual to interpersonal to institutional/structural).

So, we must ask:

- How are we learning and walking in ways that uproot settler colonialism?
- How are we shifting away from domination and towards liberation?
- How are we acknowledging harm experienced from our own and others' complicity in lethal substitutes for true community?
- What are we personally and collectively doing to heal?
- What reparations are we making?
- What structures are we questioning and re-creating?

Two examples of how expressing community can be transformative relate to:

Place-based philanthropy with a radical edge

DC is a study in contrasts. A place where Black elected officials and business and professional figures have a great deal of formal power, yet simply "breathing while Black" is often deadly. We are #1 in the nation in gentrification, specifically displacement of Black residents. #1 in the nation in Black maternal mortality. Here in DC, **Diverse City Fund** (of which I'm a co-founder) is at this moment celebrating its 10th anniversary, a decade of having grant decisions made by community residents, all Black/Indigenous/People of Color—better known as the global majority—who are involved bringing about justice. Recently, our first impact and assessment report (diversecityfund.org) generated shared insight. It offered narratives that bind us together, raise our visibility, and enhance sustainability.

Thanks to the writing of this report, we know that across roles, our community's stakeholders expressed:

1. A strong connection and appreciation for . . . redistribution of wealth and power towards community-led social and racial justice work in . . . DC.
2. A sense of trust in the DC Fund and its . . . transparency and accessibility . . . in its grantmaking . . . [and] equitable practices in . . . internal decision-making.
3. A belief that DC Fund is playing a vital and important role in both the activist and philanthropic communities.
4. A sense of gratitude because participating in or partnering with the DC Fund helps them pursue . . . personal goals of creating a more equitable city.

We found that our main impact was: "Creating a community, networking and learning space for social justice organizations, leadership, partners, and other funders."

This narrative also helped us name 3 themes to create a path forward.

1. Strengthening Communication Loops
2. Making Shared Decisions in the organization
3. Diversifying Funding & Grantee Support

and setting a gift acceptance policy that reflects the organization's values

These insights guide us forward. An example is making a commitment to expand the pool of community folks who serve on our grantmaking teams with shared political analysis that they draw from lived experience . . . especially east of the Anacostia River. And we are looking to create a communications hub for local social justice groups.

As we build community in one space, we create the conditions for broader community:

During this pandemic, DC Fund was a co-convenor in the formation of **Resourcing Radical Justice**, a group of DC-MD-VA (or "DMV") funders who center Black liberation as the key to a thriving region. Examples of our work include a survey documenting experiences of global majority people in local philanthropy that motivated us to hold a healing retreat with storytelling and original creative works (visual art* and spoken word that we commissioned (Resourcing Radical Justice). We then held three learning sessions on harm, repair and accountability; followed by small group conversations and a retreat on reimagining philanthropy. We've had intense learning experiences from dialogue and collaboration—especially weaving narratives together—that build our resilience and resolve. Another world is possible.

These forays into transforming philanthropy draw from experiences—mine and those of folks who've occupied different places in the system, all pointing toward a power shift. We look to a rich knowledge base with written work to open minds and hearts, such as

- *The Revolution Will Not Be Funded: Beyond the Non-Profit Industrial Complex* by Incite!
- *Decolonizing Wealth*, by Edgar Villaneuva
- *Operationalizing Racial Equity*, by Maggie Potapchuk

And a forthcoming book by Yanique Redwood, who is transitioning from President and CEO of A Foundation for Radical Possibility (https://www.iffdn.org) to Executive Director of the Center for Anti-Racist Research.

Consciousness and community-making require understanding what's real. Communication offers that reality check.

5. Communication is Community-Building

From the amazing spaces that this conference stitches together, the invitation is to communicate—to write and express—what contributes to a richer sense of our interconnectedness, and commitment to honor it *by any means necessary*. One means is the word—not to be worshiped, rather treated as part of a multi-hued palette to paint a world. Our focus must be on reorienting, resisting, reimagining.

We express and transform community when we join in community radio—including Pacifica's WPFW in DC, WBAI in NY. We define and take our place in community with campaigns such as #Don't Mute DC that boldly proclaim the importance of keeping DC culture in the sounds and sights on our streets.

I implore you to keep your reading expansive. Added to the illuminating work of so many gathered here, writers that fire my passion for community include:

- **Robin D. G. Kelley**, *Freedom Dreams* ("The idea of a revolution of the mind has always been central to . . . black conceptions of liberation . . . an unleashing of the mind's most creative capacities, catalyzed by participation in struggle for change." p. 191)
- **Keeanga-Yamahtta Taylor**, *From #BlackLivesMatter to Liberation* ("Solidarity is standing in unity with people even when you have not personally experienced their particular oppression." p. 215)
- **Angela Davis**, *Freedom Is a Constant Struggle: Ferguson, Palestine, and the Foundations of a Movement* ("The personal is political. There is a deep relationality that links struggles against institutions and struggles to reinvent our personal lives and recraft ourselves." p. 108)
- **Paul Ortiz**, *An African American and Latinx History of the United States* ("If American history serves as a guide, not even the president of the United States can stem the tide of grassroots freedom movements and the ability of people throughout the hemisphere to draw inspiration from each other's struggles . . . the self-activity of the most oppressed is the key to liberty…" p. 184)
- **Mariame Kaba**, *We Do This 'Til We Free Us: Abolitionist Organizing and Transforming Justice* ("We want to invite a broader and deeper conception of justice . . . one rooted in reparations, modeled on Chicago's . . . The reparations framework outlines five elements—repair, restoration, acknowledgement, cessation, and nonrepetition." p. 66)
- **Resma Menakem**, *My Grandmother's Hands* (audio excerpt at https://www.youtube.com/watch?v=hANCtQbhly4)
- **angel Kyodo williams**, *Radical Dharma*
- **Sara Trembath**, *This Past Was Waiting for Me* (" . . . teaching the truth . . . academically and then societally and psychologically, what must result . . . is *a new American Story* and with it a firmer foundation for equality and peace and healing to manifest." p. 95)
- **Mindy Fullilove**, *Root Shock* and *Urban Alchemy*

- **Chris Myers Asch & George Derek Musgrove,** *Chocolate City: A History of Race and Democracy in the Nation's Capital*
- **Alexis Pauline Gumbs, Makani Themba, N'Tanya Lee,** and more . . .

6. Moving in this moment . . .

May we all be guided by the words of adrienne maree brown *(from Emergent Strategy p.55):

> "I am living a life I don't regret
>
> A life that will resonate with my ancestors,
>
> And with as many generations forward as I can imagine.
>
> I am attending to the crises of my time with my best self,
>
> I am of communities that are doing our collective best
>
> To honor our ancestors and all humans to come."

This is our invitation, our point of possibility: To be about repair, reimagining, about writing/wording our way to community, which is to say liberation.

Works Cited

Anders, Tisa. "Combahee River Collective (1974-1980)". *Black Past.* April 23, 2012, https://www.blackpast.org/african-american-history/combahee-river-collective-1974-1980/

"Association of Black Psychologists." *Association of Black Psychologists.* https://abpsi.site-ym.com/

Association of Black Psychologists. *Defy the Lie and Embrace the Truth: Join the Movement for the Emotional Emancipation of Black People.* http://www.abpsi.org/pdf/EECCallToAction6-23.pdf

"BLM petitions D.C. demands justice for An'Twan Gilmore" *AFRO.* 30 August 2021. https://afro.com/blm-petitions-d-c-demands-justice-for-antwan-gilmore/.

brown, adrienne maree. *Emergent Strategy: Shaping Change, Changing Worlds,* AK Press, 2017.

Chimbanga, Esther. "Anna Julia Cooper." *First Wave Feminisms,* 4 December 2019, https://sites.uw.edu/twomn347/2019/06/07/anna-julia-cooper/.

Diverse City Fund. *Diverse City Fund.* https://diversecityfund.org

Diverse City Fund. *2020 Impact & Assessment Report.* https://diversecityfund.org/wp-content/uploads/2021/06/DC-Fund_2020-Impact-Assessment-Report-1.pdf

Don't Mute DC. https://www.dontmutedc.com/

Kindred Southern Healing Justice Collective. *Our History.* https://kindredsouthern-hjcollective.org/our-history/

Lee, Linda. "Kemetic Teachings: Principles of Maat." *Spirit Quest with Linda,* 10 May, 2021, https://www.spiritquestwithlinda.com/blog/principles-of-maat.

Ogude, James. *Ubuntu and Personhood*. Africa World Press, 2018.
"Reinventing Organizations." Reinventing Organizations. https://www.reinventingorganizations.com
"Resourcing Radical Justice." Resourcing Radical Justice. https://www.resourcingradicaljustice.org
Resourcing Radical Justice. *Advocate*. https://www.resourcingradicaljustice.org/advocate
Sogorea Te' Land Trust. Purpose and Vision. https://sogoreate-landtrust.org/purpose-and-vision/
Wild Seed Society. https://www.wildseedsociety.com

Author Bio

Brigette Rouson, J.D., M.A., (she/her/li/ella), principal of Rouson Associates, brings more than 30 years' experience advancing nonprofit effectiveness toward a just society. She works with the RoadMap consulting network, is a co-founder and board member of Diverse City Fund, and part of local funders' collective Resourcing Radical Justice. Brigette focuses on internal transformation, emphasizing racial justice and intersectionality, toward sustainable change in ourselves, practices, and policies. Brigette has supported 250+ groups to innovate. She is involved in local organizing and activism, including faith-based and woman-centered initiatives.

Brigette is a graduate of Howard University (B.A.), Georgetown University (J.D.), and University of Pennsylvania (M.A.) where she completed all coursework toward a Ph.D. in communications and culture.

Articles

Innovaciones y Historias: A Home- and Community-Based Approach to Workplace Literacy

Guadalupe Remigio Ortega, Alfonso Guzman Gomez, and Calley Marotta

Abstract

Drawing from Latinx studies and the literacy experiences of men employed as university custodial staff, we propose a home- and community-based approach to workplace literacy. The central goals of this approach are to allow participants to identify their professional and vocational literacies to highlight their literate assets and goals across contexts. The approach offers a humanizing lens for individuals who are often denied the opportunity to showcase their literate repertoires and desires within the context of their formal workplaces. Overall, this article calls for a broader understanding of participants' literacy experiences—not only as workers but as people who work.

Keywords

home, community, workplace, university, Latinx, critical methodologies

Introduction

I was the first boy born to my family. When I was a boy, there were lots of fiestas with people dancing and drinking and songs. The music was very good—the guitars and songs. When I was in my mother's stomach, I was looking out at the party and I remember eating bananas, apples, pears, and guava. When I was two years old, I went up to my grandfather and I held onto him by the water. It was special water. My family used it to cook and drink. While I was digging a hole, I held my grandfather and a big, heavy rock fell on us. My grandfather dropped me and stopped the rock, but I fell into the water and he could only see my leg. He pulled me out and saved me. I was passed out for an hour and my mother thought I was gone and cried. She said, "thank you for my son; I love my son." When I came back, she was very happy and all of her friends said, "the boy came again."

Fui el primer niño que nació en mi familia. Cuando era niño, había muchas fiestas con gente bailando y tomando y canciones. La música era muy

buena, las guitarras y las canciones. Cuando estaba en la barriga de mi madre, estaba mirando la fiesta y recuerdo comer plátanos, manzanas, peras, guayaba. Cuando tenía dos años, corrí hasta mi abuelo y me agarré a él cerca de un manantial. Era un agua especial. Mi familia la usaba para cocinar y beber. Estaba agarrado a mi abuelo cavando un hoyo cuando una roca grande y pesada me cayó encima. Mi abuelo me soltó y paró la roca, pero yo caí en el manantial y él solo podía verme una pierna. Me sacó y me salvó. Estuve desmayado durante una hora y mi madre pensó que me había muerto y lloró. Dijo: "gracias por mi hijo, amo a mi hijo". Cuando desperté, ella estaba muy feliz y todos sus amigos dijeron, "el niño ha vuelto."

This excerpt comes from the beginning of Alfonso's life history, a testimonio he wrote to share miracles with his church community. At the time Alfonso wrote this story, he was also participating in a workplace study with Calley, an academic researcher who was studying the literacy practices of people employed as university custodians. As a part of the study, Calley asked Alfonso about his reading, writing, and speaking experiences within the workplace, but she soon found that her questions did not adequately account for important literacies like this testimonio. Similarly, other study participants expressed a desire to discuss literacies they practiced outside of the university. As opposed to those literacies directly tied to their institutional labor, they wanted to discuss those connected to their faith, families, and intellectual and professional pursuits. They wanted to discuss literacies activated in their garages, kitchens, and church pews—their home and community contexts—because it was those conditions that supported their literate desires. In this way, participants highlight a need for literacy researchers to look beyond a single site of employment to understand the workplace literacies of people who, because of race, class, and linguistic othering, are often denied opportunities to practice their chosen work and literacies in the context of their job.

Drawing from a broader year-long qualitative study, this article focuses on the question: for men who identify as Latino and are employed as university custodians, how does understanding literacy in home and community contexts inform understandings of their workplace and community literacies? To begin to answer this question, we draw from the experiences of two participants, including their stories, videos, and photographs across home, work, and religious community contexts. We also draw from Latinx and Chicanx theories in education, writing studies, and transnational literacy studies to assert the value of understanding workplace literacies in relation to people's broader literate lives. We propose a home- and community-based approach to workplace literacy that positions these spaces as central to, rather than context for, each other. Putting these literate contexts in conversation is particularly consequential for workers like Latino immigrant university laborers who are disproportionately racialized and whose conditions too often instrumentalize and dehumanize their labor as a part of literacy production (Marko et al; Marotta). Such exploitation is upheld by racist cultural stereotypes that limit Latinx men's identities to that of labor (Molina) and thus deny them their knowledge and literacies within a public literacy institution. Considering these hypocrisies, universities have a stake in isolating workers from literacies that connect them to identities and lives beyond their institutional labor.

Literacy researchers can reinforce these problematic institutional constructions through their framing and analysis when they position home- and community-based literacies as either separate from or context for literacies practiced in a single site of paid labor. Drawing from a long history of Latinx/Chicanx and transnational literacy scholarship, we propose a home- and community-based approach to workplace literacy to analytically connect literacies activated in home and community spaces to practices and experiences in the context of paid work. This approach asks researchers to shift the lens through which they analyze workplace literacies. Rather than starting analysis with literacies primarily practiced in the context of formal employment, it asks them to use literacies participants identify as meaningful across their home and community spaces to analyze literacies practiced within a formal, paid work context. While the object of study remains workplace literacies in that the analysis and implications focus on interpretations of literacies associated with work, this approach fundamentally changes what is being centered in that analysis, so participants' literate wealth, knowledge, and priorities are positioned at the forefront.

In this article, we focus on two participants, Henry and Alfonso, whose experiences reflect a broader pattern in the research. We describe how Henry uses his home as a workspace to extend his professional knowledge that he must negotiate within his university workspace. We then explain how Alfonso leverages personal storytelling in his church but faces university work conditions that restrict those storytelling practices. Both these cases show how reading people's literate experiences in their formal workplace through practices activated in home and community contexts illuminates how they experience literacies across contexts—including that of their paid employment. This approach reveals literacies often obscured or silenced by workplace conditions and how workplace conditions that (dis)connect workers from their broader literate lives have important consequences for their experience.

Alfonso and Henry's responses align with Latinx and Chicanx scholarship in writing studies (Alvarez; Cintron; Ruiz; García and Baca) and education (Elenes, Delagdo Bernal; Pacheco) that have long claimed researchers must look beyond institutional spaces like classrooms to understand Latinx peoples' literacies. Their responses also align with transnational literacy studies research that suggests literacies are not tied to single sites but move across contexts (Lam; Nordquist; Bolt and Leander; Vossoughian and Gutiérrez; Lorimer Leonard). While it has become increasingly common for researchers studying classroom literacy to do so in the context of literacies taking place in homes and communities, workplace literacy studies still predominantly examine a formal workplace as a central site[1] (for example see Farrell; Lauer and Brumberger; Hull; Haas and Wittee; Rose; Spinuzzi; Windsor; Wardle). As such, there is a need to further examine the relationship between work, home, and community spaces in the lives of Latinx people and Latin American immigrants.

Drawing on these theories and Alfonso's and Henry's experiences, a home- and community-based approach to workplace literacy allows participants to identify with multiple work contexts and to identify which work is primary for them. Considering conditions that construct them as the lowest rank of university labor, Henry and Alfonso want to be recognized for university work, but they also want to be understood as more than labor. Alfonso and Henry's experiences show sometimes work, callings, and vocation exist beyond sites of paid employment but also impact those sites. Failing to examine literacies across contexts fails to appreciate the complex relationships between sites of work—how people negotiate their home and community literacies within their formal workspaces and how they make homes and communities their workspaces. For example, Henry's work in his garage is an extension of his role as a community member. To him, his work is much more than a paid job. For Alfonso, his role in church is part of his spiritual calling or vocation and an example of how he contributes to his community. As such, community and home contexts become important sites for understanding workplace literacies at the same time as workplaces become important sites for community literacy scholarship. Both case studies contribute to community literacy studies by challenging current definitions and perspectives which use "community" to explain all literacies that do not neatly align with educational institutions.

The central goals of this approach are to allow participants to identify their professional and vocational literacies to highlight their literate assets and goals across contexts as well as to inform more equitable workplace literacy conditions. This article calls for workplace and community literacy to inform one another so that individuals can connect their broader literate goals and repertoires across contexts. A home- and community-based approach to workplace literacy offers a humanizing lens for individuals who are often denied the opportunity to showcase their literate repertoires and desires within the context of their formal workplaces. Overall, we call for a broader understanding of participants' literacy experiences—not only as workers but as people who work.

A Home- and Community-Based Approach to Workplace Literacy

To provide a theoretical rationale for a home- and community-based approach to workplace literacy, we combine Latinx and Chicanx theories in education and writing studies with theories in transnational literacy studies. Theories in Latinx and Chicanx scholarship position home and community contexts as central sites of literacy and knowledge. And theories in transnational literacy studies conceptualize literacies as necessarily moving across contexts like universities, homes, and religious community spaces examined in this study. We use these theories to analyze how participants leverage literacies as a part of broader sociocultural and professional histories and how those histories, experiences, and repertoires can show up in their experience of university and community work.

This article extends Latinx studies and Chicana feminist scholarship in education and writing studies that have long theorized home and community contexts as sites of literacy strength. Through ethnographic research with Mexican families and communities in particular, scholars have urged researchers and teachers of literacy to account for home-based practices and knowledge (Delgado Bernal; Cintron; Elenes; González et al.; Farr and Guerra; Farr) to extend rather than erase and silence students' "ample cultural and cognitive resources" (Zepeda 140). These resources stem from "pedagogies of the home," the often informal embodied lessons learned at home and transmitted across generations (Delores Delgado Bernal)[2] and "funds of knowledge" (González et al.) or assets students carry into classrooms from home-based learning. This scholarship also highlights community-based literacies (Alvarez; Pacheco; Yosso) as central assets to the lives of many Latinx peoples. This scholarship challenges deficit-based constructions of home forwarded by many educational institutions (Alvarez).

In this article, we highlight how Henry's and Alfonso's home- and community-based literacies allow them to pursue and leverage the literacies they desire. We draw from Tara J. Yosso's theory of cultural wealth to challenge institutional perceptions that communities of color lack knowledge by highlighting their linguistic navigation and storytelling as particular sources of wealth and cultural capital. This scholarship helps us analyze Henry's ability to communicate his professional knowledge across languages and contexts as well as Alfonso's commitment to use his words and stories to offer advice to others and draw from his own life experiences to model ways of living. We also build upon these theories by expanding their focus from students and families in educational institutions to the experiences of Latino adults who work there. Expanding such theories to include adult workers highlights the knowledge participants acquire and express across the lifespan and challenge workplace conditions that often restrict or fail to recognize their experience. Like classrooms, workplaces should cultivate opportunities to leverage home- and community-based literacy practices.

Considering this scholarship, we argue that researching beyond formal paid workspaces offers an important opportunity to understand literacies within them. We draw from transnational conceptions of literacy as necessarily working across contexts because literacies are not contained by or bound to single sites but deeply connected to a variety of contexts (Marcus) in immigrants' literate and linguistic lives (Vossoughian and Gutiérrez). Following these scholars, we conceptualize literacies as moving, dynamic, connected and often in flux (Lam; Nordquist; Bolt and Leander; Vossoughian and Gutiérrez) to analyze the vast literate repertoires of people whose lives are marked by histories of movement and migration and whose literacies are constantly revalued (Lorimer Leonard) across the contexts of their daily lives. This perspective considers how home- and community-based literacies necessarily work across borders and time as Henry and Alfonso carry and transform literacies from their social histories.

Understanding literacies as dynamic also helps us analyze how institutional conditions limit participants' repertoires as a part of systems that racialize and dehumanize labor. It helps us analyze how the university "stalls" (Lorimer Leonard) participants' literacies by constructing itself as a bounded space. This boundedness prevents participants from connecting to their literacies and lives outside of the institution. As we discuss later in the text, workplace literacy policies and conditions often restrict the use of literacies that would connect participants to the broader stories of their lives. Such workplace conditions importantly reinforce racist cultural stereotypes that depict Latinx men as workers (Molina) who are limited to their immediate university labor. This system is mutually reinforcing because those dehumanizing depictions of labor then provide a rationale for dehumanizing labor conditions. While we are not arguing that anyone needs to be literate to warrant humane treatment, we are arguing that, in the case of Henry and Alfonso, their literacies can importantly connect them to contexts, practices, and identities beyond their labor in ways that are dangerous to institutions that have a stake in denying their workers' humanities.

Following this scholarship, we recognize spatial boundaries as constructs that create a false contrast between literacies *within* and *outside* workplaces. However, we use home, community, and university-based language to highlight the institutionally constructed boundaries between participants' university experiences and their broader lives and to distinguish the predominant context in which literacies are activated. We analyze how participants negotiate their literate repertoires in the university workspace and how that (dis)connects to their broader community roles. By arguing for a home- and community-based approach to workplace literacy, we neither claim that workers' draw from practices outside of the workplace to do their work better nor that they leverage workplace practices to reach goals outside of it. Rather, we argue that it is essential to read institutional practices and experiences through those that happen outside of the institution's walls.

Beyond the Workplace in Workplace Literacy Studies

Although literacy and language studies of immigrant manual laborers have long shown how work conditions can obscure workers' literacies and literate repertoire, workplace studies of literacy and communication often center the practices of workers within workplaces (for example see Brandt; Farrell; Lauer and Brumberger; Haas and Wittee; Spinuzzi; Windsor; Wardle). In some cases, scholars in literacy studies and sociolinguistics have intentionally focused on workplaces to expose skills within work deemed illiterate (Hagan et al; Hull; Rose; Windsor; Vigoroux). Scholars of Latino work in political science, Armando Ibarra, Alfred Carlos, and Rodolfo D. Torres, have also argued that studying workplace experiences is fundamental because "work conditions every other aspect of their [Latino workers'] material lives, structuring the vast majority of their experiences" (14). Recently, however, literacy studies of writing-intensive work have begun to demonstrate that contexts beyond the workplace are also important to people's experiences of work in the current information economy. These studies urge researchers to look beyond a single work or training setting to include other sites, relationships, histories, and materials that help understand people's experiences of workplace literacy.

Literacy and language studies of immigrant Latinx workers have demonstrated how work conditions tied to English and white supremacy neither reflect workers' full literate repertoire nor their motivation to learn and use literacies. Gabriela Ríos argues migrant farm workers are often seen as illiterate because of the "persistent privileging of traditional literacy," which includes the negative claims made against immigrant farm laborers due to their limited or lack of reading and writing skills as well as their inability to speak English, especially for those who have been in the US for many years. Yet farm workers in Ríos' work explain how "due to the transient nature of their labor, learning English is the last thing on the list of important needs" (60) and instead they turn to their own literate repertoires even when these are not valued in their place of work. Such was the case with Luis Valdez's El Teatro Campesino during the farmworker's strike in California during the 1960s and 70s. Current work conditions for farmworkers privilege traditional English-only literacies and thus devalue farmworkers' "knowledge as skilled laborers" and "their ability to organize themselves and build movements for social change" (Ríos 61). And in his seminal work, *Illegal Alphabets,* Tomás Mario Kalmar tells the story of Mexican migrants who create phonetic English dictionaries and translation tools to communicate and advocate to management after the death of their friend. Kalmar's scholarship shows how participants' motivation for using literacies is not tied only to their immediate work but to the racially motivated murder of a friend—an incident and context that happens beyond their workplace. These studies reveal how racism and xenophobia become tied to literacies in interlocking community and workplace experiences.

In the current information economy, recent workplace literacy studies have begun to draw from contexts outside of the workplace to better understand experiences of literacy within it. As they do so, scholars reveal how literacies and the workers who produce them are affected by broader materials, histories, and relations connected to contexts outside of work. For example, in her study of corporate ghost writers, Elisa Findlay finds that workers' experiences of writing and their identities as writers are deeply shaped by ideologies promoted throughout their schooling histories (Findlay). Deborah Brandt highlights how workers in writing-intensive positions tend to bring their writing home such that personal and professional writing boundaries begin to collapse within the current conditions of the information economy's constant demand for writing. And in his study of African American coders in a coding bootcamp program, Antonio Byrd offers ecological mapping as a method to track the materials and relationships supporting participants' workplace coding preparation amidst systemic racism and inequality. These studies demonstrate the value of examining materials, practices, histories, and ideologies that are predominantly located outside of the immediate work and training context to better understand experiences of workplace literacy. These recent examinations, however, have largely focused on roles that are writing intensive. Further examination is needed to understand how people in manual service and labor positions—those that remain deeply racially, ethnically, and linguistically stratified and are often not writing-intensive—access and connect to literacies beyond those tied to their immediate workplace labor.

In light of theories that assert home- and community-based contexts as potential sites for highlighting the literacy assets and desires of Latinx peoples, there is a need to look beyond the literacies practiced in university workplaces to understand people's experiences of workplace literacies. For Latino immigrant men who are employed as university custodians, how does understanding literacies in home- and community-based contexts inform understandings of their workplace and community experience?

Studying Workplace Literacy Practices Across Contexts

As an introduction to our methods and data, we provide brief introductions to individuals most directly involved in the creation of this article through their participation, research, and writing. We describe some of our roles and how we relate to one another.

Alfonso

Alfonso's life is motivated by his family and his faith. He is the proud father of daughters and a son as well as a grandfather to several grandchildren. He was born in a rural area of Mexico and worked on his family farm before working as a carpenter and custodian. Although he left formal education after grade school, he achieved high grades throughout his formal education. He speaks English and Spanish and is a talented and funny storyteller. He participated in the article through observations, interviews, photographs, and as an author of this article. He considers Lupe and Calley his dear friends.

Henry

Henry is a trained electrician. He immigrated from Cuba to the US as an adult after he participated in the military and attended college. He is a father and grandfather and enjoys working on electrical projects. He speaks Spanish and is also studying English. He participated in the article by sharing his lived experience and expertise through interviews, observations, and videos. Although Henry was not able to collaborate as an article author because of some personal issues that had arisen, we sent him a Spanish translation of his section and the introduction of the article by email and requested any changes and suggestions. In addition to his original permission to participate in the study, he gave us permission to include this writing about his experience in the article and to submit to this journal.

Lupe

Lupe is a dissertator in the English, Composition and Rhetoric, program at The University of Wisconsin-Madison. Lupe's identity as a researcher is heavily grounded on her lived experiences as the daughter of Mixtec migrant farmworkers in the U.S. Her position as a Mixtec woman in academia has influenced her dedication to expanding how we understand literacy by acknowledging the practices of groups and individuals beyond native-English speakers. Lupe speaks, reads, and writes English and Spanish fluently and understands some Mixtec, her parents' native language. This position allowed her the opportunity to work with Calley in interviewing, transcribing, and translating between English and Spanish. Lupe is committed to validating the literacy practices of individuals like Alfonso, Henry, as well as that of her parents in order to recognize the knowledge and values such practices can bring to our own communities.

Calley

Calley is a mother, a writing professor, and a former K-12 special educator. She was the original researcher on this project. The project grew out of her experience working in education institutions which systemically undermined Latinx and Latin American students' and families' rich literate repertoires. Calley's position as an academic provided her access to resources to modestly compensate participants, colleagues to collaborate with who have vast skills in linguistic translation, and the ability to work with management to get approval to do on site observations. Growing up Catholic also gave her access to some of Alfonso's religious teachings. But as a U.S.-born, white, monolingual English speaker, Calley lacks the cultural and linguistic intuition awarded by a shared linguistic and cultural position with participants (Delgado Bernal). In addition to learning from scholars in Latinx and Chicanx studies, Calley strives toward cultural humility and equitable participation by seeking collaborators like Lupe, Alfonso, and Henry whose relationships she has been fortunate enough to grow over several years of working together. She is grateful to call them friends and teachers.

Methodology

Context and Recruitment for the Broader Study

At a time when immigrants have and continue to experience heightened discrimination within educational institutions and workplaces (Iwama, Immigrant Legal Resource Center, Gomez), the broader study associated with this article took place at a midwestern public research university with a particularly racially and linguistically stratified custodial staff. The focal crew worked on the second shift and was made up of fifteen men and women and a lead worker while the institutional hierarchy for custodial staff managers was almost exclusively white and male. Approximately half of the specific custodial crew members were Latinx and Latin American. Six male immigrants who were born in Mexico (5) and Cuba (1) participated in the study.

After contacting all the second shift managers by email, one manager opted into the study and Calley recruited participants at his crew's daily staff meetings. Participants received materials in Spanish and English including transcripts of interviews depending on their preference. Participants were also given the option of using a Spanish translator and interpreter who facilitated three participants' interviews and translated and transcribed their materials. This article is informed by the broader study with six participants.

Methods Across Contexts

Based on participants' activities and descriptions, we define literacies here as the multimodal (Gunther and Kress; Gonzales), multilingual (Canagarajah), embodied (Haas and Witte) practices (Heath) and materials (Pahl and Roswell; Vieira) participants employed to read, write, listen, speak, and compose. To account for literacies activated in multiple contexts and to decenter the institutional gaze in the broader study, Calley used data collection and analysis methods that specifically accounted for literacies outside of participants' university work context.

1. Observations allowed Calley to trace literacy practices as participants moved across contexts like the university, cars, and churches. She observed two participants in their religious community spaces for a total of seven hours. These observations were among the seventy-five hours of observations across the study.

2. Videos (Cardinal; Konignstein and Azadegan) and photographs taken by three participants allowed them to construct, compose, and identify reading, speaking, writing, listening practices to center their perceptions. Participants were given an iPhone and, in total, submitted ten video clips ranging from one to five minutes and twenty photographs.

3. Twelve- and-a-half hours of focused interviews, each of which lasted an hour to an hour-and-a-half and were semi-structured, individual, and audio-recorded, investigated participants' literacy experiences and practices within and outside of the workplace and provided brief literacy histories (Brandt) to ground participants' workplace experiences.

Across the data collected, Calley used closed coding (Saldaña) to track the literacy context including university, home, and community. Then, to privilege out-of-workplace practices in analysis, Calley coded for purposes and audiences across home- and community-based literacies and then analyzed participants' literacies within the institutional context for overlap and divergence from those codes. Another round of coding focused on workplace conditions like policies, messages, and practices that *connected* and *disconnected* participants from other parts of their literate lives. These codes served as the basis for our argument which was shared for feedback and extended by Alfonso.

Collaborative Writing Process

The article's collaborative writing process is inseparable from its content. Amidst important differences in our relations to power and the long history of racial, linguistic, and ethnic exploitation and colonization associated with ethnographic work (Smith; Tuck; Tuck and Yang; Fine) and writing studies scholarship (Ruiz et al.; García and Baca), Calley and Lupe write collaboratively with Alfonso to be accountable to him (Patel) and to center what matters to him in the text. Alfonso follows other scholars

(Rosenbaum) by adopting a pen name to assert his essential role in the production of this article while also maintaining his confidentiality.

Writing together has been an interactive, collaborative, and recursive process. Calley and Lupe predominantly typed on a shared Google Document and Alfonso communicated over the phone using video, call, and text. Lupe translated from English to Spanish verbally, transcribed audio in English and Spanish, read aloud, and often texted paragraphs so that Alfonso could see and read the writing as well as listen to it aloud.

For each paragraph, Alfonso shared what he found most important, clarified anything that did not feel true to his experience, and added any additional relevant information in detail. For example, there were times when he stated "No se si le dije a ella (I'm not sure if I told her (Calley)," and then went on to share a long and detailed story using the opportunity of having a live translator to provide additional detail that ensured we were getting his story right. In the introduction, he wanted to highlight how important it was that so many people could not practice the work they wanted to do and how differently workers of color were treated than their peers.

On occasion, Alfonso would also call Calley and Lupe to share an idea that he wanted to incorporate. When Alfonso was not present on the phone during work sessions, Calley and Lupe typed questions to him directly in Google Notes that Lupe would then translate. Calley and Lupe also highlighted any new writing in a different color to translate. Alfonso would give feedback, Calley and Lupe would revise, and Lupe would translate again for his further review. In Google Document comments, Lupe and Calley wrote directly to each other and Alfonso and defined any academic terms in plain language so that Lupe could translate and so that Alfonso could continue to be central to each part of the text. Calley and Lupe also worked with Alfonso's daughter to give him full copies of the text by email.

Reading Workplace Literacies through Home- and Community-Based Practices

In this section, we share some of Henry's and Alfonso's home- and community-based literacy practices. We do this to demonstrate the strengths and desires they are able to activate in those contexts connected to their own professional and vocational goals. But we also do this to trace how university work conditions shape, and often limit and conceal, how those literacies can show up in their formal work context. We discuss how Henry uses self-sponsored workplace literacies in his home with the hopes of serving his local community and his university workplace. Through these literacies, Henry repositions his home as a workspace that he uses to extend his professional history and sustain his intellectual inquiries and community commitments. Then we discuss how Alfonso teaches and connects with his religious community through storytelling as a part of his broader life work. But we also share how he is prevented from using these literate talents in the university workplace. In both cases, Henry's and Alfonso's experiences in home and community spaces provide insight into how literacies become potential vehicles for integration and (dis)connection across the contexts of their lives. These experiences also highlight workplace systems and cultures that would need to change for them to pursue the broader work and community literacies they desire in the university workplace.

Taken together, these cases demonstrate the complex relations between home-, community-, and institutionally based work and how literacies become tied up in those relations. The cases present important distinctions. Henry and Alfonso hold different positions and histories in relation to paid and unpaid work. Henry's innovations are connected to his previous paid employment while Alfonso has never been monetarily compensated for his church practices. And perhaps because of these differences in position, Henry tries to integrate his home-based literacies into his university work, while Alfonso considers his church-based practices to be more separate from his job. Both cases, however, demonstrate how analyzing workplace literacies through a particular paid work context like the university offers a limited perspective on literacies related to work. Both Henry's and Alfonso's experiences highlight how university workplace conditions obscure aspects of their literate repertoires and how understanding their home- and community-based literacy practices provides insight into literacy desires across their lives. As such, these cases show that a nuanced understanding of literacies associated with work requires an understanding of literacies beyond a single context of paid employment.

Henry: Innovating at Home

While transnational literacy scholars have highlighted how immigrants' literacies are revalued by formal workplaces as they cross national borders (Lorimer Leonard, Vieira), participants like Henry shared how their homes became self- and family-sponsored workspaces where they used literacies to learn, innovate, and create local businesses in informal (Cintron) and sometimes unpaid ways. In this section, we discuss how Henry uses his home space to work on electrical projects that extend his professional and intellectual inquiry. First, in a video recording translated from Spanish and taken in his home, Henry shared projects he uses to continue to learn in a profession he does not currently work. Then, Henry demonstrated how he negotiates his university conditions to utilize and assert his professional wealth across contexts. By doing so, he expands conceptions of workplace literacy to account for practices outside of institutionally sponsored work and demonstrates how researchers can better incorporate the professional work of immigrants who are often not—at least not yet—able to practice their vocation as a part of US formal economies.

Before analyzing Henry's professional projects in his home, we will briefly describe what he explains in the video which is also reflected in Image One. Calley asked if he would take a video in his home to demonstrate some of the projects he was working on after he said he spent his weekends working on electrical projects at home. In the video, he shared images of his tools propped on top of a washer and dryer. First, Henry spans across the space to show the bulbs and wires in the broader context as he introduced what he called his "innovations." He explained the project was "a twenty-Watt fluorescent cold light lamp" that helps with energy consumption. Then he went on to teach Calley via the video step by step, first on the elements that make up the project: he said, "I'm going to stop for a moment right now so you can see. I'm going to, to start by dismounting the fluorescent lamps and the transformers…" Then he connected to the broader purpose: "It's more efficient and less expensive, and it doesn't affect the ecology either and, hence, it's more cost-effective." He explained this would make an important difference to benefit people's lives, because "it's going to be cheaper for the energy consumption in each household."

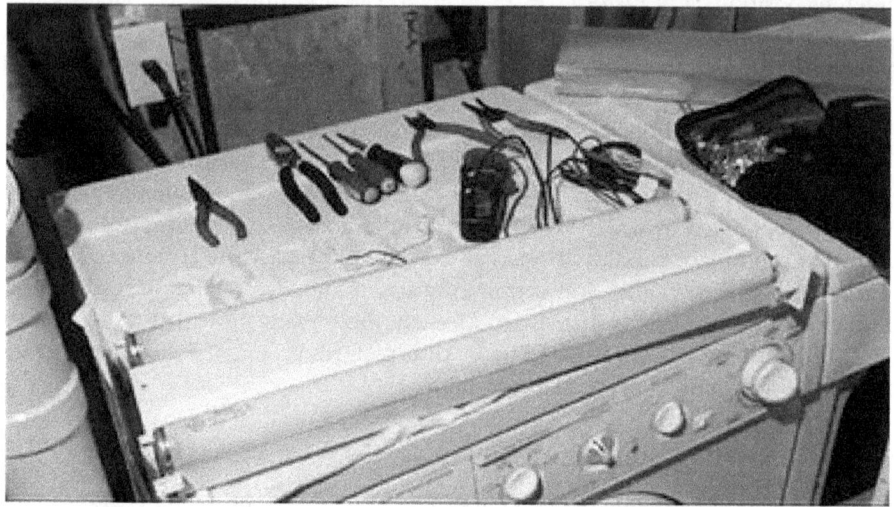

Figure 1. A still image from the video Henry took to demonstrate his electrical innovation.

In this instance, Henry's home context provides conditions to pursue his desires: to learn and teach about his electrical innovations by drawing on his professional knowledge he accumulated in Cuba. At home, he has the space and time to draw from his years of study and experience as an electrician in various professional contexts in Cuba to thoroughly explain his invention. He cultivates conditions where he can be seen and valued as he was in his country of origin, especially when current work conditions in the U.S. provide a very different experience. In doing so, he can hold on to and develop his previous profession and identity as an electrician even if he no longer practices this for a living. As he describes, this work continues to be his "vocation" even outside of formal U.S. economies and constructions of work.

This video also reflects how Henry's home workspace allows him to connect and leverage his professional experience in combination with skills he has built in the U.S. by communicating across languages. He reflects rhetorical skill developed from moving between languages and audiences (Martinez et al.) to invest Calley (his viewer) in the project's broader importance. He also draws from multimodal visual affordances of the video with the materials available to him (Gonzales) as a process of translating both the content and language for Calley, a monolingual English speaker with very little content knowledge in the area he is discussing. In other words, in his home, Henry not only demonstrates his professional literate repertoire but also the specific literate and linguistic strengths he has built from his linguistic experience—the rhetorical awareness and translation expertise required of multilingual people in his position. The video thus demonstrates how, in this case, his home allows him to express aspects of his literate repertoire that he connects to his professional literacies.

Finally, these video clips demonstrate how Henry's professional-, home-, and community-based literacies become tangled and intertwined in terms of their contexts and purposes. While Henry's home allowed him to display his electrical knowledge and the vast literacies and knowledge attached to that professional identity, this demonstration was not only about his role as an electrician—it was also about his desire to help communities, a desire he continues to act on in his current work at the university. He focused on how the project would benefit people at the household level but also the broader *ecology* and environment around them. This currently unpaid work serves not only him but a broader community. In this way, Henry's home becomes a workspace for broader community impact. His video demonstrates the variety of connections between his contexts and roles and the importance of accounting for and supporting those connections across the contexts of his daily life.

While Henry creates opportunities to express aspects of his literate repertoire and knowledge within his home workspace, he described how those aspects were consistently undermined and undervalued within the university. He shared how, within the institution, it was difficult for him to be recognized as a professional electrician because of the racism tied to his language and class of work. He said other people at the university doubted his knowledge because he was a Spanish-speaker and a Latino who cleaned. To exemplify this experience, he described an instance in the university when he saw a man working on some lights. He watched to see what he was doing and if he could help. But when the man noticed, he said, "Would you like something? Do you want to know about something?" And Henry said "No, no, no, no, no, just looking, knowing, I like electricity, I'm just looking." He told Calley he was frustrated that the man had assumed he was there to learn rather than teach—that he presumed Henry had no knowledge to share. Finally, Henry asked another worker for a pencil and drew the circuit to help the electrician. He said "Oh my God! How do you know that?" And Henry told him, "Because that's my life, I studied it, I went to University." In this way, Henry expresses how his position within the university often prevented him from showing literacies related to his formal education and profession—the literacies that he used to define himself.

Institutional conditions related to monolingual English ideologies (Alvarez; Canagarajah) similarly positioned Henry as a learner rather than a bearer of knowledge. In the institutional context, Henry was constructed as an English-learner rather than a Spanish-speaker. English was promoted through safety policies that required English reading comprehension assessments. It was also sponsored through free institutionally run English Language Learning courses. Although Henry said he had attended and appreciated the classes, he preferred to learn on his own—to engage in self-directed learning that met his specific desires and goals. Despite over half of the crew speaking Spanish, English was the language spoken by managers and thus the classes helped build communication in a way that catered to managers' linguistic repertoire as opposed to those of non-managerial workers. Within the context of his class work, Henry was positioned to go over his English homework with his manager and, during team meetings set in an actual classroom, to literally sit in the seat of students. These conditions reinforced the labor hierarchy by emphasizing English as the institutional language and positioning workers like Henry as learners. These conditions contrasted how Henry constructed himself in his videos as an inventor and teacher. Henry's home-based workplace videos highlight how institutional monolingual ideologies, not Henry's linguistic repertoire, created barriers for him to express his knowledge in the university.

A home- and community-based approach to workplace literacy makes evident how, even within university conditions that deny Henry a knowledgeable status, he uses his literate repertoire to negotiate his professional knowledge across contexts. One day while waiting for a crew team meeting to begin, Calley noticed Henry sitting at a table in the front row with a piece of cardboard in his hand. Calley asked him what it was. He walked over to her seat and held up an empty light bulb container, bending down to her level and resting the container on the table in front of her. He pointed to the wattage number explaining that the university was wasting a lot of electricity because they were using the wrong kind of light bulbs. He had brought bulbs that would save the university money and was planning to show John, the manager. Just like he had used the video to teach Calley and drew the circuit to teach the electrician, he would use the container as a multimodal teaching tool to educate John, another monolingual English speaker. This, again, shows his linguistic wealth on multiple levels. It shows the rhetorical awareness and multimodal translation work (Gonzales) he uses to draw upon materials and embodiment to make his point clear to his audience. While he could not carry his innovations in their entirety into the institutional workplace, he used the lightbulb container as a literacy prop to teach and benefit his workplace. He leveraged his professional knowledge and experience so that he could demonstrate it within a workplace where conditions so often denied him the ability to do so.

Henry's experience shows the importance of expanding workplace literacies to include those that, because of white English supremacy, cannot always be expressed in workplaces like educational institutions. To fully appreciate Henry's literate repertoires and desires in the workplace, we argue, his workplace literacies should be read through those he practices at home. From his home workspace, Henry illuminates his vast linguistic and professional wealth and how workplace conditions shape the extent to which he can share his experience and knowledge. The literacies he shared from home function to challenge the identities and literacies the institution constructs for him. While inequitable socioeconomic and ideological forces continue to shape experiences of workplace literacy, Henry's work at home positions home as an important site of workplace literacy that exists outside of the institutional gaze. His experience also encourages teachers, researchers, and employers to seek opportunities for working people to engage their full literate repertoires and define for themselves the workspaces and literacies they want to use across contexts.

Alfonso: Storytelling at Church

Similar to the way Henry utilizes his home context to engage in his desired literate practices and purposes, Alfonso pursues his chosen literacies within the context of his church community. In this section, we discuss how Alfonso leverages his religious community-context to engage in storytelling practices as a part of his broader life work. Then we explain how his university work conditions deny him opportunities to act on those particular desires. Alfonso's experiences extend Latinx studies that have highlighted storytelling as a specifical cultural and linguistic strength for Latinx peoples (Yosso; Farr; Hurtig amongst others), by showing how his religious storytelling could also be an important workplace literacy practice that potentially improves people's experience of work. Alfonso's desire and talent for storytelling have important implications for how he can connect to others and serve his life's purpose across the contexts of his life—including his university work. The section demonstrates how Alfonso's community-based literacies provide insight into his work experience because, through their absence, we can better understand the limitations of his university workplace conditions and what he might need from those conditions instead.

Alfonso sees his storytelling as a vehicle for teaching people how to pursue a good life. He explained how, in his youth in Mexico, he would "hang out with the elderly men" during community occasions like wakes or around school meetings and "they would start to tell stories, different stories, and I enjoyed listening to them." He was particularly drawn to stories with drama and danger. As he listened to these stories, he would often think about how storytellers told stories, including the different moves and choices they made and the thoughtfulness that they put into them. He began to identify as a storyteller when he realized how his stories affected others and that he could use storytelling to help people choose better "life paths." He described how, as a child, he used La Llorona—a Latin American folktale about a grieving ghost mother dressed in white—to teach other children not to be mischievous or harmful. The tale of La Llorona is vastly popular in Latin American culture and is often used by parents or adults to scare children and get them to listen or change their ways. Alfonso begins his story by describing how he convinced his cousin to help him teach other children a lesson,

> "Those kids, we are going to get rid of them because they are killing the turtle doves, and the morning doves, and we are going to scare them." And he asked me, "But how?" "No, you, you don't worry about that. I know how." We went up, there was a tree, a tree known as socono, a tree that is always good. When they were about to kill the doves, we jumped out at them with the sheets and the wind blew the sheets up and we started to scream, "oh my children." And the kids were frightened. They were going to hit us with the slingshots, but they just froze. The slingshots fell to the ground. They dropped the slingshots and stones. And it was very windy and there was a thunder of trees and branches. And we were like, "Bye my children. They killed all the small animals. They will not leave them in peace." They took off flying (Alfonso laughs). Then we got down from the tree. We got in front of

them and… it was dark. The next day at school we heard them telling others, "The other night, the Llorona appeared to us. She appeared to us. We went to the doves." And they began to tell their friends. "At night, the Llorona appeared to us. We went to kill doves to eat and the Llorona appeared to us. And we left, we came running home. We are not going back."

Here, Alfonso expressed his skill and passion for storytelling both by extending the tale of the Llorona and through his theatrical retelling of the event. In the retelling, Alfonso built suspense by withholding details of his plan until he jumps out of the tree and in his description of the boys freezing and that "The slingshots fell to the ground." He embedded symbols of goodness like the tree and the doves which emphasized the underlying themes. Laughter was audible in his voice as he shared how his friends would always say "Tu tienes unas historias que dan risa, dan alegría" (You have stories that make us laugh, that give joy). The word *tienes* indicates the stories belong to Alfonso to which he responds, "yo tengo historias buenas que contar" (I have good stories to tell). Overall, this instance reflects Alfonso's desire to use storytelling for purposes of justice in the world—to right wrongs and put people on what he considers to be the right path. He draws on the cultural tale of the Llorona to teach the boys a lesson. This instance reflects how, for him, storytelling is a deeply social act that has the potential to impact his communities for the better.

As an adult in the US, Alfonso's church has become a space where he can use his literacies to tell stories that impact his community.[3] This context gives him an opportunity to tell his story because his church community expresses how they value his knowledge and experience. In Alfonso's church, like many Latinx Protestant churches, there is a calling for believers to share the good news with others. Using one's testimony, lived experiences, especially those before coming to know God, is strongly encouraged. This work gives Alfonso an opportunity to make use of lived experience to teach others. Alfonso specifically explained how the church leaders and members recognized and valued his ideas. During Bible study, he said, the leaders asked his opinions and really listened to his response. They encouraged him to write and share his life history. And when Alfonso did give testimony in church, he felt "awe" from the audience and received positive feedback during and after he shared. Thus, the church awarded a platform for storytelling and, importantly, an audience who was moved by his testimony. These experiences demonstrate how, for Alfonso, his storytelling practice is about more than speaking—it is about being heard and affecting an audience. Much like his storytelling as a child, Alfonso hopes to use his life story as a means of inspiring others to choose a better path. He wants to achieve this purpose by drawing connections and a sense of unity between him and his audience. He evokes a definition of testimony that relies on a reader or listener with whom to share, and ultimately, to establish solidarity. For Alfonso, this work expresses the message of testimonio: that "I am you," (Beverly), or in his own words, "If I can survive, you can survive too." Alfonso's storytelling is driven by this message—a message that proves to be essential for understanding his experience of literacy across the contexts of his life.

Alfonso's experiences telling his life stories at church provide insight into his university workplace experiences and how workplace conditions limit his ability to live out his broader life's work. University workplace structures and conditions specifically undermine his position of storyteller by limiting his identity. Several institutional conditions stripped Alfonso of his broader identities and largely reduced him to his labor. For example, during new staff training, new members of the custodial staff were told to introduce themselves their shift, their crew number, and the name of their manager before their own names. This position associated workers with their immediate labor and direct supervisor while alienating them from their individual identities. And this alienation was compounded when, each team meeting, his manager explained substitutions by naming whose run or route a worker would be completing. Rather than describing the space they would clean, he said that Alfonso would *be* the absent worker. For example, if Alfonso were covering Henry's area, he would say, "Alfonso, you are Henry today." This messaging suggested that, for the institution, Alfonso's identity was interchangeable with Henry's. Alfonso expanded on this observation saying, "A lot of people have brought that up--that we should have substitutes," because custodial staff that assume another worker's responsibilities are still only compensated for a single person's work. As Alfonso explained, on one hand, these systems sent the message that he was exchangeable and even less than human. What mattered was the work, not the person doing it. And on the other, it positioned him as more than one person because he was both Alfonso and Henry. Constructed as both sub-human and super-human, these conditions threated the common humanity he sought to convey through his stories.

In contrast to his experiences at church, Alfonso's work conditions made him feel like his knowledge and experience did not matter and these conditions ultimately impacted how he could fulfill his role as a storyteller. Alfonso called Lupe and Calley one day because he wanted to include a specific instance in the article. He had been on a one-week vacation and returned to work with much more work because the person who had replaced him had not done his work correctly. Alfonso went to HR and told them they needed to talk to supervisors about this, but he felt like no one was really listening to him. He explained how this reflected a larger institutional problem of creating "more rules and less training" for custodial staff as well as a consistent feeling of not being heard when they asked for change. For Alfonso, this instance made him feel like the university did not care what he knew or what he thought because they believed he could be replaced by someone who could not complete the work. These conditions, he explained, reminded him the university views him as the lowest rank of labor. These dehumanizing conditions denied Alfonso the role of storyteller because, for Alfonso, that role required having a human story to tell.

Institutional conditions and hierarchies also prevented Alfonso from fulfilling his role as storyteller by restricting contact and connection with his potential audiences. Like most custodial staff at this institution, Alfonso works in the evenings and such regulations around time segregated him from students, faculty, and staff who work during the day. Similarly, university conditions require him to work alone and thus segregate him from other custodial staff who work on his crew. These conditions prevent Alfonso from talking to his colleagues who speak Spanish or English outside of the daily team meetings—even on breaks. In addition, institutional policies prevent him from using both his personal phone and any institutional phone in an office or institutional building without permission. He was also prohibited from using personal or institutional computers outside of work or break time. In new staff training, custodial staff are discouraged from leaving the building during shifts because doors upon exiting the buildings. Without access to keys and phones, it is difficult to arrange for others to open doors. These restrictions further limit Alfonso's contact with audiences beyond the institution and reify boundaries between within- and outside-of- university work contexts. By isolating workers from their stories and audiences outside of the university, these university literacy conditions support exploitative labor systems that define workers like Alfonso by their labor alone.

By sharing experiences at home and in his church context, Alfonso demonstrates how literacies allow him to express connections to his broader history and life's purpose. At the same time, these experiences also provide insight into how institutional conditions prevent him from drawing upon his repertoire in ways that separate him from his human story, his audience, and his role as storyteller. Examining Alfonso's experience of work at the university through his home and community-based literacy practices exposes how the absence of his desired literacies shape his experience of university work.

Looking Beyond the Institution

Extending a long history of Latinx scholarship, Henry's and Alfonso's experiences urge writing studies researchers to center home- and community-based literacies in workplace literacy studies by reading literacies that take place in the context of work through the lens of workers' broader lives. Within economic systems that exploit racialized workers and privilege English and practices associated with white middle-class culture, a home- and community-based approach to workplace writing exposes literacies that have been overlooked, undervalued, and misunderstood when researchers, teachers, and employers in higher education focus on workplaces alone. Additionally, this approach offers a way to bring community and workplace literacy studies into conversation to help people who work carry the literacies that matter to them across the contexts of their daily lives. While scholars invested in community literacy have long argued for more connection between classroom-, home-, and community-based literacies, in this article, we argue that workplaces are also an important context to apply that framework. We argue a home- and community-based approach to workplace literacy provides important possibilities for creating workplace literacy conditions that allow people to integrate their innovations and even miracles into their work experiences.

Supporting workers' literacies across contexts directly challenges systems of oppression that position people as labor so this kind of shift would require higher education institutions to stop dehumanizing and exploiting workers. The systemic nature of these problems encourages Alfonso and Henry to direct their literacy energies outside of the university workspace. Following their lead, Lupe and Calley have supported their home- and community-based efforts such as helping Alfonso share this article and broader testimonio with his church community. That is not to say that university spaces cannot be informed by this scholarship—they can and should be. Universities can start by asking participants in positions like custodial staff about the literacies they desire to practice and build space and conditions for them to practice those literacies regardless of institutional benefit. For Alfonso and Henry to practice the literacies they desire like their innovations and personal stories, the university would need systems and cultural shifts that position them as university actors with valuable knowledge to share. That would require systems that cultivate communication and trust between participants and engaged and receptive university actors. These conditions ultimately require all university actors including administrators, faculty, students, and staff to challenge the white English supremacy embedded in university culture that undermines these just literacy conditions.

Acknowledgements

We would like to thank the editors of *CLJ* for allowing us to write together while maintaining Alfonso's anonymity. Thank you to the anonymous reviewers and the copyeditors who helped us clarify our conceptual approach and supported our work toward just methodologies.

Alfonso-thanks to Calley and Lupe.

Lupe- I am grateful to Calley and Alfonso for their dedication to this article. I am so grateful to get to write with them. Thank you to the editors and reviewers of the *Community Literacy Journal* for their helpful feedback. Finally, thank you to my husband Marcus and daughter Josie Amelia for always being there to support me in every way possible.

Calley-thanks to this article's writers and participants for sharing their expertise, experiences, and friendship. Thank you to Kate Vieira for your continual support, Ana Vanesa Hidalgo Del Rosario for early interpreting and translating, Gabrielle Kelenyi and Eileen Lagman for reading, listening, and encouragement, Beth Godbee and Anjuli Fahlberg for insights about methodological equity, and Ryan Hall and Traci Salazar for Ella's brilliant care.

Notes

1. Here we are distinguishing formal from informal work taking place within homes and communities but outside of sanctioned and recognized formal US economies.

2. Following recent work by Garcia and Delgado Bernal, we do not want to romanticize or idealize home which is often the site of gender-based inequity. Rather we are arguing it is an important site to examine to better understand participants' workplace literacy experiences.

3. Transnational literacy studies have demonstrated how church spaces can be spaces to establish literate and professional identities for immigrants who are often denied that status in other institutions. See Vieira.

Works Cited

Alvarez, Steven. *Community Literacies en Confianza: Learning from Bilingual After-School Programs*. National Council of Teachers of English, 2017.

—. "Literacy." *Decolonizing Rhetoric and Composition Studies: New Latinx Keywords for Theory and Pedagogy*, edited by Iris D. Ruiz and Raúl Sánchez, Palgrave Macmillan, 2016, pp. 17-29.

Beverly, John. *Testimonio: On the Politics of Truth*. University of Minnesota Press, 2004.

Brandt, Deborah. *The Rise of Writing: Redefining Mass Literacy*. Cambridge University Press, 2015.

Byrd, Antonio. "Between Learning and Opportunity: A Study of African American Adult Coders' Networks of Support." *Literacy in Composition Studies*, vol. 7, no. 2, 2019, pp. 31-55.

Canagarajah, Suresh A. "The Place of World Englishes in Composition: Pluralization Continued." *College Composition and Communication*, vol. 57, 2006, pp. 586-619.

Cardinal, Alison. "Participatory Video: An Apparatus for Ethically Researching Literacy, Power, and Embodiment." *Computers and Composition*, vol. 53, 2019, pp. 34-46.

Cintron, Ralph. *Angels' Town: Chero Ways, Gang Life, and Rhetorics of the Everyday*. Beacon, 1997.

Delgado Bernal, Dolores. "Learning and Living Pedagogies of the Home: The Mestiza Consciousness of Chicana Students." *Qualitative Studies in Education*, vol. 14, no. 5, 2001, pp. 623-639.

Elenes, Alejandra C. "Transformando Fronteras: Chicana Feminist Transformative Pedagogies." edited by Dolores Delgado Bernal, Alejandra C. Elenes, Francisca E. Godinez, and Sofia Villenas, State University of New York Press, 2001, pp. 245-259.

Farr, Marcia. *Rancheros in Chicagoacán: Language and Identity in a Transnational Community*. University of Texas Press, 2006.

Farrell, Lesley. "Texting the Future: Work, Literacies, and Economies." *The Future of Literacy Studies*, edited by Mike Baynham and Mastin Prisloo, Palgrave McMillan, 2009, pp.181-198.

Findlay, Elisa. "When Writers Aren't Authors: A Qualitative Study of Unattributed Writers." *College English*, vol. 81 no. 5, 2019, pp. 432-456.

Flores, Barbara. "The Intellectual Presence of the Deficit View of Spanish-Speaking Children in the Educational Literature During the 20th Century." *Latino Education: An Agenda for Community Action Research*, edited by Pedro Pedraza and Melissa Rivera, Lawrence Erlbaum Publishers, 2005, pp.75-98.

Fine, Michelle. *Just Research in Contentious Times: Widening the Methodological Imagination*. Teacher's College Press, 2017.

Garcia, Nichole M., and Delores Delgado Bernal. "Remembering and Revisiting Pedagogies of the Home." *American Educational Research Journal*, vol. 58, no. 3, 2020, pp. 567-601.

García, Romeo, and Damián Baca, editors. *Rhetorics Elsewhere and Otherwise: Contested Modernities, Decolonial Visions*. NCTE, Conference on College Composition and Communication Studies Writing and Rhetoric, 2019.

Gomez, Alan. "Colleges Brace to Shield Students from Immigration Raids." *USA Today*, Jan. 2017. https://www.usatoday.com/story/news/2017/01/26/colleges-universities-shield-students-immigration-deportation-raids/96968540/.

Gonzales, Laura. *Sites of Translation: What Multilinguals Can Teach Us About Digital Writing and Rhetoric*. University of Michigan Press, 2017.

González, Norma, et al. "Funds of Knowledge for Teaching Latino Households," *Urban Education*, vol. 29, no. 4, 1995, pp. 443-470.

Guerra, Juan. C. *Close to Home: Oral and Literate Practices in a Transnational Mexicano Community*. Teachers College Press, 1998.

Guerra, Juan. C., and Marcia Farr. "Writing on the Margins: The Spiritual and Autobiographical Discourse of Two Mexicanas in Chicago." *School's Out!: Literacy at Home, at Work, and in the Community*, edited by Glynda Hall & Kathy Schultz, Teachers College Press, 2002, pp. 96-123.

Haas, Christina, and Stephen Witte. "Writing as an Embodied Practice: The Case of Engineering Standards." *Journal of Business and Technical Communication*, vol. 15, 2001, pp. 413–57.

Hagan, Jacqueline, et al. *Skills of the Unskilled: Work and Mobility among Mexican Immigrants*. University of California Press, 2015.

Heath, Shirley Brice. *Ways with Words: Language, Life, and Work in Communities and Classrooms*. Cambridge University Press, 1983.

Hull, Glynda. "What's in a Label? Complicating Notions of the Skills-Poor Worker." *Written Communication*, vol. 16, no. 4, 1999, pp. 379-411.

Hurtig, Janise. "Storytelling, or the Cultural Construction of Writers in a Mexican Immigrant Neighborhood." *Latino Language and Literacy in Ethnolinguistic Chicago*, edited by Marcia Farr, Routledge, 2005.

Ibarra, Armando, Carlos, Alfredo, Torres, D. Rodolfo. *The Latino Question: Politics, Labouring Classes, and The Next Left*. Pluto Press, 2018.

Immigrant Legal Resource Center, National Immigrant Justice Center and the National Immigration Law Center. "Funding for ICE Homeland Security Investigations (HSIs) is Funding for Trump's Anti-Immigrant Agenda," April 2019. https://www.nilc.org/issues/immigration-enforcement/hsi-backgrounder-webpage/.

Iwama, Janice A. "Understanding Hate Crimes Against Immigrants: Considerations for Future Research." *Sociology Compass*. vol.12 no. 3, 2017, pp. 1-10.

Kalmar, Tomás Mario. *Illegal Alphabets and Adult Literacy: Latino Migrants Crossing the Linguistic Border*. Routledge, 2000.

Koningstein, Manon, and Shadi Azadegan. "Participatory Video for Two-Way Communication in Research for Development." *Action Research*, vol. #, 2008, pp. 1-19.

Lam, Wan Shun Eva. "Literacy and Capital in Immigrant Youths Online Networks Across Countries." *Learning, Media and Technology*, vol. 39, 2014, pp. 488-506.

Lauer, Claire, and Eva Brumberger. "Redefining Writing for the Responsive Workplace." *College Composition and Communication*, vol. 70, no. 4, 2019, pp. 634-662.

Lorimer Leonard, Rebecca. *Literacy on the Move: Migrant Women and the Value of Literacy*. U of Pittsburgh Press, 2017.

Leander, Kevin, and Gail Bolt. "Re-Reading 'A Pedagogy of Multiliteracies': Bodies, Text, and Emergence." *Journal of Literacy Research*, vol. 45, no. 1, 2013. pp. 22-46.

Molina, Natalia. *How Race is Made in America: Immigration, Citizenship, and The Historical Power of Racial Scripts*. University of California Press, 2014.

Marko, Tamara, et al., "PROYECTO CARRITO When the Student Receives an 'A' and the Worker gets Fired: Disrupting the Unequal Political Economy of Translingual Rhetorical Mobility." *Literacy in Composition Studies*, vol. 3, no. 1, 2015, pp. 21–43.

Marotta, Calley. "Nonregulated Writing: A Qualitative Study of University Custodial Staff Literacies." *Research in the Teaching of English*, vol. 55, no. 3, 2021, pp. 289-310.

Marcus, George E. "Multi-Sited Ethnography: Notes and Queries." *Multisited Ethnography: Theory, Praxis, and Locality in Contemporary Research*, edited by Mark-Anthony Falzon, Ashgate Publishing, 2009, pp. 181-196.

Martinez, Ramón, et al. "Found in Translation: Connecting Translation Experiences to Academic Writing." *Language Arts*, vol. 85, no. 6, pp. 421-431.

Nordquist, Brice. *Literacy and Mobility: Complexity, Uncertainty, and Agency at the Nexus of High School and College*. Expanding Literacy in Education Series. Routledge, 2017.

Pacheco, Mariana. "Learning In/Through Everyday Resistance: A Cultural Historical Perspective on Community Resources and Curriculum." *Educational Researcher*, vol. 41, no. 4, 2012, pp. 121-132.

Pahl, Kate, and Jennifer Roswell. *Artifactual Literacies: Every Object Tells a Story*. Teachers College Press, 2010.

Paris, Django, and Maisha T. Winn, editors. *Humanizing Research: Decolonizing Qualitative Inquiry with Youth and Communities*, Sage Publications, 2014, pp. 223-249.

Patel, Leigh. *Decolonizing Educational Research: From Ownership to Answerability*. Routledge, 2015.

Prior, Paul, and Jody Shipka. "Chronotopic Lamination: Tracing the Contours of Literate Activity." *Writing Selves/Writing Societies: Research from Activity Perspectives*, edited by Charles Bazerman and David R. Russell. WAC Clearinghouse, 2003, pp. 180-238.

Ríos, Gabriela Raquel. "Cultivating Land-Based Literacies and Rhetorics." *Literacy in Composition Studies*. Special Issue: The New Activism, edited by Steve Parks, Ben Kuebrich, and Jessica Pauszek. March 2015, pp. 60-70.

Robinson, Cedric J. *Black Marxism: The Making of the Black Radical Tradition*. The University of North Carolina Press, 2005.

Rose, Mike. *The Mind at Work: Valuing the Intelligence of the American Worker*. Viking, 2004.

Rosenbaum, Mark. "Pseudonyms to Protect Authors of Controversial Articles." *BBC News*. 12 November, 2018. https://www.bbc.com/news/education-46146766.

Ruiz, Iris, et al. *Race, Rhetoric, and Research Methods*. WACClearing House, 2021.

Saldaña, Johnny. *The Coding Manual for Qualitative Researchers*. Sage, 2012.

Smith, Linda Tuhiwai. "Decolonizing Methodologies: Research and Indigenous Peoples." 3rd ed. Bloomsbury Press, 2021.

Spinuzzi, Clay. *Network: Theorizing Knowledge Work in Telecommunications*. Cambridge University Press, 2008.

Tuck, Eve. "Suspending Damage: A Letter to Communities." *Harvard Educational Review*, vol. 79, no. 3, 2009, pp. 409-427.

Tuck, Eve, and Wayne K. Yang. "R-Words Refusing Research." *Humanizing Research: Decolonizing Qualitative Inquiry with Youth and Communities*, edited by Django Paris and Maisha T. Winn, Sage Publications, 2014, pp. 223-249.

Vieira, Kate. "'American by Paper': Assimilation and Documentation in a Biliterate Bi-Ethnic Immigrant Community." *College English*, vol 73, no. 1, 2010, pp. 50-72.

Vigoroux, Cecil. B. "Rethinking (Un)skilled Immigrants: Whose Skills, What Skills, for What, and for Whom?" *The Routledge Handbook of Migration and Language*, edited by Suresh Canagarajah, Routledge, 2017, pp. 312-329.

Vossoughi, Shirin, and Kris Gutiérrez. "Studying Movement, Hybridity and Change: Toward a Multi-Sited Sensibility for Research on Learning Across Contexts and Borders." *National Society for the Study of Education*, vol. 113, no. 2, 2014, pp. 603-632.

Wardle, Elizabeth. "Identity, Authority, and Learning to Write in New Workplaces." *Enculturation*, vol. 5, no. 2, 2004. http://enculturation.gmu.edu/5_2/wardle.html.

Winsor, Dorothy A. *Writing Power: Communication in an Engineering Center*. SUNY Press, 2003.

Yosso, Tara. "Whose Culture has Capital? A Critical Race Theory Discussion of Community Cultural Wealth." *Race, Ethnicity, and Education*, vol. 8, no. 1, 2005, pp. 69-91.

Zepeda, Candace. "Chicana Feminism." *Decolonizing Rhetoric and Composition Studies: New Latinx Keywords for Theory and Pedagogy*, edited by Iris D. Ruiz and Raúl Sánchez, Palgrave Macmillan, 2016, pp. 137-152.

Author Bios

Guadalupe Remigio Ortega (she/her) is a PhD candidate at the University of Wisconsin-Madison where she also serves as Senior Assistant Director of English 100, UW-Madison's first-year writing program. Her research focuses on indigenous (Mixtec) literacies and knowledge, border and migrant rhetorics, and oral histories. Her current project is a collection of oral histories and testimonios of Mixtec migrant farmworkers in Fresno, California whose traditional and non-traditional literacy practices demonstrate the complexities of Mixtec literacies and how these, alongside the intersectionality of Mixtec identity in the United States, challenge current dominant discourses on literacy, illiteracy, and non-literacy.

Alfonso Guzman Gomez (he/him) is a man of faith and family. He is a proud father and grandfather. He is a storyteller and an active member of his church community.

Dr. Calley Marotta (she/her) is a writing teacher, researcher, and mother who works as a Teaching Assistant Professor at the University of Denver. Her teaching and research focus on writing and linguistic justice. Her scholarship has appeared in *College English*, *Research in the Teaching of English*, and *Inside Higher Education* and has been supported by the Spencer Foundation. She is grateful to the theorists, teachers, and students who guide her work.

The Rules of the Road: Negotiating Literacies in a Community Driving Curriculum

Rebecca Lorimer Leonard and Danielle Pappo

Abstract

This article is an ethnographic case study of a community literacy project that teaches immigrants to the U.S. how to get their driver's licenses. The article shows how perceptions of literacy change when project participants encounter the "rules of the road"—unspoken rules that are highly social, deeply embodied, and usually pitched by the powerful as clear, neutral, and necessary for survival. Based on qualitative analysis of written materials and interviews gathered during the project, we demonstrate how the community project activated analogic thinking about literacy. That is, realizing that driving rules are negotiable leads learners to realize that literacy rules are negotiable, too.

Keywords

community literacy, immigrants, literacy studies, mobility studies, multilingualism

In studies of immigrant literacy, driving is a quiet but persistent presence: immigrants in the U.S. describe the "textual vulnerability of driving" without documentation (Vieira 131); students discuss the pressures of unwarranted traffic tickets (Auerbach et al.); a custodian-college writing collaborative drives their autobiographies around town—printed and wrapped on a minivan—when the student newspaper won't print their writing (Marko et al.). These studies show that the practice of driving often inserts itself into immigrants' literate experiences, with repercussions for literacy users' papers, status, or bodies. This article proceeds from the center of this phenomenon, asking how driving shapes immigrants' literate experiences. Drawing on an ethnographic case study of a community literacy driving project, we show how perceptions of literacy change when project participants encounter the "rules of the road"—the unspoken social and literate rules that regulate literacies in the car and on the streets.

The "rules of the road" were brought to our attention at the start of our partnership with a community language school, whose students in a free English program for immigrants and refugees asked for literacy support in earning driver's licenses. In an initial interview about the driving project, a school staff member, Kathy,[1] explained that their students needed to learn about driving in the U.S. because she believed they had "trouble acknowledging the rules of the road." She explained:

> [In] different countries, people have different styles of driving, different rules—or they have no rules, which were getting in the way of them successfully driving here…You have to respect the rules, even though you think they might be stupid. We all have rules in this country that we think are stupid, but if we don't follow them, we are going to get stopped, get a ticket… They think they can negotiate; there's no negotiation.

In this staff member's understanding, driving rules are necessary for success, safety, order, and fairness; lack of rules seems to invite disorder and danger. However, our immersion in curricular design and subsequent study of the curriculum shows that road rules are saturated in complexity, with negotiation at their very center. The deployment and acceptance of rules depends on who wields and receives them; a driving context of "no rules," in fact, indicates *other* rules, often implicit and culturally normed. Thus, the "rules of the road" are belief systems through which literacy users must physically move. This means that the "rules of the road" refer to the systems of both driving *and* literacy being learned: both are highly social, deeply embodied, and usually pitched by the powerful as clear, neutral, and necessary for survival.

This article explores how negotiating driving rules leads participants to a more complex understanding of literacy, asking: What are the rules of the road? How do literacy users resist, negotiate, or change these rules? How does making literacy mobile—literally putting it on the road—shape understandings of literacy itself? Based on qualitative analysis of written project materials and interviews with project participants, we argue that the curriculum activates analogic thinking about literacy through driving. That is, realizing that driving rules are negotiable leads participants to realize that literacy rules are negotiable, too. In the sections below, we explain the driving project in full, describe our qualitative study of it, and share analytic findings that respond to each of our research questions in turn. Each section narrates the process by which project participants come to recognize rules, and then manipulate them.

A Community Driving Curriculum

Our article draws on a study of an ongoing community literacy partnership between the University of Massachusetts Amherst and the International Language Institute of Massachusetts (ILI).[2] Over four years, the partnership has engaged in several literacy projects, including the driving curriculum that is the subject of this article. Throughout the partnership, literacy projects have been guided by models of community literacy that de-center universities as the locus of language and literacy expertise, build coalitional energy at the community school, and work toward a shared vision of social change (Campano et al.; Mitchell). When ILI requested the driving curriculum, curriculum designers were drawn from Lorimer Leonard's community-engaged course that introduces undergraduates to literacy studies through the lens of language diversity.[3]

ILI's immigrant students expressed wanting a driving curriculum for reasons both pragmatic and political. Students knew that driving offers access to medical care, community classes, and events at children's schools. They also knew that living in a car-dependent region often means that "people who drive are more likely to find jobs, work more hours, and earn higher wages" (Hendricks 2). In other words, they knew well that physical mobility and social mobility are linked, with driving independence often leading to better jobs, schooling, or community support (Kerr et al.). Beyond these pragmatic motivations, students' literacy work, such as poster projects displayed in school hallways, showed that they also were aware of local advocacy around the Work & Family Mobility Act, which grants undocumented people access to driver's licenses.[4] Such advocacy efforts assert that driver's licenses ensure public safety on roads, support immigrants' economic contributions, and positively affect immigrant families' well-being (Amuedo-Dorantes et al.). Given the political moment (2018-2020) immigrant students also may have experienced a heightened racialization of their status under Trump's 2017 Executive Order on immigration, which made driving without a license a deportable offense and linked it to racial profiling.

In later stages of curriculum development, the COVID-19 pandemic made access to a car unusually important, wherein car use became differently consequential: social protests were conducted as car parades; drive-throughs were created for virus testing and vaccinations; choir rehearsals and political rallies took place by sitting on top of cars; vehicles became sanctuary for frontline workers or office space for working parents with children at home. Access to driving became more necessary for anyone wanting to engage in advocacy, social life, or healthcare. In asking for help in getting their licenses, then, ILI's students anticipated the kaleidoscope of literacy and language knowledge necessary to earn a license in this time and place. Therefore, during the fraught social conditions of 2018-2020, the driving curriculum evolved as project participants collaborated on curricular content and structure. As undergraduate participants read, wrote, and discussed literacy research and theory, ILI's staff and teachers met regularly with them, brainstorming together what a driving curriculum should include and why. While the project never aimed to eulogize a car culture that may be receding amidst climate change, or uncritically enact narratives of car-based freedom, it became clear that a politically pragmatic approach to driving meant treating driving literacies as more than speed limits and traffic signs.

Studying Driving Literacies

Even in early stages of the project, discussions of a driving curriculum revealed surprisingly complex notions of literacy. This complexity echoes across research on driving in the field of mobility studies, which frames driving as a multi-layered phenomenon in which bodies, feelings, and objects are "kinaesthetically intertwined" (Sheller 226-227). Driving requires a "disciplined 'driving body'" because drivers' "eyes, ears, hands, and feet, [are] trained to respond instantaneously and consistently" (Urry). Drivers enact civility like turn-taking through hand waves; incivility is enacted through rude gestures sometimes proudly expressed. Car communication expressed via the body like the hand wave or signal flash can involve heightened emotion, such as "anger at assumed rule-breakers," and can thus demand "the capacity to read" gestures and codes of politeness (Featherstone 12).

Because driving is "tied to patterns of gender expression, racial and ethnic distinction...national identity and transnational processes" (Sheller 236), judgments of driving norms and resulting behavior are highly gendered (Murray), racialized (Purifoye), and culturally negotiable (Redshaw and Nicoll). For example, urban sociologist Gwendolyn Purifoye notes that "even as low-income Blacks and Latinx do travel on what limited systems they do have" their movement through cities is "controlled by others through policies and rules" and "they are continually reminded that their time and comfort are of little importance to those outside their communities" (496). Such rules discipline movement across space as well as languages: in this study, participants often described racialized experiences of driving in terms of language, as when they felt judged by white listeners' assumptions of their communicative abilities. Negotiating such judgments requires literacies beyond the memorization of car parts and street signs.

The sociomateriality of driving also suggests why driving literacies are complex (Hamilton; Rowsell and Pahl; Vieira). Connecting the social nature of literacy—cultural practices, value systems—to its material—bodies, tools, artifacts, environments—suggests that the complexity of driving may be found not only in literacy learners' use of a license or car, but also in the way those materials are "endowed with energy and agency" that shapes what users can do with them (Micciche 497). For example, driver's licenses empower drivers, but social institutions determine what that empowerment means, granting primary power to the license, not to the driver. This "diffuse, unstable" relationship between literate material, literacy user, and literacy-regulating institution shows why driving literacies need to account for the complex agencies among things, people, and possibilities (Micciche 491).

Therefore, in trying to make sense of how the driving curriculum shaped participants' literacy learning, we designed an ethnographic case study to understand how the literate complexity of this driving project, including its sociopolitical conditions, shaped understandings of literacy more generally (Dyson and Genishi). Our use of case study also sought to trace how social forces and contextual conditions shaped individual participants' experiences and perceptions of literacy. In terms of driving, this meant understanding how increasing xenophobia, shifting economic conditions, and pandemic-era isolation shaped how participants understood the seemingly routine task of learning to drive. It's important to emphasize that "participants" here means everyone involved: undergraduate and community students, graduate student tutors, community and college teachers. All of these literacy users offer insight into how mobility shapes literacy because their differing positionalities cause them to move through the world in differing ways.

In pursuit of this understanding, we collected two types of data: textual artifacts such as unit and lesson drafts, curriculum meetings notes, and written reflections about the curriculum from 12 participants; and semi-structured interviews with undergraduate curriculum designers (n=3), grad student curriculum tutors (n=2), and ILI students (n=3) and staff (n=3). We also conducted one interview with a local driving instructor who is an immigrant to the U.S. for his insights into the multilingual communication that occurs during driving lessons and exams. Collected textual data tracked participants' sense-making in process, while interviews sought to elicit participants' recollections of how a driving "event in the present is informed by an ontological and/or discursive event in the past" (Merriman and Pearce 503). As researchers, our positionalities are distinct from some participants—as white, middle-class women, we likely experience driving in the U.S. in less marked ways than others—but our positions in the project also are enmeshed with participants': we taught the course and designed the curriculum alongside participants. Our analysis below is thus shaped and limited by our close and far proximity to participants' experiences of driving literacies.

Data Analysis

Our data analysis was structured through rounds of thematic and focused coding that sought to respond to our three research questions: 1) What are the rules of the road? 2) How do literacy users resist, negotiate, or change these rules? 3) How does making literacy mobile—literally putting it on the road—shape understandings of literacy itself? Each coding round was collaborative, wherein coding was conducted independently by each author and then refined through discussion.

To answer our first research question, we used deductive codes that simply cataloged different driving, writing, or language "rules." To respond to question two, we used inductive codes that characterized participants' lived experience of the driving curriculum, often in their own terms. The consistent coding of emotion, affect, and embodiment was a topic of discussion across rounds; we often used the terms and theory of affect to code the complex lived and felt experience of learning to drive. Our conversations that compared codes helped us distill them into four categories: literacy rules, mobility rules, rules of the road, and discernment. Along the way, we generated memos to make sense of how participants' literate experiences (question 2) impacted how they understood literate rules (question 1). Finally, a round of focused coding attended to our third research question: How does making literacy mobile—literally putting it on the road—shape understandings of literacy itself? Coding just for "understandings of literacy" showed us that our "discernment" category was too limited. While "discernment" had followed Lagman's use of "emotional discernment" to gather participants' critical stances toward "existing structures and ways of being" (Lagman 12-13), our analysis showed that participants' ongoing rule-breaking and making was less receptive and more active.

To make sense of this strong feature our coding left us with—namely, the physicality of negotiating rules—we turned to scholarly understandings of rule negotiation in literacy and language studies. Most traditionally, "rules" in literacy and language learning are treated as guidance by which writers can avoid error. In this conception, rule-breaking means form-breaking resulting in error, whereby error is "morphological, syntactic, and lexical forms that deviate from rules of the target language, violating the expectations of literate adult native speakers" (Ferris 3). Others suggest that engagement with prescriptive and descriptive rules can serve as content in critical language learning that "allow students to engage intellectually and personally" with rules (Curzan 878; also see Delpit). Writing researchers agree that when writers unthinkingly follow rules, they do not engage with the problem-solving or creativity of composing (Dufour and Ahearn-Dodson; Rose). In fact, critical language approaches like translinguality treat writers' engagement with rules as a space where literate innovation occurs. For example, Blommaert and Horner treat rule-breaking not as "the absence of clear and applicable norms" but as "the production of new, alternative ones" that account for "innovation and creativity" (14-15). They argue that when writing is "at odds with the hegemony and therefore continually open to negative sanctioning and misrecognition," this is not a display of error but rather evidence that the "rules do not fit the system they are supposed to direct" (14).

Therefore, negotiating literate rules can be cast as innovation, but such innovations are subject to social forces that can affect their outcome, including the social positions of those engaging in rule negotiation. As Deborah Cameron notes, "the social function of the rule is not arbitrary…rules of language use often contribute to a circle of exclusion and intimidation, as those who have mastered a particular practice use it in turn to intimidate others" (12). Flores and Rosa frame this exclusion in terms of the white listening subject, challenging claims that "being told explicitly the rules of the culture makes acquiring power easier" (Delpit 24). They instead argue that acquiring power through language depends on the willingness of those in power to provide it: "rules of the culture" are not "objective linguistic practices" but are instead "ideological phenomena" (Flores and Rosa 164-165). Indeed, the participants in this study specify the "social function" of literate rules by pointing explicitly to the bodies attempting to negotiate them. That is, the rules limit the literate innovations of some bodies, but not others (Cedillo). In our findings sections below, we offer two takes on what these conditional negotiations look like in the lived experience of the driving curriculum's participants.

Breaking Rules and Making Mistakes

Common-sense understandings of writing education follow the thinking that a writer must know the rules before they break them. This linear understanding of development, in which a rule is learned and only then challenged, also applies to more than writing. For example, as driving instructor Victor said about exceeding speed limits: "First, you have to learn how to follow the rules; then you are able to break the rules if you want." Nevertheless, the relationship between rule-breaking and mistake-making was a strong theme across the study, defined by the calculus of who was allowed to break rules and whose breakage was forgiven as a mistake.

In response to our second research question—*How do literacy users resist, negotiate, or change the rules of the road*—we found that participants engaged with rules across a range of intentionality, from breaking the rules of monolingualism in lower-stakes contexts to witnessing how "broken" English rules can have higher-stakes consequences. For the undergraduate curriculum developers who spent a semester reading critical approaches to literacy and discussing how those approaches might shape a driving curriculum, their written course materials and post-course interviews were not surprisingly imbued with resistance to language rules. One undergraduate, Marissa, wrote in a class reflection that "as a person who has a high value on my own academic literacy" she came to realize that "other forms" of literacies beyond standard Englishes "count for myself and for other people too." She wrote that she doesn't "have to be as rigid" with herself or with others regarding language standards, supporting "having the freedom to break the 'rules' and say what you need to say."

Other participants negotiated literate rules for immediate social needs. For example, during driving curriculum sessions, Amare, an ILI student from Burundi and the Democratic Republic of the Congo, created what he called his multilingual driving "dictionary." Amare's tutor, Aaron, described Amare's dictionary as a "running list that [Amare] would reference constantly," which tracked driving phrases across four columns: a visual representation, a Swahili translation, a French translation, and an English phonetic pronunciation. Both a multilingual composition and a reference guide, Amare's dictionary is reminiscent of the bilingual glossaries created by multilingual migrant workers in Tomas Kalmar's ethnography, *Illegal Alphabets and Adult Biliteracy*. In Kalmar's study, the migrants' glossaries exhibited "a paradigmatic writing system, a mental chart of relations between letters and sounds in one or more known languages," created by "collecting, manipulating, and fixing new data… [materializing] the chart into a diagram, a plan" (Kalmar 90). Just as the migrants negotiated literacy learning "between two legal systems, two economies, two sovereign states, two languages," so did Amare negotiate the rules dictated by the multiplicity of driving laws, cultural norms, and languages he used to learn how to drive (77). Importantly, in Kalmar's study it is the language learning context of a classroom and a teacher that deems biliterate glossaries as breaking the rules of English-only pedagogy. Amare's dictionary provides a counter example, created in a community language learning context for the learner's immediate self-determined needs.

Similarly, the driving instructor, Victor, negotiates both driving and language rules for self-determined social needs. Having lived in Latvia, Israel, and the United States, he described himself as a multilingual, transnational driver who both does and does not mix Russian, Hebrew, Latvian, German, and English. He explains that he uses "a set of scripts" that "are all grammatical" during driving instruction but also notes that when instructing a multilingual student, they always find shared pieces of language "to [understand] each other" often having to "stray away from the script" to discuss something more. Straying from his scripts seems not only to help Victor's teaching but also to mitigate moments when, as he says, "his English needs improvement." He explains that "every time students sit next to" him in the car, he apologizes saying, "my English is not so good, so take it easy; don't pay attention too much, or if you think it is necessary, fix my mistakes." While Victor seems to be operating from a deficit perspective about his English language use, he also is creating a careful communicative context in each driving lesson: he sets the terms for negotiation by simultaneously telling students to "take it easy" and inviting them to "fix my mistakes" if they must. He initiates a language relationship wherein his instructor position maintains power that he mitigates by offering students the English upper hand. This kind of complexity—seemingly doubled approaches to mistake making and correcting—is Victor's strategy for negotiating much of the literacy necessary to teach driving.

In fact, Victor defines mistakes as the slippage between his belief that "the rules never change" and his recontextualization of those rules into "it depends." For example, he holds tight to the notion that "if you follow the rules, you save not only your life but the life of your passengers and the people around you,"—but then admits that this "depends on the person, on his ability, on her ability, to get information, to communicate, to understand what is most important." He grants that once students "have experience as this old man" they "will be able to speed or break the rules." He reiterates that passing the driving test "depends on the person":

> The inspector can be very picky. Small mistake, and [makes a choking noise] hasta la vista, baby. Sometimes, instructor doesn't pay attention on small things, but if you repeatedly make the mistake, you cannot hope to pass ... [but] it depends on the inspector when you take the test.

During the road test that Victor conjures here, rules are deployed by an examiner but performed interpersonally. Therefore, Victor seems to locate non-volatility in the rules but not in the people who enact them. The rules persist but always depend on those who take them up with their communicative abilities, including rule-negotiation.

Indeed, this relative quality—that what is deemed an error or mistake depends on the rule-breaker—echoes across participant accounts, particularly of police interactions on the road. Because mistakes frequently came up in the context of being pulled over by police, negotiating literacy mistakes included physically knowing how to place one's body, searching for the resources to reframe mistakes as something other than error, and monitoring one's emotions in hopes that the mistake wouldn't be punished. For example, Benicia, an ILI student from Guatemala, described an incident of her husband encountering the police while she was in the passenger seat:

> A few years ago, my husband was not sure about a bus stop [and asked], 'I will go, I will stop?' So he went, when a police was there, and said 'You didn't see the bus?!' He said "Yes, but you know, what is the rule?" 'The law is you have to stop!' 'I didn't know.' 'For now, it's fine, but next time, put a ticket.' That is something he didn't know ... if the law said you need to stop or not.

Benicia narrates this incident as a back-and-forth conversation between her husband and an officer. In her role as an observer, she narrates the law her husband didn't know, the negotiation between her husband and the officer, and the officer's decision to let it go "for now." Benicia's husband broke a rule, and the officer treated it as a mistake.

In contrast, Riya, an Indian American undergraduate curriculum designer, describes her mother's recalled interactions with police as emotionally intense and rule-bound, with mistakes marked as "scary":

> My dad for driving ... just always followed the rules, never got caught ... but my mom—she was telling me the first time she got into an accident, she start-

ed crying and I was in the backseat, and she didn't know what to do and she got really nervous because the police came . . . I used to always get so frustrated with her, being like, you know English. You know this protocol. Why are you stumbling? Why are you getting so flustered? Why can't you just speak normally? You know how these words work.

In her interview, Riya explains that recalling this incident while working with other participants on the driving curriculum heightened her empathy for her mother, saying that such conversations about language and literacy changed Riya's understanding "from me not wanting to understand, to, oh wow, that's like super scary, for anyone if you get into an accident, but especially when…you think someone's not gonna understand you and you made a mistake."

As Benicia and Riya's examples show, the social context of mistake-making contains distinctly uneven power relations between driver and officer, in which the officer decides what constitutes a mistake, as well heightened fear and worry stemming from not knowing the rules or the outcome of breaking them. Both Riya and Benicia are observing the scenes they describe from another seat in the car; they watch their loved ones' attempts to navigate the car even as they navigate perceived communication errors. In this context, mistakes exist along a sliding scale of consequence: sometimes "it's fine" and other times it's "scary." Knowing, as Riya says, "how these words work" gives literate dimension to how mistakes are treated. Everybody makes mistakes, but not everybody is given the same leeway.

Embodied Literacy and Racialized Rules

Participants' disparate experiences of rules often pointed them directly to, as Riya says, "The people, the people!" This means that in response to our third research question—*How does making literacy mobile shape understandings of literacy itself*—our study shows the extent to which the rules of the road are not only metaphorical, but are experienced in the body, in motion.

As Mimi Sheller notes, drivers "not only feel the car" but feel the world "through the car and with the car" (228). Driving studies show how cars place bodies—"who sits where, beside whom and with their back to whom"—in ways that condition inner car communication (Laurier et al. 9). Spatial arrangement restrained by seats and seatbelts impacts eye contact, turn-taking, topic choice and change (Laurier et al. 20). Our study concurs with mobility scholars' claims that the "bodily competencies" built by learning to drive include intertwined "motion and emotion, movement and feeling" (Kerr et al. 26; Sheller 226-227). The traumatic repetition of police killing Black drivers during traffic stops specifies such feeling to include real, imminent danger.

Data in this study show the extent to which such intense physicality and literacy learning are linked. For example, in reflecting on their driving curriculum experiences, ILI students Araceli and Benicia shared stories primarily focused on bodies in danger, treating driving as an inescapably embodied act. When asked about their memories of driving, Benicia shared a story about a car not stopping for her son in a parking lot, while Araceli shared a deeply tragic explanation of her markedly physical experience of learning to drive in the United States. Araceli explained that as she moved through the driving curriculum's lessons, she was simultaneously processing the loss of her brother due to a motorcycle accident in Colombia six years prior. After this loss, Araceli "stopped driving" and hadn't "touched a car since." Araceli expressed being rendered immobile, both physically and emotionally, but also described a forward motion dependent on both driving and immigration status:

> My brother is not going to come back. I am building my new life in the U.S., and to get along and to get forward with that, I need a driver's license. So I say, I need it at this time. Next month is going to be his sixth anniversary; I say, I think it's time. I will be a better driver than the person.

Araceli's motivation to learn to drive is indeed pragmatic, but also highly symbolic for her and embedded in concepts of independence, citizenship, happiness, and the "good vibes" she often evoked. Learning driving literacies for Araceli is an opportunity to "get along and to get forward" in building her new life. She expresses conviction that through this literacy learning she "will be a better driver than the person" who broke the driving rules that ended her brother's life on a road.

In this way, participants' experiences learning to drive underline the extent to which literacy learning is associated with and experienced in the body. Further, across the study's data, negotiating rules often was described as a process by which one's or others' bodies became racialized. For example, for undergraduate curriculum designers, race-based police violence shaped how they understood what it meant to teach the literacies necessary to drive within, as one undergraduate said, "the current climate and what's happening right now with police and immigrants and driving." In research interviews, several explained that ongoing racist incidents involving driving and cars directly impacted their conversations about what belonged in a driving curriculum. One student wrote a reflection that described his growing awareness that literacy "can be this physical thing, too, and then become embodied in us" and how "what our bodies are doing…can be forms of navigating the world" that also depend on literacy. Eventually, undergraduate curriculum designers began to explicitly include considerations of racialization in the curriculum's lessons. Undergraduate curriculum designer Riya explained that while they started with just "this fun diagram, and this little tutorial, whatever," their growing awareness of how "where you're from, how good your English or language skills are, the way you look" began to ground lessons in lived experience inflected by race. She said, "Once we actually thought about the physical people, and picturing, at least for me, myself in a car…putting people into the equation changed everything." For example, undergraduate curriculum designer Marissa, who identified as a white student from Texas, explained how race-based understandings of driving were connected to literacy and language:

> The things we tried to think about with the driving curriculum, when you can have a lot of interaction with authority or police that can be dangerous or very nerve-wracking…When you're doing something that's already a little bit inherently physically dangerous, and then to encounter a person who is also physically dangerous. It felt very high stakes…[for] immigrants who

cannot just truthfully, for a lot of reasons that are horrific, cannot afford to misspeak to a police officer. Cannot afford to be pulled over by a police officer, because they don't know what "use yah blinkah" means.

The phrase "use yah blinkah," a Massachusetts-ism that winks at a New England accent as well as the region's proud flouting of driving rules, was displayed on highway alert signs around the state at the time of curriculum design. The curriculum designers discussed how multilingual language users new to the region might misunderstand such a written version of a New England accent and its assumptions of in-group humor. Shared personal experiences of encountering this sign and other powerful codes on the road, including "their interactions good and bad with police and getting stopped" were pooled among curriculum designers and compiled "as a central [curricular] theme of being misunderstood on a very basic level." Curriculum designers realized that driving students' "being misunderstood" would not be an "arbitrary" slip in communication but might instead be a communicative tool of powerful, often-white listeners—examiners, instructors, police—who may use misunderstanding to maintain "exclusion and intimidation" during car-based communication (Cameron 12). As Riya wrote in a class reflection, "It seems as though the rules are created with restrictions to further define and distance people who are simply trying to live respectfully by these very rules."

Curriculum tutoring sessions between ILI student, Amare, and his tutor, Aaron, a white graduate student from Connecticut, further demonstrate the racialization of both driving and literacy rules due to the physicality involved in learning both. Aaron worked one-on-one with Amare on each of the curriculum's lessons over the course of several months. Amare recounts appreciating this personalized learning as he learned "vocabulary, organization, news, and writing" in English language discussions about driving. But Amare and Aaron's interactions during the lesson on driving fines also showed Aaron sorting through his white-privileged experiences of fines, tickets, and police encounters while discussing these topics with Amare.

Amare was motivated to seek language support in preparing for the driving test because his brother's experience with the examiner during his own test had been "rude" and had involved "language discrimination." Amare wanted to know "how to be in the car with the guy" during the test, so he and Aaron created a norm in their sessions of making literacy learning physical, using techniques like role playing to prepare for the test. Aaron explained that they practiced "the actual actions of all the things you do when you're in the car," from the "motions you have to make" for a "three-point turn" to "remember your blinkers" to enacting the "combative presence" that can be a norm on Massachusetts roads. In later sessions, Amare and Aaron conducted sessions sitting in Aaron's car. Recalling his experience with the driving test, Aaron remembered that to pass, "it's not just performing the maneuvers, it's moving your body that performs the maneuvers in the right way."

The racial aspects of such driving performances were brought into focus during the curriculum's lesson on fines, which introduced the concept of being pulled over by police. Following the physicality enacted in previous sessions, Aaron said he "parodied" for Amare what to do "when you get pulled over." He explained to Amare, "they [the police] want your hands where they can see them." In his interview, Aaron provides more context for choices he was making throughout the lesson:

> This is also in the middle of a time when it's very clear that the rules for getting pulled over for a white person are very different than the rules for getting pulled over as a Black person. And it came up a bit. If he wanted to talk more about it, we could have gone down that road, but I'm not going to be the one to be like, 'How do you, a Black man, deal with getting pulled over?' Although, we did talk about the fact that it's different.

Aaron was frank in thinking through what he felt he should assume in his conversations about racist police interactions with Amare. He sought to follow Amare's lead, noting Amare did not often raise race-based issues or questions. But Aaron also felt a responsibility to explore the racial tensions around driving given the contemporary political context and his resulting conclusion that the literacy rules of driving are "built in all these secrets," one of which is the racialization of the social and physical mobility promised by a driver's license. In Aaron's thinking, a license is "protection against…political infractions" that inhibit mobility, but accessing a license "opens you up to other" forms of immobility in that "once you are on the road, you're subject to more policing."

Although Amare's original request for language support was informed by the linguistic discrimination his brother experienced during the driving test, his desire to know "how to be in the car with the guy" moves beyond the "objective linguistic practices" of driving rules, toward the "ideological phenomena" the rules also entail (Flores and Rosa 165). Amare wants to know how to *be* in a car: how to precisely adjust mirrors, turn to look, or reach for something or stay put; alongside the disproportionate, sometimes violent, reactions to errors in such moves; alongside knowing what to say or not say in English to powerful others while moving. Learning about driving makes it impossible to ignore the physicality of these layers of literacy.

Conclusion: Negotiating Literacy's Layers

In its current form, the driving curriculum is fully designed and available online, with ten lessons sequenced as individually paced tutor-learner sessions, culminating in a lesson that features critical reflection on the entire curriculum. In accordance with its goals, the curriculum treats driving literacies not only as vocabulary items to be learned but also as social practices upon which drivers should critically reflect. The curriculum teaches language and literacies related to driving but includes opportunities to critically consider the ways that driving situations and literacies can intersect to marginalize people. For literacy users whose bodies and language are racialized every day, thinking about the body in relation to literacy is not optional but a given. In this way, the study suggests that linguistically and culturally responsive community-based literacy projects should include considerations of literacy's intense physicality.

Further, the rule negotiations demonstrated in the two findings sections above suggest that treatments of negotiation in literacy theory also should include analysis of the people who are negotiating. To say that literacy's rules are embodied is to stress that the act of literate negotiation happens not only between a writer and imagined readers on the page, but also among physically present literacy users negotiating with and through text. Intentional theoretical inclusion of the last aspect means analyzing not just texts, or texts in context, but also "positions of enunciation and reception"—the social positions of those creating and receiving the texts—particularly of "marginalized speakers' shared, racialized positions of enunciation and particular listeners' hegemonic positions of reception" (Flores and Rosa 172).

One participant, graduate student tutor Victoria, thought of this phenomenon in the context of teaching driving literacies as navigating "layered literacies." Speaking about her experience tutoring ILI students through the driving curriculum's lessons Victoria said, "There's just so many different layers of literacy happening":

> It's part of what makes this curriculum and tutoring . . . more complex than it seems on the surface. [It's] not just that you're helping [tutees] understand what a no right on red symbol means, you know? You're also helping them understand that . . . these words mean something, but there's also this physical driving action that relates to those words, and . . . this social context, where if you don't do this thing, you might get pulled over, what does that mean for you and your body that's unjustly marked linguistically and racially.

Resonant with literacy's chronotopic laminations (Prior and Shipka) as well as literacy's "layered simultaneity" (Blommaert, *Discourse*), Victoria's literacy "layers" include facets that recall sociomateriality: a material or textual layer, such as textual "words" like signs; a social layer, which includes cultural and linguistic norms mediated through social interactions and exchanges; and a physical or embodied layer, including senses and feeling. Moving through the driving curriculum alongside immigrant literacy users helped Victoria to see that "those layers [of literacy] happen in a very lived way." Victoria explained that she and her tutees were "always negotiating these three things, that balancing act of understanding the rules but also critiquing [them]." In other words, literacy theory must consider embodiment, of course, but also must consider how embodiment is an extricable element of literate negotiation, not just in but around texts.

Scholars note that negotiating language rules in texts is difficult due to the lack of paralinguistic cues and the fixed temporal dimension of writing (Canagarajah "Multilingual"; Canagarajah "Negotiating"; Donahue). They further note the difficulty of negotiating the expectations of multiple unknown readers across wide-ranging "literacy regimes" (Blommaert, *Grassroots*). But we have yet to fully explore writing-related negotiation around a text, including the role that bodies play in these negotiations. While driving, for example, literate negotiations occur in response to texts (highway signs), in the enactment of read texts (following directions), during the production of texts (deciding to keep silent while police write a ticket). In experiences of driving, multiple literate negotiations happen all at once. By considering how people enact literacy in real time with others in motion—during driving, marching, migration, or other mobile activities—the concept of literate negotiation expands to include physical experience.

Acknowledgements

The authors are deeply grateful for review feedback from Kate Vieira and another anonymous reviewer, as well as to this study's generous participants, including the wonderful staff and students of the International Language Institute of Massachusetts.

Notes

1. All participant names are pseudonyms.
2. The International Language Institute of Massachusetts (ILI) is a non-profit community language school whose mission is to promote intercultural understanding and strong, diverse communities through language instruction and teacher training.
3. For a full description of this course, see Lorimer Leonard, Rebecca, Danielle Pappo, and Kyle Piscioniere. "Course Design: English 391ml, Multilingualism and Literacy in Western Massachusetts." *Composition Studies*, vol. 48, no. 1, 2020, pp. 103–114.
4. For example, see https://miracoalition.org/get-involved/drivers-licenses/.

Works Cited

Amuedo-Dorantes, Catalina et al. "Labor Market Impacts of States Issuing of Driver's Licenses to Undocumented Immigrants." *Labour Economics*, vol. 63, 2020, pp. 1–41.
Auerbach, Elsa et al. *Adult ESL/Literacy from the Community to the Community: A Guidebook for Participatory Literacy Training*. Routledge, 2013.
Blommaert, Jan. *Discourse: A Critical Introduction*. Cambridge University Press, 2005.
—. *Grassroots Literacy: Writing, Identity and Voice in Central Africa*. Routledge, 2008.
Blommaert, Jan, and Bruce Horner. "Mobility and Academic Literacies: An Epistolary Conversation." *London Review of Education*, vol. 15, no. 1, 2017, pp. 2–20.
Cameron, Deborah. *Verbal Hygiene*. Routledge, 2012.
Campano, Gerald, Maria Paula Ghiso, and Bethany Welch. *Partnering with Immigrant Communities: Action through Literacy*. Teachers College Press, 2016.
Canagarajah, Suresh. "Multilingual Strategies of Negotiating English: From Conversation to Writing." *JAC*, vol. 29, no. 1, 2009, pp. 17–48.
—. "Negotiating Translingual Literacy: An Enactment." *Research in the Teaching of English*, vol. 48, no. 1, 2013, pp. 40–67.
Cedillo, Christina V. "What Does It Mean to Move?: Race, Disability, and Critical Embodiment Pedagogy." *Composition Forum*, vol. 39, 2018.
Curzan, Anne. "Says Who? Teaching and Questioning the Rules of Grammar." *PMLA*, vol. 124, no. 3, 2009, pp. 870–79.

Delpit, Lisa. *Other People's Children: Cultural Conflict in the Classroom*. The New Press, 2006.

Donahue, Christiane. "Negotiation, Translinguality, and Cross-cultural Writing Research in a New Composition Era." *Literacy as Translingual Practice*, edited by Suresh Canagarajah, Routledge, 2013, pp. 149-161.

Dufour, Monique and Jennifer Ahern-Dodson. "Good Writers Always Follow My Rules". *Bad Ideas about Writing*, edited by Cheryl E. Ball & Drew M. Loewe, WVU Libraries, 2017, pp. 121–25.

Dyson, Anne Haas and Celia Genishi. *On the Case: Approaches to Language and Literacy Research*. Teachers College Press, 2005.

Ehret, Christopher. "Propositions from Affect Theory for Feeling Literacy Through the Event." *Theoretical Models and Processes of Reading*. 7th ed., edited by Donna E. Alvermann et al., Routledge, 2018, pp. 563–581.

Featherstone, Mike. "Automobilities: An introduction." *Theory, Culture & Society*, vol. 21, no. 4-5, 2004, pp. 1–24.

Ferris, Dana. *Treatment of Error in Second Language Student Writing*. University of Michigan Press, 2002.

Flores, Nelson and Jonathan Rosa. "Undoing Appropriateness: Raciolinguistic Ideologies and Language Diversity in Education." *Harvard Educational Review*, vol. 85, no. 2, 2015, pp. 149–71.

Hamilton, Mary. "Imagining Literacy: A Sociomaterial Approach." *Beyond Economic Interests Critical Perspectives on Adult Literacy and Numeracy in a Globalised World*, edited by Keiko Yasukawa and Stephen Black, Springer, 2016, pp. 3–18.

Hendricks, Sarah E. "Living in Car Culture Without a License." *American Immigration Council*, 2014, americanimmigrationcouncil.org/research/living-car-culture-without-license.

Kalmar, Tomas Mario. *Illegal Alphabets and Adult Biliteracy: Latino Migrants Crossing the Linguistic Border*. 2nd ed. Routledge, 2015.

Kerr, Sophie-May et al. "Diverse Driving Emotions: Exploring Chinese Migrants' Mobilities in a Car-Dependent City." *Transfers*, vol. 8, no. 2, 2018, pp. 23–43.

Lagman, Eileen. "Moving Labor: Transnational Migrant Workers and Affective Literacies of Care." *Literacy In Composition Studies*, vol. 3, no. 3, 2015, pp. 1–24.

Laurier, Eric et al. "Driving and Passengering: Notes on the Ordinary Organization of Car Travel." *Mobilities*, vol. 3, no. 1, 2008, pp. 1–23.

Marko, Tamera et al. "Proyecto Carrito—When the Student Receives an 'A' and the Worker Gets Fired: Disrupting the Unequal Political Economy of Translingual Rhetorical Mobility." *Literacy in Composition Studies*, vol. 3, no. 1, 2015, pp. 21–43.

Merriman, Peter and Lynne Pearce. "Mobility and the Humanities." *Mobilities*, vol. 12, no. 4, 2017, pp. 493–508.

Micciche, Laura. "Writing material." *College English*, vol. 76, no. 6, 2014, pp. 488–505.

Mitchell, Tania D. "Traditional vs. Critical Service-Learning: Engaging the Literature to Differentiate Two Models." *Journal of Community Service Learning*, vol. 14, 2008, pp. 50–65.

Murray, Lesley. "Motherhood, Risk and Everyday Mobilities." *Gendered mobilities,* edited by Tim Cresswell and Tanu Priya Uteng, Routledge, 2008, pp. 61–78.

Rose, Mike. "Rigid Rules, Inflexible Plans, and the Stifling of Language: A Cognitivist Analysis of Writer's Block." *College Composition and Communication,* vol. 31 no. 4, 1980, pp. 389–401.

Rowsell, Jennifer, and Kate Paul. "The Material and the Situated: What Multimodality and New Literacy Studies do for Literacy Research." *Handbook of Research on Teaching the English Language Arts,* edited by Diane Lapp and Douglas Fisher, Routledge, 2011, pp. 175–81.

Prior, Paul, and Jody Shipka. "Chronotopic Lamination: Tracing the Contours of Literate Activity." *Writing Selves, Writing Societies: Research from Activity Perspectives,* 2003, pp. 180–238.

Purifoye, Gwendolyn Y. "Transit Boundaries: Race and the Paradox of Immobility within Mobile Systems." *Mobilities,* vol. 15, no. 4, 2020, pp. 480–99.

Redshaw, Sarah and Fiona Nicoll. "Gambling Drivers: Regulating Cultural Technologies, Subjects, Spaces and Practices of Mobility." *Mobilities,* vol. 5, no. 3, 2010, pp. 409–30.

Sheller, Mimi. "Automotive Emotions: Feeling the Car." *Theory, Culture & Society,* vol. 21, no. 4-5, 2004, pp. 221–42.

Sheller, Mimi. & John Urry. "The City and the Car." *International Journal of Urban and Regional Research,* vol. 24, no. 4, 2000, pp. 737–57.

Urry, John. "Inhabiting the Car." *Sociological Review,* vol. 54, 2006, pp. 17–31.

Vieira, Kate. *American by Paper: How Documents Matter in Immigrant Literacy.* University of Minnesota Press, 2016.

Author Bios

Rebecca Lorimer Leonard is Associate Professor of English at the University of Massachusetts Amherst where she teaches undergraduate and graduate courses on language diversity, literacy studies, and research methods. She has published in *College English, Journal of Language, Identity, & Education, Journal of Second Language Writing,* and *Research in the Teaching of English,* among others.

Danielle Pappo is a PhD candidate at the University of Massachusetts Amherst where she teaches first-year writing and is the Assistant Director of the Junior Year Writing Program. In 2021-2022 she joined the Herstory Writers Network as a CCW/Jacob Volkman Human Rights Fellow, and is now a Herstory consultant focused on communications and curricular development. She has published in *Composition Studies* and *Reflections: A Journal of Community-Engaged Writing and Rhetoric.*

Crash Encounters: Negotiating Science Literacy and Its Sponsorship in a Cross-Disciplinary, Cross-Generational MOOC

Stephanie West-Puckett

Abstract

This article examines how scientists, classroom teachers, poetry educators, and youth negotiated the domains of science through their engagement in a two-year Massive Open Online Collaboration (MOOC) funded by the National Science Foundation. To make sense of learners' unconventional and interdisciplinary writing and the cultural and disciplinary conflicts that emerged around it, I offer a reframing of science literacy as a series of crash encounters. Such a reframing prompts literacy practitioners to anticipate fallout when diverse bodies, objects, and rhetorics collide and, therefore, to better design and participate in interdisciplinary networks to create more dynamic and vibrant approaches to science literacy.

Keywords

OOC, science literacy, multimodality, interdisciplinary writing, crash encounters

A Vignette

On a brisk November morning in 2014, an unlikely group of museum scientists, classroom teachers, and spoken word poets met by the black waters of the Scuppernong River to design a radical science learning opportunity for underserved youth in rural eastern North Carolina. No one was quite sure what form this project might take or how each partner's expertise might contribute to building a collaborative learning experience, but they all knew it would be an experience no one partner could design and deliver alone. Nervous apprehension warmed to excitement, however, when one of the scientists presented each member of the group with a pair of plastic goggles, delicate glass vials, graduated cylinders, natural specimens, isopropyl alcohol, and a mixed surfactant—the seductive stuff of science.

To demonstrate the museum's approach to interactive science, the microbiologist led the group in using low-cost everyday household materials, like the aforementioned alcohol and dish detergent, to extract DNA from a specimen of wheat germ. Each member of the group followed along diligently during the procedure, carefully listening, measuring, and agitating the liquids in their vials. The conversations among the groups became more organic as they passed chemicals back and forth and compared the progress of their extractions. Soon each person held a mucus-like glob of DNA on the end of a wooden coffee stirrer, and the scientist praised the group's veritable success. Looking unimpressed at the scientist and the snotty blob on the stick, one of the teachers questioned, "So what? What do we do with this?" The scientist was clearly confounded and replied, "It's the genetic code of life!" But the teacher wasn't satisfied and pressed, "Yes, I see that. I get that. But why does it matter?"

There was an awkward pause before one of the poets suggested that everyone take a few minutes to write a short poem personifying the snot-like blob. "This makes me very uncomfortable," the scientist countered. "We are trained to avoid the humanization of things that aren't human. It's a dangerous practice." But the poets, led by a highly charismatic and persistent director, insisted, and the group, including the reluctant scientists, set to writing haikus and rhyming couplets. Spurred by the spoken word poets, both teachers and scientists shared a few silly and provocative lines, and the poems opened a robust discussion about the significance of DNA extraction. From there, they brainstormed several learning pathways that young people could pursue to make meaning out of this strange matter. The discussion meandered around both fiction and nonfiction texts that take on the implications of hacking the A-C-T-G codes of DNA. It surfaced the cloning of extinct or nearly extinct animals to increase biodiversity à la *Jurassic Park*, medical research involving extracted DNA cell lines as explored in *The Immortal Life of Henrietta Lacks*, and forensic science applications such as those that helped authorities find the infamous Green River Killer. Together, the group began to see how the push and pull of objects and discourses around objects could make matter matter for themselves and for the young people they teach, a realization that resulted from the melding of their diverse disciplinary backgrounds and expertise.

Introduction

The previous vignette represents just one of the many moments of conflict that emerged as formal and informal educators negotiated the domains of science literacy from multiple disciplinary and institutional vantage points. Brought together through a National Science Foundation grant, these diverse practitioners eventually designed and delivered a large-scale, youth-facing, open, online science literacy program titled *Remix, Remake, Curate*. During the program's design and development stage, numerous tensions surfaced among practitioners in the sciences and those in the humanities as well as among youth participants and adult facilitators, and these conflicts played out across physical and digital spaces. Cultural and disciplinary ways of knowing, doing, and writing (Carter 387) were disrupted by the clash of disparate epistemological and ontological traditions. From these "crash encounters," a term coined by Jane Bennett to describe the ways meaning and matter emerge out of conflict (119), non-hierarchical ways of knowing, doing, and writing science as well as sponsoring science literacies emerged.

In this article, I apply Bennett's notion of crash encounters to community literacy work. This application allows me to account for the disruptive processes as well as the unpredictable, uncomfortable, and often untapped potential to create new forms of meaning *by way of difference* in heterogeneous literacy networks. These impacts have the potential to unsettle frameworks that structure cohesive meaning-making and allow new forms of science literacy sponsorship to emerge. A framework of crash encounters prompts practitioners to pay more attention to the diverse materialities, bodies, and experiences that construct science learning and to better anticipate the fallout of those collisions for both literacy leaders and learners. To illustrate the need for reframing science literacy through a crash encounters framework, I discuss the contrasting ways science literacy has been constructed, consider the role of both formal and informal educators in sponsoring science literacy in a digitally networked society, and note that research must attend to how we better prepare facilitators for engaging in this contested work. Next, I provide a rich description of the *Remix, Remake, Curate* programming and analyze moments in which epistemologies, ontologies, and the technē that construct them collide. Here, I focus on two micro-cases—*50 ft. Shark* and *Eagorilla and Other Mashups*—to illustrate young people's capricious and undisciplined composing processes and detail facilitators' divergent reactions to those practices that thread through online and offline spaces. By analyzing these moments and anticipating such crash encounters in diverse and distributed learning environments, I argue that literacy scholars can better equip themselves to design and participate in more vibrant approaches to sponsoring science literacy. I then conclude with practical suggestions for how literacy scholars might form broader coalitions to do so.

Constructing Science Literacy and Sponsorship

Science literacy, as it has historically been understood in Western societies, encompasses the knowledge of scientific principles and theories (such as the principles of evolution, laws of general relativity, or the big bang theory, to name a few); an understanding of scientific methods (hypothesizing, experimenting, collecting data, analyzing data, etc.); and an ability to integrate this knowledge into personal, civic, and professional life (refusing single-use plastics because one understands detrimental environmental impacts; using data regarding sea level rise to inform community planning; preparation for technology-driven work environments, etc.). Science literacy is central to U.S. American economic success and military security, and the renewed focus on science, technology, tngineering, and math (STEM) in U.S. American schools is generally lauded as a strong return on investment; however, the significance of science literacy extends beyond enterprise and national concern. Science literacy and the human actions informed by it impact Earth's ecological sustainability, the quality of life for its inhabitants, and our own survival as a species (Clough 1).

Research suggests that while science literacy in U.S. America has increased modestly in the 21st century, recovering slightly from its plunge at the end of the 20th century, nearly three-fourths of adults lack a "civic scientific literacy" (Miller). In addition, many U.S. American youth experience only surface engagements with science in K-12 classrooms because science curricula, particularly in elementary schools, have tended to privilege breadth over depth. Furthermore, formal science learning often struggles to meet the needs, interests, experiences, and motivations of a wide range of diverse students and can therefore fall short in exciting curiosity and promoting sustained inquiry and engagement. Falk and Dierking argue that "an ever-growing body of evidence demonstrates that most science is learned outside of school" in contexts such as museums, afterschool programs, and community centers (Falk and Dierking 483). That does not mean, however, that formal schooling has no value for the science learner. Formal classrooms can help learners grasp generalized concepts that learners can build on through lifelong, free-choice science learning (Falk). Most importantly, efforts to coordinate science learning across formal and informal contexts hold great promise for supporting lifelong learners and building civic scientific literacy (Falk et al.).

While only a small fraction of U.S. Americans consider themselves well-versed in science and technological advancements, many citizens are unsettled by the ethical issues that are raised by innovation in life sciences such as human and animal cloning (Siang). Such concerns about ethics underscore the problem of disciplinary siloing in U.S. American institutions. Scientists asking questions of "What, when, and how?" haven't traditionally engaged humanists asking, "Why and for whom?" And if these engagements do take place, they often take the form of humanities scholars reacting to scientific practices with questions of *meaning* being taken up after questions of *matter*. Feminist physicist and philosopher Karen Barad argues that this kind of siloing, across or even inside disciplines, is the wrong approach. Barad cautions, "... the notion of consequences [of scientific research] is based on the wrong temporality: asking after potential consequences is too little, too late, because ethics of course, is being done right at the lab bench" (qtd. in Dolphijn and van der Tuin). In other words, we can't afford to ask *retroactively* of science and technology "Why?" or "For whom?" Those questions of ethical responsibility, the kinds of questions that humanists are good at asking and exploring, must instead *inform and guide* scientific and technological research, practice, and literacy sponsorship. Given these ethical challenges, it is apparent that interventions aimed at increasing science literacy need to not only coordinate efforts across learning spheres but also coordinate learning across disciplinary terrain.

In addition to exploring the geographies of learning spaces and disciplinary terrain, researchers argue that we must pay attention to how particular people in particular places and times operationalize the concept of science literacy. In contrast to the more abstract and acontextual notions of science literacy posited by the professional and governmental organizations at the beginning of this section, environmental educators and literacy researchers point to materiality, embodiment, and everyday practice as key aspects of science learning. Drawing on training in environmental biology as well as indigenous cultural knowledge, Anishinabekwe scientist Robin Wall Kimmerer argues for an approach to science that foregrounds "restorative reciprocity" ("Restoration" 260). Restorative reciprocity holds that our scientific knowledge of the natural world is born from our relationship with it. To deepen knowledge, then, is to deepen a reciprocal relationship that involves both caring for and being cared for by the earth. For Kimmerer, science literacy does not arise from objective study but instead grows from being with a diversity of bodies—plant, animal, spirit, human—who have their own stories to tell (*Braiding*). Likewise, Ortoleva's ethnographic study of the Narragansett Indian Tribe's ecological relationship to the Narragansett Bay reveals how embodiment can serve as a catalyst for scientific literacy as well as grassroots environmental advocacy and action. Ortoleva identifies this instantiation of science literacy as "biospheric literacies of the body" (59) and describes its conditions as "transformational moments when body and place connect and the literacy acts that result from this connection" (59). Drawing on Indigenous ontologies, Ortoleva's theory, like Kimmerer's, grounds the material dimensions of science literacy and points to the processes of building science literacy from the individual to the ecological scale. Complementing the everyday practices of science learning such as braiding sweetgrass and bathing in saltwater, Briseño-Garzón et al. found that members of marginalized communities read and write science-informed texts as an ongoing process of building their lifeworlds. Their study found that motivations for engaging in science reading and writing practices outside of formal schooling include, but are not limited to, the human need to be more entertained, informed, equipped, and challenged. Briseño-Garzón et al. argue that traditional approaches to science literacy foreground discrete skills, knowledge, and acontextual understandings of scientific contexts and practices while ignoring science literacy as a lifelong and life-sustaining practice that is "…always contextualized and meaningful when related to the specific needs and realities of people" (103). The approaches described in this paragraph point to the material, embodied, and quotidian nature of science learning informed by culturally diverse perspectives, the likes of which have not traditionally been foregrounded in discussions of science literacy and how to best sponsor it.

Relatedly, as Internet technologies have proliferated over the last quarter century and the World Wide Web has transitioned from a read-only to a more participatory read/write web, both formal and informal science learning organizations in the United States have wrestled with how to sponsor science literacy in networked environments. Semper argues that this shift requires rethinking the concept of a museum. He writes, "Our first challenge may be to get beyond the physical notion of what a museum is. Rather than thinking of ourselves as isolated institutions, we need to think of museums and our audience as nodes in a net of connections." Since the early twenty-tens, science museums across U.S. America have been experimenting with such programming, while researchers have focused on best practices in informal (aka "free-choice") science learning as well as how those best practices lead to better learning outcomes (Ennes and Lee). In this vein, writing studies scholars Sackey et al. investigate an online science literacy program sponsored by the Science Museum of Minnesota (SMM). Their findings illustrate a set of conditions that promotes transformative online science learning, including the careful choice of technological platforms; the design of open-ended activities to prompt participants to become more aware of themselves and their physical, social, and cultural environments; and embedded opportunities for participants to share related perspectives, reflections, content, and media that they encounter in their daily lives. Sackey et al. also highlight the importance of engaged facilitators who are adept at leveraging the capabilities of chosen technologies; proficient in promoting and encouraging critical awareness; and skilled at prompting learners to reflect on new information and perspectives to think differently about science. They argue that such facilitation, as a practice of rhetorically constructing online learning environments through specific writing strategies, can be "seen, taught, and learned" (122).

Pinpointing these specific moves, as Sackey et al. have done, is essential to understanding the performative work of online community facilitation; yet, cultivating the orientations and abilities they have identified is, in practice, a difficult task. It becomes more difficult when online science literacy programming is attempted across formal and informal settings, disciplinary terrains, diverse cultural backgrounds, distributed platforms, and real bodies in particular times and places. As demonstrated in this review of literature, there are a host of discursive and material bodies with different orientations, experiences, and emotions at play in such initiatives. Given these material realities, a purely discursive approach to considering the performance of facilitation moves may struggle to shed light on the embodied experiences, emotions, and motivations of facilitators and learners. Related to this, Palloff and Pratt (2007) argue that focusing solely on the textual performances in online learning communities runs the risk of disembodying learners and leaders. They argue that to ethically build and study online learning communities, we should foreground embodied presence and the ways that such presence can "personalize and humanize" online learning and its scholarship. To be clear, I don't think Sackey et al. are guilty of disembodying their research participants, but I am suggesting that a multiple-methods approach to studying online communities, which I describe in the following section, is useful as scholars seek to learn more about how both facilitators and participants navigate the challenges, conflicts, and crash encounters of vibrant science learning.

Multiple Methods Study Design

The findings shared in this article, which point to the importance of more dynamic and vibrant metaphors and practices for sponsoring science literacy, were analyzed and interpreted from multiple data sets collected between January and May of 2016. These data sets include semi-structured interviews with facilitators; publicly available data on the *Remix, Remake, Curate* online platforms; grant applications, reports, and facilitator notes; as well as experience narratives written by the scientists, spoken word poets, and classroom teachers who designed and delivered this open-ended science literacy programming (MOOC). Borrowing from work in grounded theory (Magnetto; Farkas and Haas), I (with the help of my dissertation director, William Banks) engaged in three practices of data analysis: qualitative coding, reflecting through the co-production of coding memos, and creating 3D representations of the coding schemes. Most important for this article and for the methods that allowed a crash encounter framework to emerge, I employed selective coding to identify and taxonomize participants' affective valences. Affective valence, as I employ the term, refers to the relative comfort or discomfort of experience, and, as Chang et al. argue, affective valence is central to how individuals perceive their agency in each context. In response to prompts that invited participants to elaborate on both positive and negative orientations toward the material aspects of networked production of science literacy, a host of negative valences, particularly anxieties, were expressed. Axial coding methods revealed that these anxieties were overwhelmingly linked to feelings of ill-preparedness in addressing hybrid, ambiguous student compositions. The two micro-cases shared in this article were constructed developing linkages across data sets and provide empirical evidence that suggest that science literacy might be better understood, practiced, and sponsored by frameworks that acknowledge that literacy acquisition is just as much, if not more, about disrupting, crashing, smashing, and breaking as it is about adding to an already existing set of knowledges and practices.

Remix, Remake, Curate MOOC: Context

Recognizing the responsibility of community partner organizations in increasing science literacy, as evidenced in the two-year partnership between the Association of Science and Technology Centers and the National Writing Project funded by the National Science Foundation in 2014, the purpose of this partnership was to engage formal and informal educators in designing science literacy programming that would thread through in- and out-of-school contexts. This funding opportunity, informed by the principles and practices of connected learning (Ito et al.), galvanized the North Carolina Museum of Natural Sciences, the Tar River Writing Project at East Carolina University, and the Poetry Project to imagine online learning opportunities for rural eastern North Carolina youth, primarily low-income youth of color, who had limited access to local or regional science centers.

These imaginings eventually produced the *Remix, Remake, Curate* Massive Open Online Collaboration (MOOC), a variation on the for-credit MOOCs phenomenon that trades the *course* construction for a focus on *collaborative*, social learning and network building across institutional boundaries (West-Puckett et al.). From 2014 to 2016, seven museum scientists, thirteen K-higher education faculty, and six spoken word poets facilitated fifteen weeks of intensive online science programming with more than fifteen hundred youth across grade levels and educational contexts. *Remix, Remake, Curate* was informed by the principles and practices of citizen science, a branch of participatory science that promotes collaboration between scientists and the general public and that fosters public appreciation for scientific knowledge-making (Trumbull et al.; Brossard; Cronje et al.). However, unlike dominant approaches to citizen science, which primarily cast public participants in data collection roles for large-scale scientific inquiry, the *Remix, Remake, Curate* MOOC was designed to afford manifestly divergent, critical, and context-specific participation options.

To span vast geographical distances, age, and experience levels, facilitators designed online opportunities for young people to contribute to ongoing research projects and share science writing produced as part of those research projects. For example, in one community invitation, youth were invited to document flora and fauna in their neighborhoods or on their school campuses with the iNaturalist mobile application. Similarly, young people were encouraged to compose, perform, and digitally record spoken word poetry. Using the museum's in-house application SoundSee (figure 1), students were prompted to upload their recordings to the museum's public collection of human voice files, which enabled participants to visualize the waves that compose the unique timbre of each human voice.

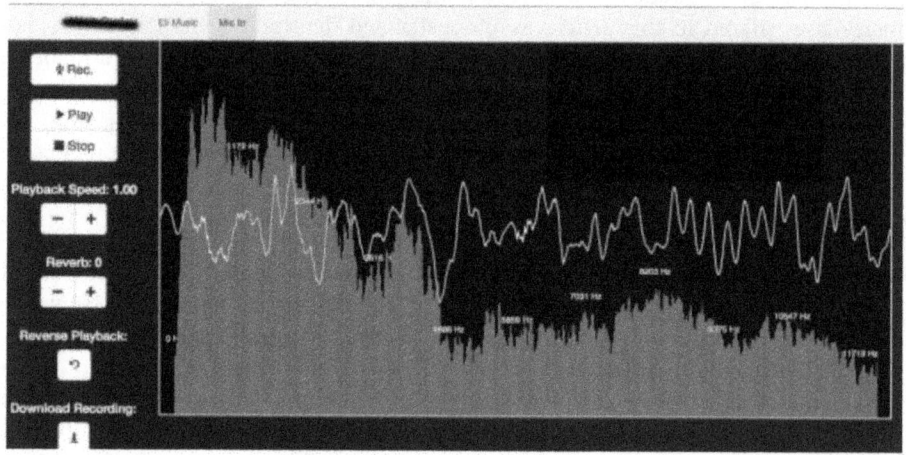

Figure 1. SoundSee application screenshot.

To prioritize access and accessibility, the *Remix, Remake, Curate* team not only used everyday materials to make science but also used openly networked digital tools like WordPress, Twitter, and Google+ to overcome geographical and economic boundaries and connect classroom and youth learners across the state. Each *Remix, Remake, Curate* facilitation team included at least one poet-educator, one scientist, and one classroom teacher from the elementary, middle, and secondary or college level. Each facilitation team designed and facilitated one writing and making unit during each year of programming. The first year, these units lasted one week each; however, the second year, facilitation teams extended the duration to two weeks to allow more time for youth and facilitator engagement. The units focused on the following areas of inquiry:

- biodiversity and backyard citizen science
- the art and physics of sound
- collecting and curating nature and memory
- exploring the microworld of crystals
- insect and arachnid anatomy and physiology
- biotechnology and life codes
- computer programming languages and coding meaning on the web

These units were largely determined by the participating scientists' expertise as well as their affiliation with a particular public science lab at the museum. The poets and teachers chose to work with the scientists based on their own personal and professional interests. Over the two-year project span, facilitation teams met for four extended planning and debriefing retreats and collaborated through hundreds of phone calls, group messages, emails, and collaborative online tools like Google Documents and Google Hangouts.

Scientists and poets participated alongside students and teachers during each unit. They developed and shared video tutorials and poetry performances that showed them working on similar inquiry projects in both their labs and their living rooms. They responded to youth makers' science and poetry compositions, which were shared in the Google+ community. They engaged in live Google Hangouts and Twitter Chats with participants by answering questions and discussing their research and writing. They posed big questions about ethics and responsibility, and they modeled curiosity, engagement, and, at times, failure in open online spaces.

Remix, Remake, Curate MOOC: Design and Delivery

While planning the make cycles, facilitation teams foregrounded three domains of literate practice, which they mapped across the disciplines of science and writing studies: *concepts, practices,* and *values*. These domains provided the basis for open and flexible curriculum pathways in each make cycle. For example, during the first make cycle of year two, which focused on biodiversity and citizen science, facilitation teams developed programming to lead participants in tracing biodiversity (*natural science concept*) by having students document and observe (*natural science practices*) the life forms that assembled around their porch lights by taking field notes (*scientific writing practices*). Participants used their field notes to draw conclusions about the relationships between weather and insect behavior (*scientific practices*) as well as to personify, craft, and perform dialogic poetry between various life forms they observed (*creative writing practices*). Young people and their adult mentors, including classroom educators, youth leaders, and family members, shared their observation notes, photos, videos, drawings, questions, problems, hypotheses, and poem drafts in the various online forums of *Remix, Remake, Curate* (*peer review practices common in both science and creative writing*). Through generous feedback on the participants' shared compositions, facilitators celebrated close attention and curiosity, two *values* that were shared by both scientists and poets. Facilitators also explicitly named and labeled the use of poetic devices such as hyperbole and exaggeration, noting how these strategies created rhetorical significance but were ill-fitting devices for scientific inquiry as they lacked *accuracy* and *precision*, values that undergird effective meaning-making in the sciences. By providing a space for combining poetic, rhetorical, and scientific language practices, youth participants were encouraged to develop critical literacy practices that grapple with disparate ways of knowing, doing, and being across disciplines.

Over the course of two years, the *Remix, Remake, Curate* Google+ community engaged 377 Google+ users as members, with 148 considered "active," meaning they posted at least once in the community. The community doubled its reach in year two by increasing membership in the Google+ community by 65%. Facilitators and participants logged a total of 453 posts in the Google+ community, 590 +1 "like" or "recommend" responses, and 1,098 comments on participants' posts. Appendix A includes a representative listing as well as photos of select science media that were posted and shared in the community as responses to the open-ended invitations to the make cycles. Open-ended invitations were posted on the homepage of the WordPress blog (https://trwpconnect.wordpress.com/) and emailed to participants at the start of each make cycle. They were titled "Welcome to Make Cycle . . ." and signaled transitions to new shared foci within the MOOC. While far from complete, the artifacts in Appendix A indicate the diversity of individually and collaboratively composed products that materialized in the MOOC network in response to such invitations.

These compositions were assembled from a variety of digital and analogue matter threading across online and offline places. In the digital places of the MOOC, they are flattened into code and translated into bits and bytes that can travel across the World Wide Web. It's important to remember, however, that all of these compositions are both material and discursive, as they engaged composers' bodies, other objects, hardware, software, and infrastructures of delivery, as well as the material and embodied practices of meaning-making (Grabill; McKee and Porter; Palloff and Pratt; Banks and Eble; Fleckenstein).

As demonstrated in Appendix A, youth composers shared several playful poems, silly mashups, as well as outrageous science- and science-fiction-inspired compositions. These compositions engendered uneasy tensions between youth and adult desires as well as humanistic and scientific literacies. Throughout the duration of the MOOC programming, facilitation teams struggled with how to respond to unconventional science writing and making. In the two examples that follow, I describe these compositions and discuss how their impacts reverberated through *Remix, Remake, Curate*. These reverberations produced multivalent affective responses including anxiety and dissociation and prompted interventions that would help facilitators cope with the fallout of interdisciplinary and intercultural collision.

Remix, Remake, Curate Micro-case Study: 50 ft. Shark

The anxieties and behaviors around an elementary student's posting in year one became a flash point for the group. During the "Collecting and Curating Nature and Memory" make cycle, a student shared a memory about visiting an aquarium and learning about a shark, using the digital composing tool ThingLink to create an image with embedded digital content (figure 2). The student's teacher, a participating facilitator, posted a link to the student's digital composition, which included a photograph of the student holding the paper drawing with one line of anchored text that reads, "He is about 50 feet long." The teacher added the following comment to the post: "This is [student's] nature story about a shark he saw at the aquarium. We are going to double check on the size of the shark. He may still do some editing so feel free to ask questions and he can add them to his digital story. . . ."

Soon after the posting, two teachers commented on the composition, appreciating the student's work with digital literacy tools and nature narrative; yet there was no response from the scientists. When questioned during a subsequent facilitator meeting about the absence of their feedback, the scientists acknowledged that they were not comfortable responding to digital texts, as their previous educational programming was largely enacted in face-to-face settings with students producing science experiments as opposed to science texts. Beyond their discomfort with responding to student compositions in public forums, the scientists were also unsure how to promote scientific thinking and communication practices in this creative space. "Is it our role in this MOOC," one asked, "to tell the students they are wrong? Do we just let these kinds of inaccuracies go, or should we be correcting them?"

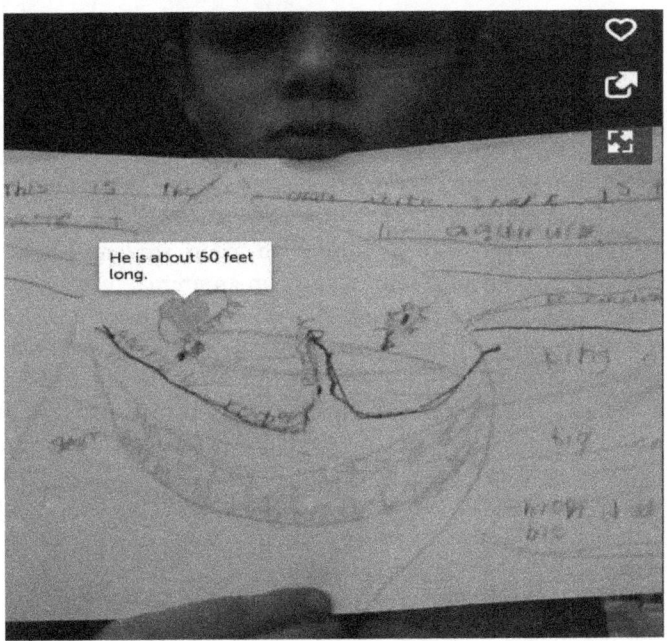

Figure 2. 50 ft. Shark

The case of *50 ft. Shark* exemplifies how youth composers brought together disparate material and discursive domains to make meaning about experiences with other bodies in the natural world. As is characteristic of informal science learning centers such as aquariums, the author of *50 ft. Shark* engaged a material, embodied, and affective encounter with a different species from the natural world, processes described by Ortoleva's notion of biospheric literacy. Clearly, the student was impacted by this engagement, and, I conjecture, the elementary student's understanding of the shark's size is likely understood in terms relative to his own body. In communicating with others in the MOOC about his encounter, the student mashes multiple discourses—visual, narrative, digital, numeric, embodied, and scientific. The resulting text can be read as a collision of discursive, material, affective, and disciplinary ways of knowing and doing science. The student's classroom teacher later reported that the student was eager to conduct secondary research to determine if the initial size estimation was correct, and, ultimately, the student revised the text to represent a more accurate length. The revised draft, however, was never shared in the MOOC community platforms. Teacher facilitators reported this was common, as the more sustained engagement with revised thinking, writing, and making was often shared in the classroom but not necessarily reposted publicly. These reports indicate that while *Remix, Remake, Curate* was effective at prompting crash encounters that foster openness, curiosity, flexibility, and creativity, classroom educators played a key role in leveraging those collisions in their local contexts to promote persistence, responsibility, and critical reflection on students' processes and products.

Remix, Remake, Curate Micro-case Study: Eagorilla and Other Mashups

Another example of these crash encounters can be seen in ways youth composers participated in "bursting" as they rapidly iterated on each other's compositions in the "Biotechnology and Life Codes" make cycle in the spring of year two. According to Anna Smith et al., "bursting" or the "burst effect" is a networked composing phenomenon that occurs when there are "sharp increases in participant production for a short period of time" (9). During this make cycle, high school students began rapidly producing visual mashups of fictional animal and human-animal mutations using Adobe Photoshop. Those compositions exemplify how youth composers were making meaning of their experiences extracting DNA from wheat germ as the facilitators did in the introductory anecdote. The classroom teacher leading these physical and digital experiments posted to Google+ early that day stating that the class was engaged in "Extracting DNA in a Dreamweaver class. Exploring the connection in Science, Writing/Poetry, and Graphic Design." During that same school day, sixteen different animal mashup images were posted, including two of the most popular posts of all time in the Google+ community (figures 3 and 4).

 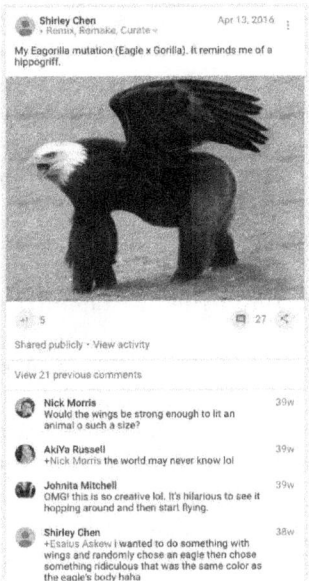

Figure 3. Turtle Kangaroo. Figure 4. Eagorilla.

These posts were re-shared more than any others in the Google+ community, and they received the most comments from other participants, with *Turtle Kangaroo* (figure 3) receiving 16 comments and *Eagorilla* (figure 4) receiving 27 comments, mostly from other student participants. In the comments section of each post, students asked questions about the mutated animals, prompting the youth mashup artists to compose fictional texts about the animals' anatomy, diet, and mating behaviors. These scientific concepts and natural science discourses threaded through from the previous make cycle about insect and arachnid anatomy and demonstrate how youth transferred learning across their MOOC experience. In addition to this language appropriation, the youth composers also re-appropriated scientific discourse as parody. Their language play created a comedic effect that was recognized and picked up by other students. One student noted that *Eagorilla* is the "definition of America!!!!" and several students agreed and included the hashtag "#murica" in the comments. These students were clearly familiar with the popular (at that time) Internet meme "Murica," which invokes the rural pronunciations of "America" that are often associated with deeply held values of nationalism, patriotism, and American strength. The meme is ambiguous in nature, as it is used to both support and criticize a particular Southern American stereotype, and students' use of the hashtag remains ambiguous as well. It is unclear whether students were expressing support or leveling critique, but what is clear is that they were blending science with Internet culture generally and meme culture more specifically to create a viral mashup sensation.

In response to this activity, a teacher commented, "I love these so much precisely because they seem so impossible. It's the stuff of science fiction . . . ," but that comment was dropped as students ignored the teacher and continued the extended banter among themselves. Another student commented, "If I saw this I would probably take a selfie with it! lol." Another of the participating teachers commented that these mashups invoked questions about authenticity and ethics. The teacher then used the tagging feature of the Google+ platform to invite the make cycle's facilitating scientist into this lively discussion. The classroom teacher asked the scientist to address the plausibility and implications of these fictional life forms; however, the scientist did not respond. The scientist neither engaged the conversation around this post nor commented on any of the related animal mashups or human-animal mashups. This is a peculiar silence considering the same scientist had commented on other posts shared during the same unit, particularly the photos of DNA extraction that were shared concurrently with these Photoshop mashups. While timing may be partially responsible for the silence, this is also likely related to the scientist's expressed frustrations about responding to imaginative content that fell outside the parameters of descriptive science writing and science making. Instead of seeing this as a fault or failure of the participating scientists, we can see this absence as more indicative of a flawed design process that did not adequately prepare facilitators to navigate the unexpected crash encounters that emerged in these Photoshop mashups.

Like the elementary composer of *50 ft. Shark* whose ways of making meaning of the natural world were located at the nexus of multiple modes and discourses as well as embodiment and affect, the high school participants were also demonstrating literacy practices sponsored by the collision of diverse nodes in the *Remix, Remake, Curate* network. The high school students' material and embodied encounters with DNA extraction, digital photo-manipulation tools, and Internet culture prompted them to imagine new life-forms that were framed through cultural, social, and political discourse. As both viral sensation and science that is just/barely fiction, *Eagorilla* demonstrates the adolescent composer's expansive and integrated literacy practices, which are layered and accelerated by emotional valences.

Historically, these emotional valences, including humor, sarcasm, and silliness, have not been embraced as important components of literacy, especially science literacy. The classroom teachers and the poetry educators who are more proximate to students' everyday literacy development were more willing to examine and work through these affective results of collisions and the creative products they engendered; however, even they found it difficult to leverage these crash encounters as a means of approaching more critical examination of issues such as ethics and power that were raised in students' writing and making. For example, none of the facilitators prompted students to contextualize "#murica," to define the ways they were using the term to support or critique or to consider how or why the hashtag could be problematic or offensive to other members of the community.

Remix, Remake, Curate Response Protocol as Conflict (re)Mediation

In response to this unconventional science making, facilitation teams—including scientists, poets, and educators—worked during the intercession of year one and year two to build a student response protocol. The protocol, included in Appendix B, was intended to make the practice of responding more participatory and distributed and to help facilitators guide youth participants to examine and reflect on the rapid production and iteration in the network. The protocol includes three techniques for responding to students' interdisciplinary writing and making across distributed platforms: noticing, appreciating, and encouraging. Facilitators drafted sentence stems that helped them to name the meaning-making moves commonly employed by poets as well as those employed by scientists. They also included options for noticing the disconnects between meaning-making in the humanities and in the sciences with prompts such as, "How might a scientist look at _____ differently than a poet? What would the scientist focus more on here? What about the poet?" In addition, the protocol prompted facilitators to value the unconventional texts students produced and permissioned them to dispense with ranking and evaluating in favor of appreciating. This proved to be one of the affordances of working in informal science learning contexts, as classroom teachers could untether themselves from the common practices of judging and quantifying judgments in the form of grades that are required in formal education contexts.

The final technique embedded in the response protocol provided language to prompt contextual connections and position youth writing and making as the beginning of broader conversations about the value of science literacy in a time of rapid technological advancement. All too often in formal education settings, a student's composition is treated like an artifact or a relic of their learning, but this practice represents a temporal error in thinking about literacy acquisition. Shifting the temporality privileges the messy and undisciplined making, doing, producing, writing, juxtaposing, and experimenting and recognizes composition's potential to serve as a catalyst for more reflective and critical literacy. In discussing the aims and pedagogical actions related to critical literacy, Vasquez et al. note that critical literacy is nurtured when learners produce texts for diverse audiences and "let the texts do the work" (307). In this case, "the work" of *50 ft. Shark* and *Eagorilla and Other Mashups* was disruption. Teachers expressed anxiety. Scientists retreated. More could have been done by facilitation teams to address adult anxieties and absences so that youth composers became more aware of those impacts, but, again, this speaks to the possible limitation of informal science learning. Teachers reported that some of these conversations happened in the classroom; however, details of those experiences are not captured in the data collected for this study.

Arguably, the most valuable aspect of the response protocol was its invitation to facilitators to express a diversity of embodied and experiential reactions to youth writing and making. The protocol foregrounded interpretive difference as facilitators developed language to name and communicate their divergent embodied and experience-driven responses to unorthodox science writing. The protocol enabled facilitators to move beyond binary notions of "right" and "wrong" and prompted them to both acknowledge their own embodied and affective experiences of writing and making science as well as those of the youth participants. By drawing attention to the different vantage points from which readers approach texts, the classroom teachers and the poetry educators demonstrated how to think critically about a text's impact on different audiences. Unfortunately, however, the scientists' viewpoints and reactions were largely missing from some of these conversations, leaving young people unable to access important feedback about what the scientists themselves might appreciate or critique. Ultimately, the protocol could not solve the problem of retreat and avoidance. While valuable, the intervention was enacted late—perhaps too late—during the partnership and programming. As such, *Remix, Remake, Curate* did not fully leverage the impacts of crash encounters as a catalyst for the critical work of reasoning around how wild science-fiction fantasies are not so far removed from the foreseeable future and its formidable realities.

Implications and Suggestions for Facilitating Vibrant Science Literacy Programming

Reframing science literacy through the metaphor of crash encounters places particular emphasis on the reciprocal transformations that occur when bodies of knowledge, discourse, and organic and inorganic materials collide. Such a dynamic notion of literacy works to empower learners to move across contexts, disciplines, cultures, media, and modes. In addition, a crash encounter framework can help scholars and practitioners follow learners and composers across those modes, even when the disciplinary and cultural territory is unfamiliar and uncomfortable. At the same time, it's important to keep in mind, and to prompt scholars and practitioners to consider, the risk inherent in metaphors that encourage impact and collision. Just as the world's largest particle collider, the Large Hadron Collider, creates high-energy radiation-emitting particles and the potential for small-scale nuclear damage, literacy colliders like *Remix, Remake, Curate* can create incidental impairment, particularly in the form of cognitive dissonance and conflict retreat, as is demonstrated in the examples of *50 ft. Shark* and *Eagorilla and Other Mashups*. Practitioners engaging in such crash encounters should prepare for unintended consequences of such destabilizing labor and develop contingency plans for engaging its fallout. To leverage crashing as a catalyst for more critical interdisciplinary literacy, practitioners in the sciences and the humanities might learn to follow youth composers on these collision courses and develop their capacity to facilitate sustained conversations regarding the relations of power that are embedded in the texts they create.

Recent scholarship in the field of literacy studies posits that mobility is a more important concept for understanding literacy development as learners are perpetually moving through a variety of online and offline media, knowledge domains, as well as formal and informal learning contexts. Literacy learners are also moving with a diversity of people, languages, objects, and ideologies and are carried and directed by multivalent affective currents that structure meaning beyond rational and linguistic domains (Compton-Lilly; Stornaiuolo et al.; West-Puckett). This article builds on theories of movement by attending to the crash encounters that are inevitable in such busy literacy learners' lives. Through these encounters, learners impact and are impacted by a host of others. As a result of these impacts, learners remix and remake themselves, creating new ways of knowing, doing, and being. When learners are allowed and encouraged to pursue such crash encounters, their experiences also have the potential to act back on the disciplines—*if* we are willing to re-examine and rethink what counts as poetry or what counts as science.

As demonstrated, there is great promise in interdisciplinary, open, online programming such as *Remix, Remake, Curate* to prompt more dynamic, flexible, and vibrant approaches to science literacy; however, certain changes to program design and delivery may be useful to promote and leverage crash encounters and foster more critical engagement with the tools, processes, and values of scientific inquiry. First, program developers and educators need time to create sustainable partnerships across institutional and disciplinary contexts. While two years may seem like an ample duration to build and plan programming, *Remix, Remake, Curate* facilitators were pressed to develop both new curricula and open-source digital platforms to deliver the curricula within the timeframe. As a result, the interpersonal work of negotiating roles, articulating commitments, discussing communication preferences, and making space for frequent debriefing and processing of experience was given too little attention. For example, facilitation teams were never prompted to discuss what to do when teammates retreat or disassociate and could have benefitted from concrete strategies to call collaborators back into these difficult public conversations. In undertaking this interpersonal work, program developers and facilitators should expect multivalent affective orientations to composing through difference, and they should acknowledge, appreciate, and discuss those emotional responses straightforwardly. The goal of discussion is not to smooth over difference or reframe negative valences. As I demonstrated with the anxieties around youth composing that led to the creation of protocols, negative feelings can prompt important work. Honest conversations can help educators become more attentive to how affect is essential to literacy work for both teachers and learners. Having these conversations and producing accords, like that of the response protocol described in the last section, might prove more effective if positioned earlier rather than later in the partnership development.

Second, program developers should work with partners to bring youth composers into the planning, development, and delivery of programming. In hindsight, an excellent use of grant funds would have been to provide stipends for youth mentors to work with each facilitation team. Science centers may have junior docents or camp counselors, and participating schools may have poetry and robotics clubs from which to recruit youth mentors. Such a move to fully integrate young people in planning and development would help to center their experiences, interests, aims, and motivations in open science education initiatives. As anyone who teaches peer review knows, youth, too, can benefit from learning to give meaningful feedback to difficult texts. If youth facilitators had been involved in negotiating the response protocol, the protocol may have been more effective in prompting critical conversations.

Finally, if the goal of science literacy is to prepare young people to effectively address critical global issues such as biological conservation, health disparities, and viral pandemics—both locally and globally—perhaps we might start with these real-world problems instead of the "problem" of science literacy. The *Remix, Remake,*

Curate programming foregrounded composing interdisciplinary texts instead of composing solutions through interdisciplinary processes and frames. In contrast, youth composers and facilitators might collaboratively identify problems, issues, and concerns that are at the forefront of their own anxieties, interests, and passions and build programming that engages others in sustained cross-cultural and cross-disciplinary inquiry. Instead of linear programming that mimics the ways students march through curricula in formal education settings, facilitators should consider offering writing and making units that run concurrently for a longer duration and ask participants to self-select a particular group that focuses on a local or global issue that they investigate using the tools and techniques of science and poetry. Research that explores the impacts of free-choice and motivation in science learning supports this intervention (Falk; Falk et al.; Miller). Falk et al. note that a broad approach to science literacy does not consider the specific experiences, questions, and personal interests that motivate people to learn science across their lifetime. They also note that when investigating science literacy among professional scientists, few have a deep knowledge of science outside of their area of expertise. This is not a deficit for professional scientists or the science learner, they argue; it is simply the consequence of living and learning in an information age in which "…access to content- and context-specific information is readily available" (464). Promoting free-choice and supporting science making and communicating that are more personally motivated could still provide space for collisions of the *50 ft. Shark* and *Eagorilla* kind; however, more time would allow facilitators to better make sense of the fallout and drive students toward more critical thinking and composing.

By taking up these suggestions, program developers can support literacy practitioners in relaxing resistance to matter and objects and encourage partners in the sciences to do the same regarding discourse. This means we must embrace the impact of crash encounters, rather than seeing science and humanities as two different lenses, if we are to grasp what that snotty blob of DNA is as well as what it means for the future of our world. Thus, we should not just *look at* but also *listen to* and *feel* the material and embodied world of science composing, approaching critical questions about both *matter* and *mattering* (Barad 3). While I'm certainly not advocating here that scholars dispense with rigorous, discipline-specific methods of investigation and knowledge-making, I am suggesting that we understand those methods differently when we see them diffracted through other disciplinary ways of knowing, doing, and being. What's more, through cultural and disciplinary intra-activity, we can approach a new space of science + literacy that acts back on each discipline and transgresses boundaries that restrict integrated meaning-making. These transgressions can enable educators to sponsor more dynamic and meaningful science literacy initiatives and cultivate lifelong learners who engage science as life-enriching and life-sustaining quotidian practice.

Works Cited

Banks, Will, and Michelle Eble. "Digital Spaces, Online Environments, and Human Participant Research: Interfacing with Institutional Review Boards." In *Writing Studies Research in Practice: Methods and Methodologies*, edited by Lee Nickoson and Mary P. Sheridan, Southern Illinois UP, 2012.

Barad, Karen M. *Meeting the Universe Halfway: Quantum Physics and the Entanglement of Matter and Meaning*. Duke UP, 2007.

Bennett, Jane. *Vibrant Matter: A Political Ecology of Things*. Duke UP, 2010.

Briseño-Garzón, Adriana, et al. "'To Learn about Science': Real Life Scientific Literacy across Multicultural Communities." *Community Literacy Journal*, vol. 8, no. 2, 2014, pp. 81-107. *Project Muse*.

Brossard, Dominique. "Scientific Knowledge and Attitude Change: The Impact of a Citizen Science Project." *International Journal of Science Education*, vol. 27, no. 9, 2005, pp. 1099-1121, Taylor & Francis Online, doi:10.1080/09500690500069483.ah.

Carter, Michael. "Ways of Knowing, Doing, and Writing in the Disciplines." *College Composition and Communication*, vol. 58, no. 3, 2007, pp. 385-418. *JSTOR*.

Chang, Yen-Ping, et al. "Affective Valence Signals Agency Within and Between Individuals." *Emotion*, vol. 17, no. 2, 2017, pp. 296–308. *PubMed*, doi.org/10.1037/emo0000229.

Clough, G. Wayne. *Increasing Scientific Literacy: A Shared Responsibility*. Smithsonian Institution, 2010. www.scifun.org/news/Increasing-Scientific-Literacy-a-Shared-Responsibility.pdf.

Compton-Lilly, Catherine. "Introduction: Conceptualizing Past, Present, and Future Timespaces." *Time and Space in Literacy Research*, edited by Catherine Compton-Lilly and Erica Halverson, Routledge, 2014, pp. 1-16.

Cronje, Ruth, et al. "Does Participation in Citizen Science Improve Scientific Literacy? A Study to Compare Assessment Methods." *Applied Environmental Education & Communication*, vol. 10, no. 3, 2011, pp. 135-145. doi:10.1080/1533015X.2011.603611.

Dolphijn, Rick, and Iris van der Tuin. *New Materialism: Interviews & Cartographies*, Open Humanities P, 2012. hdl.handle.net/2027/spo.11515701.0001.001.

Ennes, Megan, and Imani N. Lee. "Distance Learning in Museums: A Review of the Literature." *International Review of Research in Open and Distributed Learning*, vol. 22, no. 3, 2021, pp. 162-187. *ERIC*. doi.org/10.19173/irrodl.v21i3.5387.

Falk, John, and Lynn Dierking. "The 95% Solution." *American Scientist*, vol. 98, no. 6, 2010, pp. 486-493.

Falk, John, editor. *Free-Choice Science Education: How We Learn Science Outside of School*. Teachers College P, 2001.

Falk, John, et al. "Investigating Public Science Interest and Understanding: Evidence for the Importance of Free-choice Learning." *Public Understanding of Science*, vol. 16, no. 4, 2007, pp. 455-469.

Farkas, Kerrie, and Christina Haas. "A Grounded Theory Approach for Studying Writing and Literacy." *Practicing Research in Writing Studies: Reflexive and Eth-*

ically Responsible Research, edited by Christina Haas and Pamela Takayoshi, Hampton P, 2012, pp. 81-95.

Fleckenstein, Kristie. "Faceless Students, Virtual Places: Emergence and Communal Accountability in Online Classrooms." *Computers and Composition*, vol. 22, no. 2, 2005, pp. 149-176. doi: 10.1016/j.compcom.2005.02.003.

Grabill, Jeffrey. "Community-based Research and the Importance of a Research Stance." *Writing Studies Research in Practice: Methods and Methodologies*, edited by Lee Nickoson and Mary P. Sheridan, Southern Illinois UP, 2012, pp. 210-219.

Ito, Mizuko, et al. *Connected Learning: An Agenda for Research and Design*, BookBaby, 2013.

Kimmerer, Robin Wall. *Braiding Sweetgrass: Indigenous Wisdom, Scientific Knowledge, and the Teachings of Plants*, Milkweed Editions, 2020.

—. "Restoration and Reciprocity: The Contributions of Traditional Ecological Knowledge." *Human Dimensions of Ecological Restoration: Integrating Science, Nature, and Culture*, edited by Dave Egan, Evan E. Hjerpe, and Jesse Abrams, Island P, 2011, pp. 257-276.

Neff, Joyce M. "Grounded Theory: A Critical Research Methodology." *Under Construction: Working at the Intersections of Composition Theory, Research, and Practice*, edited by Christine Farris and Chris M. Anson, Utah State UP, 1998, pp. 124-135.

McKee, Heidi, and James E. Porter. "The Ethics of Digital Writing Research: A Rhetorical Approach." *College Composition and Communication*, vol. 59, 2008, pp. 711-749.

Miller, Jon D. "Civic Scientific Literacy in the United States in 2016: A Report Prepared for the National Aeronautics and Space Administration by the University of Michigan." smd-prod.s3.amazonaws.com/science-red/s3fs-public/atoms/files/NASA%20CSL%20in%202016%20Report_0_0.pdf.

Nisbet, Matthew, and Dietram Scheufele. "What's Next for Science Communication? Promising Directions and Lingering Distractions." *American Journal of Botany*, vol. 96, no. 10, 2009, pp. 1767-78. doi: 10.3732/ajb.0900041.

Ortoleva, Matthew. "Narragansett Bay and Biospheric Literacies of the Body." *Community Literacy Journal*, vol. 4, no. 1, 2009, pp. 59-72, doi:10.25148/clj.4.1.009454.

Palloff, Rena M., and Keith Pratt. *Building Online Learning Communities: Effective Strategies for the Virtual Classroom*. Jossey-Bass, 2007.

Sackey, Donnie, et al. "Constructing Learning Spaces: What We Can Learn from Studies of Informal Learning Online." *Computers and Composition*, vol. 35, 2015, pp. 112-124. doi: 10.1016/j.compcom.2015.01.004.

Semper, Rob. "Nodes and Connections: Science Museums in the Network Age." *Curator: The Museum Journal*, vol. 13, no. 20, 2010, doi.org/10.1111/j.2151-6952.2002.tb00046.x

Siang, Sanyin. "Americans Concerned About Ethics, Morality of Scientific Research, Survey Shows." *Journal of the National Cancer Institute*, vol. 93, no. 24, 2001, pp. 1841. doi.org/10.1093/jnci/93.24.1841.

Smith, Anna, et al. "Remix as Professional Learning: Educators' Iterative Literacy Practice in CLMOOC." *Education Sciences*, vol. 6, no. 1, 2016. doi.org/10.3390/educsci6010012.

Stornaiuolo, Amy, et al. "Developing a Transliteracies Framework for a Connected World." *Journal of Literacy Research*, vol. 49, no. 1, 2017, pp. 68-91.

Trumbull, Deborah, et al. "Thinking Scientifically during Participation in a Citizen-Science Project." *Science Education*, vol. 84, no. 2, 2000, pp. 265-275.

Vasquez, Vivian Maria, et al. "Critical Literacy as a Way of Being and Doing." *Language Arts: The Journal of the Elementary Section of the National Council of Teachers of English*, vol. 96, no. 5, 2019, pp. 300-311.

West-Puckett, Stephanie. *Materializing Makerspaces: Queerly Composing Space, Time, and (What) Matters*. 2017. East Carolina University, PhD dissertation. *The Scholarship*, hdl.handle.net/10342/6344.

West-Puckett, Stephanie, et al. "The Fallacies of Open: Participatory Design, Infrastructuring, and the Pursuit of Radical Possibility." *Contemporary Issues in Technology and Teacher Education*, vol. 18, no. 2, 2018, pp. 203-232.

Appendix A

Science Media Examples

Student poem about tree growth and time.

Student blackout poems, made from informational texts about DNA.

Student insect painting, observed during from porch light science.

Student six-word poem coded in HTML using Mozilla Thimble

Photo of students extracting DNA.

Video of a youth participant singing about butterflies while playing the ukulele, available on YouTube at https://youtu.be/zSZ3tZE-1Jg.

Poetry how-to video created by a poet facilitator, available on YouTube at https://youtu.be/1pxvaT07uDk.

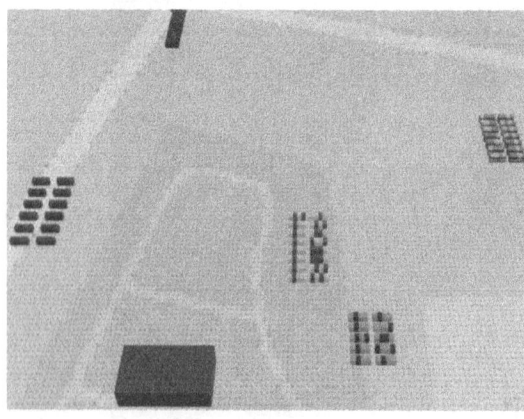

Screenshot of a digital landscape of student names coded in binary with digital Legos.

Appendix B

Facilitator Response Protocol

Noticing the science:
I notice...
You did _____ like a scientist. I know this because you_____.
I see the science of _____ here.
I think it's interesting that you said _____. Do you have any ideas why that happened?
I like how you connected...
Have you thought about which systems...
I like how you've thought about the system of_____.
What else do you want to know?
Wow! That's an interesting observation, and I'm curious because I've never seen or heard of a _____ (do or look like or be as big as, etc.) _____. They are typically more like _____.
Here's a good resource to learn more about...
Tell me more about your practices of (observation, documentation, experimentation, etc.)...

Noticing the poetry:
I noticed you used ___ like a poet. I really like _____ (these words or phrases or lines) because...
I see how you are using poetic (language, concepts, or practices) in these lines and wonder if...
Your use of _____ in the poem was really powerful. It made me think of or remember...
Your word choice in this line _____ was really accurate and precise. As a reader, that's important to me because...
Here's a good resource to learn more about...
Here's an example of a poem similar to yours that uses, discusses, demonstrates, etc....

Noticing dis/connections between science & poetry:
Both scientists and poets appreciate or use _____. I like or am wondering about how you used _____ to create this piece. Tell me more.

How might a scientist look at _____ differently than a poet? What would the scientist focus more on here? How about the poet?

Appreciating creativity:
I like how you described ____ by doing/saying_____.
I like how you used (sensory details-sound, sight, touch, smell, taste) to describe _____.
You did a great job describing your feelings/actions/observations. I noticed_____.
I like that you chose to represent your findings using a (voicethread, poem, graph drawing, etc). Tell me more about how you composed that...
That's such an interesting connection you made between...

Appreciating the content:
I like how you_____.
You did a great job of_____.
I like your____ because_____.

Encouraging deeper thought or extension:
Have you thought/or considered about _____?
Did you know that____?
What else do you want to know now?
I wonder____?
What did you have to learn about to (draw, write, compose, perform) this piece?

Author Bio

Stephanie West-Puckett (she/her) is an assistant professor of writing and rhetoric at the University of Rhode Island, where she directs the First Year Writing Program. Her research generates critical theories and practices for transforming the teaching and assessing of writing in the classroom as well as in community literacy settings. Her scholarship has been published in journals such as *College English, Journal of Adolescent & Adult Literacy,* and *Education Sciences* as well as in several edited collections. Her forthcoming book, *Failing Sideways: Queer Possibilities for Writing Assessment* (co-authored with Nicole I. Caswell and William P. Banks) with University Press of Colorado/Utah State University Press, is expected in spring 2023.

Interview

Democracy, Pedagogy, and Advocacy 2022

Steve Parks and Srdja Popovic

For the past two years, Steve Parks and Srdja Popovic have been engaged in a discussion on the global state of democracy. Parks has spent the past thirty years working with democratic advocates locally, nationally, and internationally to support their goals for increased political rights, work which has led to the creation of New City Community Press as well as Syrians for Truth and Justice. Popovic began his advocacy work through co-founding OTPOR!, an organization widely credited with toppling the Serbian dictator Slobodan Milošević in 2000. Since that time, he co-founded and directs the *Center for Applied Nonviolent Actions and Strategies* (CANVAS), which has offered training to advocates in over 50 countries. In 2021, these conversations resulted in the creation of the *Democratic Futures Working Group*, an international alliance of academic and global democratic advocates exploring how new democratic models of organizing and governance are emerging from the grassroots interaction of indigenous traditions and the legacy of Western-colonialist rights paradigms.

In the following discussion, Parks and Popovic begin by discussing the current state of democracy, both within and beyond the United States. Within this context, they focus on the need to create new public narratives about the value of democracy which operate on a local, national, and global level, often drawing off non-Western paradigms. Such narratives, however, only gain power if they exist within broad coalitions of individuals, communities, and organizations, often requiring uncomfortable alliances and compromise. And it is unclear, to Parks and Popovic, whether the current scholarly and pedagogical frameworks of the university are capable of teaching students the knowledges and skills to create such narratives and alliances. For them, the question becomes whether classrooms focused on democracy require a fundamental revisioning of who should teach and who belongs in the professoriate. Ultimately, they pose the question of what "professional credentials" qualify someone to develop a pedagogy and a writing classroom premised on democracy and advocacy.

***

Parks: We recently co-taught several writing courses whose primary theme was democracy and human rights; whose primary requirement was for students to undertake political analysis and write as public advocates on an international context; and whose primary goal was to connect such written work to actual strategies to build nonviolent democratic campaigns for justice. We were fortunate to have global human rights activists join our conversation, often though Zoom, such as Slobodan Djinovic, *OTPOR!/CANVAS*; Husam

Alkatlaby, *Hakuna Movement*/Aleppo, Syria; Dani Ayers, CEO of *MeToo*; Andre Henry, *Black Lives Matter*, CA; Johnson Yeung, former convener of the *Civil Human Rights Front* and Secretary-General of the *Hong Kong Federation of Students*, and Myo Yan Naung Thein, a leader of the democracy movement in Myanmar. Given the fact these courses occurred during and in the aftermath of the January 6th insurrection, we found ourselves wondering about the current state of global democracy, the type of advocacy which was being created to push back against a rising authoritarianism, and, ultimately, who is best suited to teach such skills to university students. Which means we returned to our usual topic: Is there any reason to be optimistic about democracy? How do we understand the organizing now occurring? How do we teach it to our students?

Popovic: In terms of global democracy trends, we are in the worst place since 1992 per the *Freedom House* report (Repucci and Slipowitz). You can take one look at that report and conclude democratic movements have become less successful. But this is a bit of a false conclusion. True, *statistically*, the movements have become less successful, but this statistical decline is a result of there being more democratic movements (Chenoweth). Instead of 100 movements and 56 (56%) successful movements, there are 500 movements and 160 (32%) of them are successful movements. More important than such statistics, I believe the Dictatorship-Democracy dynamic is the core concept to notice. According to this report, the most dramatic change in democracy is in the places considered to be democratic countries. When you look at the largest chunks of the global population, democracy shrunk in India, democracy shrunk in the U.S. This happens due to the phenomena of "Erdoganzation." You have a politician who's democratically elected, like Erdogan in Turkey. That elected leader starts packing the media with their people, the courts with their people, who then collectively start pushing the "party agenda" (De Witte). At this point, you have the *How Democracies Die* situation, as discussed by Steven Levitsky and Daniel Ziblatt, where democracies die slowly as institutional prisoners of autocratic leaning rulers and political parties (Levitsky and Ziblatt).

Parks: My sense is the Trump administration was a failed attempt (or test run) at "Erdoganzation." And I think quite a few folks were shell shocked over the speed at which democratic traditions seemed to be weaponized on Trump's behalf. There seemed to be just too much trust in a large segment of the nation that "institutions" and "traditions" would block the excesses of Trump's presidency. But it became clear that our nation-state's strong independent institutions were fortified primarily by tradition, not legal structures. And we witnessed the weakness of those traditional "checks and balances" in Congress as a result of hyper partisanship and weak politicians (as Levitsky and Ziblatt demonstrate). What we discovered is that when a political figure, such as Trump, gains power, "Erdoganzation" is more possible than most would like to think. And I think we need to understand the Republican push to limit voting rights nationally as an attempt to set the stage for the next "Trump-Erdogan" to succeed in dismantling fundamental democratic guardrails against authoritarian political leaders. This is one reason that the protests and public actions against these moves are so important.

Popovic: This highlights a central conclusion of the *Freedom House* report; not only are we witnessing one of the darkest moments in decline of world democracy – the number of countries where democracy has shrunk rose to unprecedented levels - but also that this decay comes mostly from previously "democratic" countries sliding down on guaranteed freedoms to "hybrid regimes" and "semi democracies." It is sad to see the U.S.A., India, and my own homeland, Serbia, leading this list of "bad students" of democracy. If these past several years have taught us anything, we need to understand that the time is now - more than ever - to find ways to mobilize participation of the people in "democratic" countries, and to prevent "Erdoganzation," where general apathy and low participation enabled power hungry (and originally democratically elected leaders) to topple down democratic institutions from above.

So what is the response? First, you don't take democracy for granted (Friedler). Second, you stress participation. Any positive social change starts with understanding that you need community, a collective commitment. And if you want to succeed, you need all sorts of people. You need all these different players, different talents, and different qualities. That is, both science and empiric experience teach us that to succeed, democratic movements need coalitions (Goldstone). You need both numbers and diversity to succeed. So, the very nature of nonviolent social change is actively promoting the idea of horizontal connections within a community. Social networks are central intermediary structures on which individuals and groups construct solutions that allow them to cope with the deficiencies resulting from the formal system (Adler-Lomnitz-Lomnitz and Sheinbaum).

If you are a fan of George Orwell's *1984* – the anti-utopia playbook of effective totalitarianism - you get the clear idea how these types of governments are trying to cut this type of horizontal relationship. They want you to report on your brother if he misbehaves. This is because in an autocracy, the people are lonely, lost, isolated. They only look up to their boss or down to their subordinates. Autocracies don't want people to look left and right because, if that happens, people can figure out they have the power to create change. They can figure out that five of them can change one policy in their building; 50 of them can change issues on the street. For an authoritarian status-quo, that's a very dangerous line of thinking because, ultimately, that means 500,000 of them can change the government. This is exactly why autocracies discourage horizontal networks, group civic action, and any form of independent collective action initiatives.

Parks: I agree coalition-building is a central concept about nonviolent organizing to protect and expand democratic culture and governance. Such coalitions seem to face particular difficulties at this particular moment. There are always tensions caused by attempting such work. For instance, I have heard you argue that to create change, "You have to make the police your friends. You have to bring them over to your side." Given the brutal treatment police have enacted on Black communities and their failure to often protect Asian/Asian-American communities, I've seen how such a suggestion can appear to deny the reality of such abuse. Yet, all evidence points to the necessity of such alliances. Here I'm thinking of a story told by Pumla Gobodo-Madikizela, who was on the *South African Truth and Reconciliation Commission*. She speaks to how a particularly brutal police officer was finally released from prison. She made the point that the final moment of the process of the "truth discovery" that led to someone being held accountable was reconciliation – to call them back into the culture, allow their humanity to be recognized (Marchese). I think such reconciliation is very difficult to achieve right now. In my experience, it is very difficult to state, "I'm going to work with someone who has a polluted past." And this is despite any acceptance of consequences of past acts by that individual. There's a notion of purity that blocks the actions required to enact collective change. And if the goal is to create the coalitions that create the change you want to see in the world, notions of purity within organizing efforts are ultimately a form of self-aggrandizement.

Popovic: Insisting on "Moral purity" damages the possibility of change. Whenever you see a movement that was successful throughout history, the movement succeeded through the diversity of its allies. I always cite the environmental movement since, at least in Europe, it is "the least political" movement. It's also where my own degree in environment/biology gives to me some insights. Environmentalism started as a set of crazy folks tying themselves to nuclear power plants (Yeo). They would talk about moral purity and would never talk to the companies. How did the movement end up? How did it advance? It was when *Greenpeace* began sitting at the same table with the "other" stakeholders, such as environmental protection agencies, the fossil fuel industry, and solar panels industry. The lesson here is not to look at people as individuals to like or dislike, to determine their morality. Instead, the lesson is to try to understand where their values might overlap with your campaign's values. Rather than total purity, you should try to discover situational alliances that move your stated values and goals forward. At one point in life, you need to decide whether you want to be right or successful. And being successful very often means making compromises.

Parks: At some point, through engaging in collective organizing, you need to learn that your personal opinions, your own purity, are not as important as creating systemic change that directly impacts the material reality of those too often on the side of privilege. So, I think part of what is required at this historical juncture by advocates, by Composition and Rhetoric faculty (to speak from my own position) is to work to create public narratives that enable coalitions to produce change. And as we take up such work, we need to build into that public narrative a global perspective. This new "public" must demand an international concept of democracy and democratic rights that disallow certain actions by the United States.

And to repeat what many others have said, this work also entails replacing a neoliberal national and international framework focused on market and morals, where morality is replaced with economics. As long as you allow capitalism to move unfettered from national, international, and collective rights-based concepts, there's this sense that politicians are acting ethically by meeting with dictators to expand "markets." In that world, quality, human rights, all those concepts that organize people around a common fate, get washed away. That said, I don't want to be seen as romanticizing the United Nations or past declarations of international rights. Too often, those rights have been used to historically mandate Western concepts to non-Western nations. To some extent, if we want to reimagine democratic organizing, democratic governance, emerging in the cracks of neoliberalism, we also need to support global efforts to reimagine human rights as emerging not only from "the West" but from Indigenous and non-Western frameworks. We need to try to understand (and not just blithely and insincerely accept) the actual possibilities decolonial articulations of communal responsibility and shared governance might offer.

Popovic: I would only add that frameworks to understand the interconnection of democracies should not be the domino state-by-state effect, the argument used to perpetuate the Vietnam war and other global conflicts. Rather, the interconnection must be a set of norms and values as well as international charters, starting with human rights, freedom of the press, and so on. The need for such global norms seems vital – even if they must be renegotiated in the current moment. This is because if global opinion in times of globalization becomes that such value-based concepts are stupid, bureaucratic shit, that we only care about how much we earn, you will have silence on the human rights atrocities occurring in Myanmar by the military ruling authority. You will have Obama being very democratic, but at the same time, being in bed with dictators. You will have Trump's silence and public admiration of guys like Kim Jong Un or Putin. So, there is a need to reset to international norms. It's not inventing the wheel because we have already signed up for the concept of such norms and already have some useful norms in place. It's re-inventing a more inclusive and just set of norms.

I would also add such work is necessary to re-establish belief in the moral value of democracy over authoritarianism. In this international context, I think such work has broader meaning. It is connected to people's view towards "truth." It is not because people don't believe CNN is "telling the truth" that democracies are failing. It is because people don't believe in democracy. So, the very evil nature of the poison coming from Mother Russia and other places is the stance that "Oh, democracy, autocracy doesn't matter. It's the same shit." The "same shit" is the real danger. If you kill values, then all these documents and norms, which were based on values, they don't work. If you say, the United Nations is just a bureaucratic mechanism of the world dominance of the U.S. or China or whoever, actually you are erasing these values adopted after bitter lessons of two world wars from history. You are erasing the possibility of such collective values guiding our global community. You are making everything very relative. Democracy can't work without values. Human rights are based around values. Equality is a value category first, that application of the simple truth that all men and women regardless of race, ethnicity and religion or sexual preferences are born equal.

Parks: To go to my earlier point about the need for new public narratives, I'm not convinced such a language of shared values exists. Instead, I would say we are living during the moment of this new public narratives' invention, where such discourses are integrating into (and altering) how networks of power can operate. We can point to new identity terms; expanding freedom to choose pronouns for ourselves; the infusing of counter-stories within educational institutions as positive signs. James Carville, though, has criticized such "woke culture" for pushing away white working-class voters and has argued that "wokeness" effectively kills the chance for large political coalitions. And the Republicans are clearly using elements of this new narrative to animate elements of the white working and middle-class against such tools as critical race theory, leading to school libraries banning books by African American authors. The issue becomes how do you reanimate an ethics of communal responsibilities, grounded in new possibilities instead of historical systems of exclusion, in the language available in the present moment? In some ways, such language is local, in some ways it's national, in some ways international. But undergirding it all is the concern of creating a process that enacts the positive daily benefits, the enhanced material reality possible, in the face of brutal political and cultural assaults on the very communities doing this important work.

Popovic: I think it's a two-way process. One, we are talking about educating people about their power to tackle injustice of any kind. Go back to the environment. Environment is always a good case because my kids are more environmentally aware than I am. And, of course, I'm far more environmentally aware than my parents. So, we might look at how this generationally expanded understanding worked. Part of it is that we gained access to more information. Part of it is that science took a stance. The most important part of it, however, was gaining an immediate connection between the concept and the reality, and that happened through the educational system (Ellsmoor).

To make durable change in how people connect with democracy, then, one must embed it into education, but not only by teaching people about the values, but actively practicing those values and processes.

Parks: I think we are trying to do some of that work with our new course, an entry-level required writing course co-taught with Myo Yan Naung Thein. In that course, we began by having students read theoretical materials on the value of nonviolent organizing by scholars such as Gene Sharp and Erica Chenoweth. That is a pretty typical move, I think, for an academic course. We then supplemented those readings by having students take part in CANVAS training materials that focused on how nonviolent movements utilize a set of skills to create a unity of vision, map the political terrain, and analyze the pillars of power that are supporting authoritarian regimes. (We were fortunate that in a diminishing COVID world, you were able to travel and actually work with the students directly.) When they read Bartholomae's "Inventing the University," then, that essay became a piece about how students should use nonviolent theories and strategies to actually re-invent, alter, the pillars of power that keep certain voices and heritages intentionally excluded from classrooms. Somewhat oddly, "Inventing" became a manifesto for change, an opportunity for students to test out how the skills/concepts they were learning could transform their own education.

Again, though, I realize that elements of this course might also be somewhat typical of an entry-level required writing course. I think where we moved to have students "actively practicing those values and processes" as in our partnership with Myo Yan Naung Thein, who is a nationally recognized democratic advocate from Myanmar. When the military recently led a coup to topple the democratically elected government, Thein had to flee the country to escape certain arrest, torture, and death. Since that time, I have been working with him to create the Burmese Democratic Futures Working Group (BDFWG), which sponsors research to support democratic advocates resisting the coup. By bringing the work of this group into the class, our students were able to take their sense of academic writing, nonviolent theories of social change, and CANVAS organizing materials to produce work for the BDFWG. Some of these materials are still being developed, but essentially, the students are creating a publication of personal narratives of how the coup has impacted the lives of Myanmar citizens, coupled with a brief overview of Myanmar history. Many of those who were interviewed had to flee to the Thailand border to escape arrest after protesting the coup. These narratives also highlight the need to respect all ethnicities in Myanmar, an important element emerging within the resistance movement. This book will be published in the Working and Writing for Change series and our hope is that it can be used in a variety of writing and rhetoric classes, as have other such books in the series.

More than just produce a book, though, students are using the CANVAS strategies to develop a "curriculum" to support/encourage students across U.S. universities to hold a day of "protest" in support of democracy in Myanmar. Here the students are blending their sense of academic research and public writing to create materials which will bring in participants. They are mapping the terrain, understanding what pillars within a university might be brought into supporting Myanmar participants, then providing tactics and strategies for other university students to use on their campuses. In some ways then, our course is attempting to not just provide our students with the skills to actually practice the skills and processes of democracy and nonviolent change; we are also asking our students to become "teachers" to other students. I think our hope is that such work will translate into their being able to undertake similar projects within their own U.S.-based communities as well.

In fact, one of the more interesting elements of the course has been the discussion on how creating a public narrative in support of political change in Myanmar has led students to think about political change narratives in the U.S. There seems to be a sense that political change here is occurring through individual networks activating themselves rather than some unified organization. This is somewhat the case in Myanmar, which is a larger and different discussion, but in Myanmar, you have a national government in exile which at least as a rhetorical trope is framing the endpoint of the resistance movement. That is, the goal is a new democratically elected government in Myanmar.

I'm not sure such a unified "group" or "organizing" shapes today's political narratives or campaigns in the U.S. today.

Popovic: I think we are experiencing a moment where the connection between public narrative and political change movements are undergoing a transformation. When you look at the history of movements, such as the *Solidarity* movement, the core of it was a big organization, namely *Solidarity*. It was the labor union, but it was also a big organization. You want to look at the Civil Rights Movement of the late 20th century. The core of it was a coalition of organizations, including its radical wing party called the Black Panthers. What is interesting with the new contemporary movements, according to Carne Ross, is that movements have changed their shapes. According to Ross, what distinguishes new social movements is there is no spine of the organization (Ross). You can't really say, "Okay, this is the *Indivisible* group that got the manual and then learned how to build coalitions with local groups, then they start exercising strategies and tactics or whatever." Today, organizing occurs more on the *Occupy Wall Street* horizontal model.

Here we can add in the work of Benjamin Press at Carnegie, who runs the *Protest Tracker*, an interactive database of anti-government protests in the last three or four years (Press). It looks at public triggers and how such triggers have changed organizing. That is, the first thing that connects individuals within this new strain of movements is a trigger. They start with a trigger, not an organization. And in the internet era, such triggers spread horizontally with a lot of speed. They tend to replicate across a vast terrain of geography very fast. So, they start in Minneapolis, but 15 days after that, you have public marches in New York, Philadelphia, in Florida, in Louisiana, everywhere. They spread horizontally like wildfire. It's not only numbers. It's also territorial cover. Given this context, they are very difficult to control and very difficult to suppress because they are unpredictable.

Such trigger movements are not typically created by existing organizations. So, being leaderless gives them speed and spread, as well as making them less capable of being oppressed. For instance, the real trouble for Putin is not 10,000 people defending Navalny in Bolotnaya Square in Moscow. It is the fact that you have 150 people in a tiny town in Siberia, which an ordinary person can't find on the map, which came out to march at -15 Fahrenheit (see "Russian Protestors"). This is the real problem for a dictator because he can't predict these people. He can't trace the organization. He can't corrupt, repress, blackmail, co-opt, and put the leaders in jail. Because contemporary movements are horizontal, they are very difficult to decapitate, because there is no head.

But I would argue that the lack of an organizational structure also makes such movements less effective and more difficult to coordinate from the side of the movement itself. It's different than the normal structure of the movement. In those movements you have recognizable stages – the emerging phase, building phase, engagement phase, exponential phase. And then somewhere, you have bureaucratic costs, whatever, and then the numbers go down if you succeed, if you get co-opted, if you get tired, if you get repressed, whatever. With new movements you have a different algorithmic curve. New movements start with large numbers under the banner of a term, a hashtag, not a fully realized public narrative linked to a strategy. That is, the numbers are there before the organization. The reason why many of these movements fail is that the numbers are there before a forward-looking strategy. It is connected to triggers, so by its very nature, it's doomed to fail because it's reactive.

Successful movements typically share an understanding of a common goal, that understands these are the numbers we need to mobilize, these are the pillars of power, the institutions that need to be swayed to our cause, and these are the institutional changes we want to achieve, such as desegregate schools or legalize gay marriage. It doesn't matter the topic. New movements are not issue based. They are event based. They become issue based as a new public narrative about that trigger gains traction. So, the police kill an unarmed Black man, and you have millions of people using hashtags to show communal commitment to justice. Then one hashtag, such as BlackLivesMatter (BLM), gains dominance. Now BLM is in the position to build a manifesto, an agenda. But unlike the *ANC Freedom Charter* which guided the anti-apartheid movement, BLM doesn't start with such an articulated vision/strategy. The movement ends up with very disciplined protests of BLM people in places like LA and then more join, more form protests. Some of these protests will be in front of Trump's hotels. Some will do actions which are very strategic, because locally they were very strategic, actions which reflect an emerging manifesto for change. And then you have local tactics which harm the strategic purpose, like 20 angry activists who have burned down a *Wendy's* in Atlanta. You have angry activists with helmets who barricade themselves starting the "Battle of Portland." All these actions, done under the name of the hashtag BLM, enabled their opponents to label the whole movement as "sick and deranged Anarchists & Agitators." And potentially damage their just efforts at systemic reform.

Parks: First, I should note the fact that we are two white men discussing a movement initiated by a Black women's hashtag and leadership. We probably do not want to position ourselves as "explaining" what should have been done by BLM advocates. I think, in fact, we can learn a lot about the complexity of creating new inclusive structures for advocacy through considering their impact and organization. For instance, you're saying that those movements are less successful, but I'd argue that what BLM did was to shatter the public narrative around police. Fifteen years ago, the public rhetoric was the police were a "thin blue line" against outbreaks of crime and expanding drug culture. Every politician wanted to stand next to police for a photo-op. There was a romanticization of police and a demonization of minority and immigrant communities in large cities that politicians actively utilized in their campaigns. I could argue that these spontaneous, spread-out, geographically dispersed movements actualized resistance at such a scale that it broke that public narrative, that hegemonic consensus. Such a cultural shift in public narrative is a success.

I understand it's not as initially successful in terms of local changes in policies – though I'm sure research would show legislative and policy impact. But re-invoking your discussion of the Civil Rights movement, thinking about its early days in the late 1950's, I would argue part of the success of the Civil Rights movement was the public shift in narrative about what was going on in the South. The visual images of the protesters being attacked by dogs and water hoses shattered a certain consensus. I think that one way to think about *BLM* or *Occupy* is that they shattered the public narrative, which is all to the good. But what Occupy, as a movement, was less successful in achieving was a positive public narrative—a beyond-critique stance. To my thinking, they remained only at a level of triggered, of oppositional, not productively coalitional. As you argued, *Occupy* lacked a coherent "spine" to produce actual change in systems of power—legislative or economic.

Popovic: Agree and not, we need to distinguish between two things. One thing is the argument that public awareness rising always has a positive impact on an issue, whether that issue is racism, such as police abuse or legislators denying people equal access to vote in a place like Georgia. When we talk about the success or failure of a movement, the question is whether the demands *were met*. Take Egypt. Everybody can argue Egypt is in a worse place now under Sisi than it was under Mubarak, but this counts as a successful movement. These people wanted to replace Mubarak. They succeeded and then something else happened, but this is history. This is not looking at one movement.

If you look at the goals of the movement, like BLM, they came after the trigger. Again, the goals of BLM appeared after the numbers were reached, at which point, it becomes very difficult to define whether or not the movement has succeeded. You may argue that it brought large numbers of people to be involved. You may argue also they brought a lot of people from the political middle. For instance, you will find even in a conservative place like Colorado Springs, whole neighborhoods have a BLM sign in their yards. This is a very White town, a totally White town, perhaps having only 6% of its population being Black. So, even in very White, conservative places, it engaged audiences. This is not the question of participation. Once again, the numbers are high. So, it's not disputable that the numbers are huge. Because these numbers were reached before defining the strategy, because these numbers are produced around vague ideas, or things connected to the triggers, these movements are less likely to achieve their demands because these demands are not clear and start appearing after the momentum is lost. That doesn't necessarily mean that movements like BLM are not going to be turned into a longstanding organization, which will eventually shift power; I think it will, but I'm just generalizing about the new structure of movements.

And the reason for such a hope returns us to Benjamin Press' fourth element in his analysis. Element number one was trigger, not issue or organizational based. Element number two was horizontal super spread, super decentralized in decision-making. Number three was that such movements are very difficult to suppress, very difficult to predict, very difficult to manage. The fourth thing, which is interesting, because it's decentralized, carries a characteristic which was very important in my movement, *OTPOR* in Serbia. This is the characteristic of ownership. In Serbia, it was a reaction to the fact that people were sick and tired of leaders, political leaders. So, we said, "This is not the movement of members. This is the movement of leaders." So, everybody is the leader. That was our reaction to Milosevic's attempt to decapitate our movement. That was the way to produce more local leaders. That was the reason we invested a lot in training of these people. We wanted the movement to be local because every day, we expected the top 15 people in OTPOR! to end up in jail or worse. That was the reaction to the situation. We said, "We will make it horizontal because this guy is getting more oppressive by the day. It's only a matter of time before he's going to go after us." And we want the machine to keep going, whatever happens to the 10, 15, 30 people who started the show.

This is the reason we trained people for public speaking, because we knew he's going to go after people who go public. This is why I never gave a public speech in two years of the movement. I did not give a single speech. I mean, it made more sense for me to train tens of people to do public speaking. When these people are public speaking, people were seeing young faces and more people thought that they can public speak as well. And more people aimed for public speaking. This is how you got thousands of people who can jump on a trash can and do a ten-person rally, which is once again very complicated to oppress because there are plenty of trash cans. This is how you develop ownership. Because there is no structure, organization or visible leaders, people tend to feel belonging to the movement. People feel like shareholders. So, this thing is not owned by someone else. It's not a family-owned business. It's not organization, corporation-owned business.

Parks: I agree that ownership of the movement is a key feature. I live in Chestnut Hill. It's like 90% white. It's a very low stake thing to put a *Black Lives Matter* sign up because we're all "liberal." It doesn't really mean that much that you've put it up in some ways because there's no risk associated with it. But as we put the signs up, we talk as neighbors about how to buy the signs, pick the posters. Don't you think part of what the result of movements like *BLM* is, then, is the formation of local networks that develop local agendas on how to implement something like *BLM*? So, in a way, such a movement does spread out geographically very quickly. It doesn't appear, at first, to have a central leader. In this new model, one of the results, successes, would be that you had these locally defined groups and actions confronting the local officers who were doing the damage in their communities. It's not a success in that you get a federal intervention. But in the US where it's all state's rights and the police are all locally hired, that BLM ethos spread and distilled into community moments that do produce change. Right? I think it is a success if police are surrounded by a culture that holds them accountable, a community that actively witnesses and responds to their behavior, even if the actual policies are still being reformed. As Ben Kuebrich notes in "White Guys Who Send My Uncle to Prison," police suddenly feeling the need to call a community member "Mr. Bonaparte" represents the beginning of shifts in power (Kuebrich). It's that ground up communal change, perhaps triggered by a hashtag, that creates the actualized power base from which real negotiations with political leaders can begin. Which is why I was wondering why they are not seen as successful earlier in our discussion.

I also think we need to recognize that Alicia Garza, who created the BLM hashtag, had significant organizing experience prior to BLM (Garza). She worked in California, the Bay area, in a variety of roles and organizations. This had given her experience in traditional organizing as well as the need to control the public narrative. I think it had also given her, perhaps not a list of specific legislative goals, but a clear sense of the historic demands and current issues in which those demands were being articulated within Black communities. And not unimportantly, Garza had direct experience in how "organizing" was too often premised on excluding Black community members from leadership, particularly Black women. Her decision then to organize BLM with a decentralized structure (with consensus building moments among the distributed leaders) was a strategic decision to both give ownership of the movement to individuals who were typically excluded from leadership roles, such as African American women, as well as an attempt to avoid the "charismatic" leader syndrome, who as she notes are typically understood as men. And, as she also notes, movements often fail once the charismatic leader is gone, through personal decision or assassination.

What I'm pointing to, then, is that the traditional structure of a movement "spine," has also operated to position some individuals as leaders, some as followers, often along lines of race, class, and gender. This intersectional structure of exclusion might not be as evident in Poland, which is not as racially diverse as the United States, but I think the attempt to create new movement structures needs to be understood as addressing such issues. Garza acknowledges there are some weaknesses in this model, such as quick decision making, but, my sense is, other important goals are being achieved. In a sense, with BLM, we are watching new forms of organizing, of democratic processes, being reinvented.

In fact, I initially reached out to you because of your experience doing grassroots education with democracy advocates across, what, over fifty nations. I had this sense that what I had understood as "activism" was premised on an ad hoc consolidation of leftist academic theory and historical case studies. In a way, I felt that what I was teaching, the skills and practices of advocacy, were no longer representative of what work was actually being done on the ground. My knowledge, such as it was, was disconnected from the new knowledges about community, organizing, democratic structures being created by advocates within social movements. And to a great extent, after working together for several years, I think my concerns were well-founded.

Popovic: I'm not a scholar and maybe this is my personal bias and disappointment about the futility of much of the academy's approach to everyday issues, but what we are doing now in schools, I believe, is the equivalent of teaching people the theory of climate change without teaching them how to recycle or compost things. That is, when it comes to democracy, you can find the amazing courses, the great theory, the super cool research, the whole top-bottom thing. In academia there is no lack of it. There are zillions of experts for constitutional rights who will tell you exactly how certain types of constitutions are more resilient to attempted dictatorships. And there is research that will explain to you how countries that depend only on one commodity, like fossil fuels, are more likely to end up being authoritarian. There is no lack of these resources. There's plenty of courses where this research is read. What is not being taught is the practical skill of recycling, what is not being taught is the practical skill of self-organizing, of changing your environment through collective action.

Parks: You're dead-on that the vast majority of college courses are theoretical investigations, but there are a growing range of community partnership or service learning courses within the university where as part of the course, students would go tutor after school, help clean up a park, or go work at a nonprofit. My sense is this type of engagement came to be how the university thought of itself as teaching democracy – teaching civic engagement as reformist volunteerism. Though clearly, many in my field of Composition and Rhetoric pushed back against such a limited vision of engagement. Still, I do think much of this work, even the oppositional work by white scholars such as myself, emerged within an assumed belief structure that "democracy worked" in the United States. The pillars supporting that democracy (voting, etc.) weren't really placed into question. That being the case, you could have your students sponsor a fish fry on Friday and believe you were teaching them important civic engagement skills (and often a racial blindness to their privilege).

Today, post-January 6th, post George Floyd's murder, such models seem woefully inadequate (if they ever were adequate). The stakes are higher now, and I'm not convinced that the academy has the skillset to train people how to actively defend democracy. I'm not convinced that the traditional models of scholarship, pedagogy, or partnership that mark most graduate students' education enable them to teach their students to defend democracy. And our students need models to not just defend democracy but to expand its participatory practices beyond the supremacist structures in which they emerged. That's why you and I have worked to ensure that individuals, like Andre Henry from BLM- California, can teach students about the work of securing racial justice. That's why we have someone like Dani Ayers, *MeToo* CEO educate students about organizing for gender equity. That's why someone like Myo Yan Naung Thein is needed to place democratic advocacy within a global context. And in some ways, that's also why we created our course with Myo Yan Naung Thein as we did. I think more hands-on active involvement with democratic struggles is vital.

The academy has been structured to ensure that the current privilege of the few remains acceptable, that democracy's maintenance of the status quo is a success. In a world where democracy is being attacked openly by white supremacists, where communities of color are refusing to accept a return to the status quo, new forms of democracy need to be built, drawing from Indigenous, Western, Global, and Decolonial knowledges. And, in my experience, the academy is not set up to produce such engaged public facing research/pedagogies. They've never been in the business of developing students in such skills. That's why I think advocates need to be brought into the university as teachers, as researchers. We need to be less infatuated with a PhD and more engaged with the expertise that might create the world our scholarship theorizes about.

Popovic: This is my world. I teach people *how to do* stuff, not *what to do* stuff. I think there is plenty of *what to do* stuff, and very little of *how to do stuff* when it comes to democracy -at least when it comes to democracy and advocating of human rights. And to learn *how to do,* you need exposure and experience. This is something that an expensive education can't buy, but it is something everyone needs to learn.

Parks: I clearly agree with you, but I want to push back a bit. I see you framing this issue as "faculty = knowledge" and "advocates = skills." I would argue that such a framing is a very university-based way to talk. Such a framing positions the university as having all the knowledge, which then frames advocates, such as yourself, as only having skills. I would argue, though, that when you talk, when Alicia Garza talks, when Myo Yan Naung Thein talks, there's a real theoretical knowledge base behind it. There's a theory of what community should entail, what it means to work in common respect for each other. There is a theory about how public space should operate, a theory of collective justice, equal rights. It's just many of those skills and derived theories critique how the university operates, which is modeled on elitist knowledge circulating to create a power nexus which only allows for certain forms of political change.

I think part of what a democratic-informed classroom would teach students, what I hope our current class with Myo Yan Naung Thein teaches students, is not to denigrate the advocate as possessing only skills, but to recognize how their education has stopped them from understanding the emergent theories being deployed to create structural change. The idea is to teach students that if they understood advocates as intellectual theorists with knowledge, they would gain an understanding of more robust possibilities inherent in democracy, in participatory processes. You would understand that theories have greater power, greater importance, and greater circulation than to just appear in an assigned essay or academic journal.

Popovic: Or to be instilled with a sense of duty that you can only implement your education in such venues if you want to be "serious," "scholarly."

Parks: Agreed. Typically, I would argue, a university education positions change as tweaks in the pillars of existing power, not fundamental changes to power. Advocates, such as the ones just mentioned, they are saying "No, there is a need for larger structural changes in terms of structural racism, structural economic inequality." And that work requires a different set of skills. There are the skills to exist within existing structures. And then there's the skills to change those structures. They seem different to me. But I also think it is a difference that the university, as a system, wants to maintain by supporting only the weakest vision of democratic engagement. And they will maintain this difference, exclude these new forms of democratic education, even if only to make sure advocates don't become professors, that professors don't become advocates.

Popovic: Even if this is a very "revolutionary" idea to some administrators, I believe it only makes sense that democratic organizing skills are a central element of a students' education. It makes no sense to me as a liberal, not to you as a liberal, not to me as an activist, to you as an organizer, to divorce commitments to democracy as theory from the skills which protect its existence. My natural science structured brain says you change things by trying and failing. You learn how to take function by trying to replicate it in an experiment. You learn how a fish works by cutting it open, studying its parts – learning why a dolphin is not a fish based on its internal workings. This is how you learn any natural science. If these teachers encourage you to do such hands-on work in the natural sciences, and they make a program to equip you in the natural sciences, how come when it comes to learning about democracy, learning how to create robust democratic structures, this is politics? Why is this a politicization of the classroom?

Parks: I think the trick the academy plays upon you is to say that by teaching the 5,000 Latin terms to define democracy, you are teaching your students how to operate on democracy. But what they're really doing is they're teaching a very narrow spectrum of what democracy means, hence Latin not Indigenous roots for what collective means, what the role of government is and so on. They're saying you don't need to open the fish to see how it works. Just inject some red dye which will expose a small part of the workings. Keep your eye on that part, ignore everything else. Whereas I would argue a real education would be to break democracy down into components, understand its full workings so well you can "heal the fish" or, perhaps more accurately, discover what we thought was a fish was a dolphin all along – that there are different, better, more inclusive ways to structure our public space. What if democracy can mean more than we were ever taught to imagine?

What if there were suddenly hundreds of Professor Srjda Popovics, Professor Alicia Garzas, and Professor Myo Yan Naung Theins? How might that change our students' education? How might it change my field's sense of professional responsibility? I think maybe it's time some of us more privileged professors took on the institutional work to find out.

Works Cited

Adler-Lomnitz-Lomnitz, Larissa and Diana Sheinbaum. "From Reciprocal Social Networks to Action Groups for Market Exchange: 'Spontaneous Privatization' in Post-Communist Hungary." *REDES-Revista hispana para el análisis de redes sociales*, vol. 21, no.11, 2011, http://revista-redes.rediris.es

Chenoweth, Erica. "The Future of Non-Violent Resistance." *Journal of Democracy*, vol 31. no. 3, 2020, pp. 69-84.

De Witte, Melissa. "Populism is a Political Problem that is Putting Democracy at Risk, Stanford Scholars Say." *Stanford News*, 11 Mar. 2020, https://news.stanford.edu/2020/03/11/populism-jeopardizes-democracies-around-world/

Ellsmoor, James. "Environmental Education Will Shape a New Generation of Decision-Makers." *Forbes*, 25 Aug. 2019, https://www.forbes.com/sites/jamesellsmoor/2019/08/25/environmental-education-will-shape-a-new-generation-of-decision-makers/?sh=395d004d4e31

Friedler, Delilah. "He's Advised Pro-Democracy Activists in 50 countries. Here's His Advice for Americans." *Mother Jones*, 20 Nov. 2020, https://www.motherjones.com/politics/2020/11/srdja-popovic-democracy-movement-trump/

Garza, Alicia. *The Purposes of Power: How We Come Together When We Fall Apart.* One World, 2021.

Press, Benjamin. *Global Protest Tracker.* Carnegie Endowment for International Peace. https://carnegieendowment.org/publications/interactive/protest-tracker

Goldstone, Jack. "Cross-Class Coalitions and the Making of the Arab Revolts of 2011." *Swiss Political Science Review*, vol. 15, no. 4, 2011, pp. 457-462.

Kuebrich, Benjamin. "'White Guys Who Send My Uncle to Prison': Going Pubic within Asymmetrical Power." *College Composition and Communication*, vol. 66, no. 4, 2015, pp. 566-590.

Levitsky, Steven and Daniel Ziblatt. *How Democracies Die.* Crown Press, 2018.

Marchese, David. "What Can America Learn from South Africa About Healing?" *New York Times Magazine*, 11 Dec. 2020, https://www.nytimes.com/interactive/2020/12/14/magazine/pumla-gobodo-madikizela-interview.html

Repucci, Sarah and Amy Slipowitz. *Freedom in the World 2021: Democracy Under Siege.* Freedom House, 2021, https://freedomhouse.org/report/freedom-world/2021/democracy-under-siege

Ross, Carne. "How to Create a Leaderless Revolution and Win Lasting Political Change: In an Age of Insurgency, Legitimacy is Crucial to Harnessing the Energy of Protest." *The Guardian*, 13 Dec. 2018, https://www.theguardian.com/profile/carne-ross

"Russian Protestors Brave Detentions, Freezing Cold in Siberia, Far East." *Radio Free Europe*, 31 Jan. 2021, https://www.rferl.org/a/russia-regions-siberia-far-east-navalny-protests/31078822.html

Yeo, Sophie. "How the Largest Environmental Movement in History was Born." *BBC Future Planet*, 21 Apr. 2020, https://www.bbc.com/future/article/20200420-earth-day-2020-how-an-environmental-movement-was-born#:~:text=On%2022%20April%201970%2C%202020,the%20Earth%20taken%20by%20astronauts

Author Bios

Steve Parks is an Associate Professor in the Writing and Rhetoric Program, Department of English, University of Virginia. He is a co-founder of *Syrians for Truth and Justice* (stj-sy.org), which works with in-country Syrians to record the human rights abuses of all parties in the conflict. He is currently serves as the Chair of the *Dem-*

ocratic Futures Working Group, a collective of academics and advocates researching emergent new forms of democracy being developed by social movements globally. Srdja Popovic and Myo Yan Nuang Thein are current members of this working group. His publications include *Class Politics: The Movement for a Students' Right to Their Own Language*; *Gravyland: Writing Beyond the Curriculum in the City of Brotherly Love*; *and Writing Communities*, a textbook designed to support writing classrooms become a site of community collaboration and publishing. In 2020, Parks was awarded the *Conference on Community Writing Distinguished Engaged Scholar Award*.

Srdja Popovic is a Visiting Researcher and founding member of the *Democratic Futures Working Group* at the University of Virginia. He was a founding member of the Otpor! ("Resistance!") a nonviolent movement crucial to bringing down the Milosevic regime in Serbia. He then co-founded CANVAS, an organization designed to support nonviolent campaigns for democracy globally. Popovic's educational work has also extended to teaching courses on nonviolent strategy at universities, such as NYU, Harvard or University of Essex. He is the author of numerous articles in publications such as *Slate*, *The Guardian*, and *Foreign Policy Matters* on the topic of nonviolence, as well as author of *Blueprint for Revolution*. Over the past decade, Popovic has also been awarded *Poul Luritzen Human Rights and Democracy Award*, Tuft University *Global Citizenship Award*, and *The Lawrence and Lynne Brown Democracy Medal*, presented by the *McCourtney Institute for Democracy* at Pennsylvania State University.

Project and Program Profiles

Stories from the Flood: Promoting Healing and Fostering Policy Change Through Storytelling, Community Literacy, and Community-based Learning

Caroline Gottschalk Druschke, Tamara Dean, Margot Higgins, Marissa Beaty, Lisa Henner, Robin Hosemann, Julia Meyer, Ben Sellers, Sydney Widell, and Tenzin Woser

Author Contributions

Gottschalk Druschke, Dean, and Higgins are listed as primary, secondary, and tertiary authors, respectively, to reflect their contributions to conceiving of, drafting, and revising this manuscript, as well as to curricular development and support for Stories from the Flood. Beaty, Henner, Hosemann, Meyer, Sellers, Widell, and Woser are included alphabetically after that to reflect their shared contributions to drafting and revising this manuscript, to curricular development, and to development of the Stories from the Flood project.

Abstract

This profile features the authors' shared work to co-create both a community literacy project, Stories from the Flood, and the undergraduate community-based learning courses that supported the effort. Stories from the Flood works to assist community members in southwestern Wisconsin to share their flood experiences, aiming to support community healing and serve as a resource for future conversations about flood recovery and resilience. Our collaboration on Stories from the Flood demonstrates the importance of non-university expertise and aims to daylight and correct structural asymmetries that render these rural watersheds both particularly vulnerable to flooding and absent of government intervention.

Keywords

community literacy, community-based learning, flooding, oral history, reciprocity, rural, trauma

Reciprocity is meant to sit at the center of community-university partnership (Powell and Takayoshi, Cushman et al.). Scholars over the last decade have done important work to articulate what reciprocity might actually look like and mean in community literacy and community-based learning (Miller et al., Opel and Sackey, Carlson, Weir et al.). Here we build from a framework of dynamic reciprocity—what Sibyl W. Diver and Margot N. Higgins defined as an ongoing, reflexive, time- and context-dependent practice that aims for more equitable distribution of benefits—to highlight our own ongoing collaborative process. We take inspiration from the process-oriented and critical approach of Shane Bernardo and Terese Guinsatao Monberg, who recently argued:

> Enacting reciprocity asks us to slow down in time and do the work repeatedly over long durations of time. To see ourselves as reciprocal beings means we see ourselves not as separate from and working with community members; we see ourselves instead as community members invested in making structural asymmetries legible and open to deep revision. (85)

Here we—a "we" that includes university faculty members, board members of a writing-focused non-profit, and former students involved in the first iteration of a university course based on this work together—detail our efforts at dynamic reciprocity as we collaborated to create a community literacy project, and the community-based university courses that supported it, to work towards community healing, student learning, and structural change.

That community literacy project—Stories from the Flood—was initiated by the all-volunteer non-profit Driftless Writing Center in southwestern Wisconsin in late 2018 after the latest in an accelerating series of catastrophic floods hit the area, leaving a trail of material and psychological damage in this rural and underresourced region. Stories from the Flood works to assist community members to share their flood experiences, aiming to support community healing and serve as a resource for future conversations about flood recovery and resilience. Stories from the Flood also serves as the central focus of a community-based writing course at the University of Wisconsin-Madison, two hours away in the state capitol, and a community-based environmental studies course at the University of Wisconsin-La Crosse, thirty minutes to the west. These courses center the goals of Stories from the Flood, while focusing on the intersectional drivers of trauma experienced and understood by those impacted by area flooding. In so doing, they enlist students in the ongoing support of the project, offering them unfiltered connections with community organizers and storytellers; opportunities for developing empathy and practicing collaboration; shifted understandings of universities' often fraught impacts on community residents; and growing awareness of the responsibilities for undoing that damage and building partnerships that center community knowledge.

We argue here that the success of this community literacy project—and the community-university collaboration that supports it—has much to do with dynamic reciprocity: our shared work to slow down, do the work repeatedly and adapt flexibly over time, and build community together across community partners, community members, university faculty, and students. And we have been doing all this with a shared purpose to demonstrate the importance of non-university expertise and to support project goals—to aid community healing and advocate for the inclusion of these grounded stories in ongoing flood policy discussions—while exposing and working to revise structural asymmetries that render these rural watersheds both particularly vulnerable to flooding and absent of government intervention. We hope our collaboration might undermine these damaging and persistent realities.

Stories from the Flood and Catastrophic Flooding in the Upper Midwest

Wisconsin's Kickapoo River and Coon Creek watersheds have experienced at least one one-hundred-year and two fifty-year magnitude floods in just the last decade, even as climate forecasts predict this pattern will intensify. The 2018 flood caused an estimated twenty nine million dollars in damage to businesses, homes, and public infrastructure in Vernon County, Wisconsin alone, almost one thousand dollars per person in a county with a 14.1% poverty rate (Lu, U.S. Census Bureau). Although the immediate aftermath of the flooding made state and even national news, external attention—and external funding—quickly turned elsewhere while residents continued the long process of recovery. In light of this flood damage, and because of their focus on providing literary and educational opportunities for writers in the area, board members of the all-volunteer non-profit Driftless Writing Center—all of whom were affected personally by area flooding—decided to intervene in flood recovery in the way they knew best: supporting their fellow community members to tell their stories. Board members Tamara Dean, Jennifer Morales, Lisa Henner, and Robin Hosemann hatched a plan to co-produce thorough accounts of what people, municipalities, and the environment in the Kickapoo River and Coon Creek watersheds have endured as climate change alters their lives and landscape, naming that effort Stories from the Flood.

Stories from the Flood took shape around twin goals: to promote community healing through storytelling and create the foundation for an urgent community conversation about flood resilience. Stories from the Flood aimed to support two hundred community members to share written and oral stories about their flood experiences; to create a public-facing booklet that highlighted those stories; to place the oral history audio files, transcripts, and related indexes with the Vernon County Historical Society and the Oral History Program at the University of Wisconsin-La Crosse's Murphy Library; and to produce policy reports for area decisionmakers that better account for on-the-ground experience. The proposed gathering, archiving, and distribution of these stories was a massive undertaking that required support from individuals and institutions inside and outside the affected watersheds. And so, in late 2018, Dean reached out to UW-Madison professor Caroline Gottschalk Druschke to propose serving as the required university collaborator on the submission of a $10,000 Major Grant proposal to the Wisconsin Humanities Council. When it was awarded in early 2019, that funding—alongside support from individual donors and from the John D. and Leslie Henner Burns Family Foundation, La Farge Lions Club, Vernon Communications Cooperative, Vernon Electric Cooperative, and Westby Co-op Credit Union—helped launch the project.

With initial funding in place, Stories from the Flood kicked off in early spring 2019. Licensed clinical social worker Gil Hoel, journalist Tim Hundt, and professors

Margot Higgins and Christine Lemley provided two facilitator trainings for volunteer story gatherers, and Hoel, Hundt, and Higgins, along with historian Brad Steinmetz and project manager Carly Frerichs, remained central partners on the project. Because many coordinators and volunteers involved in the project were novices in oral history, facilitator trainings featured an introduction to oral history methodologies and perspectives, including practices like pre-interview research, informed consent, ethics, and establishing rapport and trust, alongside strategies for eliciting detailed stories. Trainings also included a focus on critical oral history, which builds from perspectives in culturally relevant pedagogy (Ladson-Billings), to consider how oral history practices can do more than simply record events; instead, oral history projects can offer opportunities for individuals to tell their own stories in ways that empower, humanize, restore dignity, and work towards transformative justice (Lemley). The project also benefited from the oral history expertise of the Wisconsin Historical Society, whose release form we adapted for the project, of Tiffany Trimmer, Director of The Oral History Program at the UW-La Crosse Murphy Library, and of Troy Reeves, Head of The Oral History Program for the UW-Madison Libraries.

In addition to this focus on oral history practices, trainings were grounded in informed responses to disaster, trauma, and recovery. For example, Hetti Brown of Couleecap, a non-profit that provides disaster outreach services in the Kickapoo Valley, offered foundational insight into community needs after historical and current flooding, with a particular focus on mental health imperatives. Hoel then presented on the psychological phases of disaster response, detailing Leonard M. Zunin and Diane Meyers' classic work on how people who have experienced such trauma individually and collectively respond, moving through the pre-disaster phase, to the impact phase, the heroic phase, the honeymoon phase, the disillusionment phase, and finally to reconstruction (qtd. in DeWolfe). Crucially, individuals and communities can cycle through these phases within and over years, a situation made all the more complicated, in our instance, by the imminent threat of additional flooding in the area. Discussion of the psychology of disaster response was followed by an emphasis on the connections between storytelling and healing, including the importance of taking control of traumatic histories through story (Pennebaker & Smythe, DeSalvo).

With that training in hand, focus shifted to the story gathering effort, which relied heavily on local libraries and historical societies. Twenty-six story gathering workshops were scheduled at the Vernon County Historical Society and libraries across the Winding Rivers Library System and Southwest Wisconsin Library System from April to July 2019, publicized through press releases, local fliers, and word of mouth; these sessions resulted in approximately thirty-five audio stories. Library partners and the Vernon County Historical Society acted as community liaisons and ambassadors, vouching for the project. In addition to publishing story gathering events, they also offered physical space for story sharing. Librarians knew their local patrons—after all, they were "local" themselves—and personally recruited individuals who had been affected by the floods to share their stories. Stories from the Flood grew very much as a community effort, with local contributors, volunteers, donors, educators, and storytellers working together to get the project off the ground, many of them cycling between roles: story gathering volunteers and librarians recorded their own flood stories; flood storytellers educated others about the project; community members offered financial contributions large and small.

In summer 2019, to accommodate individuals interested in telling their stories in more intimate settings, the project moved to in-home story gathering. Dean gathered many of those stories herself in August 2019, at which point we shifted emphasis to university students as ideal collaborators. Since then, undergraduates in Higgins' environmental studies course at UW-La Crosse, "Occupying the Driftless: Culture, Place, and Environment," have continued to support the project. Further, Stories from the Flood has served as the central focus for Gottschalk Druschke's UW-Madison undergraduate English course, "Writing Rivers," taught each semester. We focus in this article on curricular details for Writing Rivers given its community-based writing focus, but we share lessons from both courses as they feature several overlapping projects, events, and outcomes, built upon a common pedagogical interest in the ways that communities form stories and values in place.

Community-Based Learning to Support Community Literacy and Flood Recovery

Writing Rivers is a community-based learning designated section of ENGL 245 Seminar in the Major at UW-Madison designed around Stories from the Flood, with the first iteration taught in fall 2019. UW-Madison's Gottschalk Druschke and Driftless Writing Center's Dean talked frequently through spring and summer 2019 to consider how undergraduates in Writing Rivers could support the Stories from the Flood effort. With guiding input from Higgins, Steinmetz, Henner, Hosemann, Morales, and others, they worked together to shape the course around the community effort. In addition to students' contributions to the project, we sought to support the Stories from the Flood effort through an additional influx of funding from UW-Madison sources, including a Course Development Grant from the Morgridge Center for Public Service, an Outreach Fellowship from the Robert F. and Jean E. Holtz Center for Science & Technology Studies, and from the Department of English and the College of Agricultural and Life Sciences' Kickapoo Valley Reforestation Fund. Meanwhile, we wanted to position Driftless Writing Center volunteers, community members, and storytellers as expert teachers to guide student learning. We hoped the experience would equip and inspire undergrads to

- Ethically engage with off-campus communities;
- Hear and feel how people express the complexity of their relationships to their environments, and consider their own;
- Apply the tools of rhetoric to solve problems and take action;
- Partner with others to address timely problems and create change;
- Enact the Wisconsin Experience: cultivating empathy and humility; relentless curiosity; intellectual confidence; and purposeful action.

That fall 2019 student cohort, many of whom are included here on the authorship team, dealt gracefully with a huge amount of uncertainty. Their initial course syllabus was extremely light on descriptive details and included a mention of a future grading contract that would be agreed upon in the second or third week of the semester. Students were essentially told on day one that they would be supporting and learning from a community-based project called Stories from the Flood, that Gottschalk Druschke couldn't yet tell them exactly when, where, and how that would happen, and that students would have to trust her and the unfolding partnership. It was a huge ask.

While we don't suggest that the vagueness of the first day syllabus was indicative of pedagogical best practices, we do think the story captures the very real uncertainty of trying to build a community-university collaboration in real time as events were unfolding. It speaks, also, to the labor of being intentional about the long, slow process of reciprocity. Gottschalk Druschke and Dean knew that there would be no shortage of writing and thinking work to be done by students, as well as a series of oral history story gatherings to be scheduled with community storytellers, but we simply didn't know exactly how that work would happen. There was value in emphasizing improvisation, flexibility, and comfort with ambiguity for students, and we tried to make space for students' own needs, interests, and flexible responses to the project so that students could pursue topics, approaches, and modes of expression that best suited them. Autonomy led to discovery and surprise, which we argue led to a more memorable and meaningful learning experience for students.

Ultimately, uncertainty was an ethical choice; we dismissed some of the structures, expectations, and demands of the university and prioritized the evolving needs of community members, the community literacy project, and students' responses to it. This purposeful decentering enacted dynamic reciprocity, prompting students to question the typical privileging of academic expertise and opening space for them to consider Driftless Writing Center partners and Stories from the Flood storytellers as the real experts in our partnership. Students who stuck with the course indicated that they did so because of their faith in the empathy and support of Gottschalk Druschke, Dean, and the full Stories from the Flood team. Through mutual trust, uncertainty became an opportunity to adjust to needs as they arose and to look forward to being part of something beyond the classroom. In other words, we worked, as Bernardo and Guinsatao Monberg directed, to model for students the capacity to see themselves, "as reciprocal beings … not as separate from and working with community members … instead as community members invested in making structural asymmetries legible and open to deep revision" (85). We tried to model that emphasis through concrete details of the course.

The Mechanics: What Students Did and What They Learned

While admittedly light on specifics, the first semester syllabus of Writing Rivers offered the basic contours of a course structure that has persisted over time. Students were expected to:

Participate in

- **classroom sessions**, seventy-five minutes, twice per week
- a full-day weekend **orientation** trip to the Kickapoo River watershed

- community-based **story gathering**—at least two, in-person
- a **community celebration** of the project—optional

Complete

- **transcription** of at least one oral history recording
- comprehensive **thematic analyses** of the existing oral history archive to support the creation of a public-facing booklet
- a student-designed, collaborative **research-based intervention** based on the Stories from the Flood archive—e.g., a series of maps marking storytellers' homes alongside FEMA flood designations, flood-related lesson plans for area schools, guides to mental health and flood-borne illness resources
- a **creative project**—e.g., original songs, artwork, playlists, dialogues
- a final course **reflection**

UW-Madison students—and their UW-La Crosse counterparts in spring 2020 and spring 2021—completed this work for Stories from the Flood while creating weekly pieces of reflective writing in response to prompts prepared by undergraduate community-based learning (CBL) interns from the Morgridge Center for Public Service, alongside learning from content prepared by the Morgridge Center including: introduction to different principles of community engagement; connections between positionality, knowledge construction, and intellectual humility; cultural humility and self-awareness; recognizing root causes; systemic and institutional bias; equitable partnership; active listening; applying an equity lens; and trauma-informed care. In both courses, students read an overlapping suite of offerings about the ongoing history of project watersheds, including explorations of their deep Ho-Chunk history, white settlement and settler impacts on land use and flooding, racial and political dynamics, and flood recovery and response. Writing Rivers students concluded the semester reading Elizabeth Rush's *Rising: Dispatches from the New American Shore* and then tried their hand at writing a community profile that integrated demographic data, flood history, and Stories from the Flood narratives to highlight past and future challenges and possibilities for responding to area flooding.

The increasing formality of the course over time meant that we lost some of the organic magic of that first semester. This relative formality and structure also meant we were better prepared to ride through the massive disruption of COVID-19, which forced the spring 2020 sections of both courses online in mid-March, and demanded that the fall 2020, spring 2021, and fall 2021 sections of Writing Rivers be taught online. While a "community-based" learning course taught online—and asynchronously online in fall 2020 and spring 2021—may seem like an impossible contradiction, it has worked reasonably well by continuing to place students in close proximity to the recorded voices, if not bodies, of community storytellers; supporting the ongoing systemic goals of the project by shifting from story gathering to policy intervention; and offering the chance for students to grow as writers and humans in a project that is larger than just one student, class, or semester.

Semester to semester, in person and online, students have completed essential work to support Stories from the Flood. Spring 2020 and fall 2020 Writing Rivers students, in tandem with Higgins' UW-La Crosse spring 2020 undergrads, quality controlled approximately seventy transcripts from approximately one hundred storytellers to prepare them for delivery to UW-La Crosse's Oral History Program and the Vernon County Historical Society. Writing Rivers students completed thematic analyses of the full Stories from the Flood archive and created community profiles that highlighted each community's flood response alongside flood stories gathered in each village, town, and subwatershed. In spring 2021, UW-Madison and UW-La Crosse students prepared indexes for each oral history to finalize the work necessary for archival placement in university and community libraries. They also prepared community profiles and short audio clips to be embedded into a public-facing map highlighting the outcomes of the project. At the time of this writing, fall 2021 students in Writing Rivers are generating thematic tags for the audio clips that will populate the public-facing map, creating audio transcripts for accessibility, and collaborating on project findings reports focused on various communities throughout the watersheds.

Students' continued focus on the needs of Stories from the Flood and community storytellers as the central compass for their academic coursework helped to reinforce the idea that project expertise lay primarily in the hands of community members and community-based coordinators of Stories from the Flood, not in the university. It also helped to reinforce the idea of dynamic reciprocity, emphasizing timely, contextualized response that encouraged a more equitable distribution of benefits across project storytellers, project coordinators, and university faculty and students. Project storytellers got the chance to tell their flood stories—some for the first time—to engaged and empathetic listeners, to take control of their stories, and to put them in community with so many others. Project coordinators got the chance to meet their goal of supporting community healing through interpersonal relations and systemic intervention. Faculty got the chance to be part of something larger than themselves and larger than academia, while supporting students' personal growth. And students benefited, as well.

Many students talked about the course as intellectually but also emotionally challenging and described their experience as both career-changing and life-changing. They continually discussed their gratitude at all they'd learned from Driftless Writing Center staff and community storytellers. As students explained, these face-to-face, intimate interactions with community storytellers were completely unique in their university experience and were, therefore, especially meaningful. Many students found this incredibly uncomfortable at first, but as community partners and storytellers welcomed students into their stories and lives, students committed themselves to the course and the project because, as one student put it, referring to community storytellers and organizers, "anything less was not what they deserved." Students weren't performing for the teacher or for a grade, they were trying to learn from, respect, and honor the experiences of community members and the labor and vision of Stories from the Flood founders.

This experience changed the way students thought about university—and community—expertise and highlighted for them the need to undo past damage inflicted by the university. While students had been taught to take pride in what's known as

"The Wisconsin Idea," the long-standing tradition that work at UW-Madison should impact the lives of those around the state, they had never been presented with the real potential for university intervention to cause harm in off-campus communities or with approaches for minimizing those harms (Cruz and Bakken). "Writing Rivers" students became aware that UW-Madison participation in Stories from the Flood was charged for some residents because of the lasting damage of university intervention over 150-plus years. Community members had become understandably suspicious of university-types after a history of exploitative studies, so extra caution was important. As one student reflected on that process:

> This course brought to my attention a lot of the bad parts about community-based research, then made every possible effort to avoid making the same mistakes. It showed me that a lot can get done when the university takes a back seat and allows community experts to call the shots, then points resources toward said experts' decisions … I think this project is a step in the right direction.

Meanwhile, student work on thematic analyses, the celebration booklet, community profiles, and public facing maps supported the project's work to communicate to decision makers at the local, state, and federal levels that the residents of these vulnerable and economically underresourced watersheds are in desperate need of support, and that these communities also contain a huge amount of strength and that community members have created tightly knit, watershed-wide networks of mutual aid to support future flood resilience. Student contributions to this collaboration worked towards correcting the structural asymmetries that mark these communities as especially vulnerable in the first place. Students worked together with faculty, community organizers, and storytellers to strive towards a vision of dynamic reciprocity. That's a huge task, of course, but this work is continually underway.

Lessons Learned and Future Directions

Our collaboration has resulted in the gathering of over one hundred stories as of this writing. Our work has been featured by Wisconsin Public Radio, the *Wisconsin State Journal*, and the *La Crosse Tribune*, and in podcasts created by the Wisconsin Humanities Council ("Power of Experience") and the online magazine *Edge Effects* (Wilson), and served as a foundation for a recently awarded National Science Foundation grant focused on community-based flood resilience in these watersheds. With funding from the Wisconsin Humanities Council, the UW-Madison College of Agricultural and Life Sciences, the Morgridge Center, and private donations, we have been able to professionally transcribe each of these flood stories, prepare them for archiving, and deliver that archive to both the Vernon County Historical Society and the Oral History Program at UW-La Crosse's Murphy Library. We are working now on the public-facing map highlighting Stories from the Flood storytellers that will be included in the redesigned Kickapoo Valley Reserve Visitor Center in La Farge, Wisconsin and hosted online for wider access, as well as on a project findings report to share with local and state decision makers, highlighting urgent needs for mental health resources, flood recovery funding, emergency communication, and flood-borne illness prevention across the watersheds. We plan to continue story gathering in person as soon as COVID-19 allows.

Meanwhile, many fall 2019 students continued their Stories from the Flood work into future semesters and beyond graduation. For example, Ben Sellers and Sydney Widell gathered oral histories after the semester ended, continued their mapping and analyses with funding from the Morgridge Center and the Kickapoo Valley Reforestation Fund, and are now pursuing graduate study (Widell) and research positions (Sellers) on flood recovery in project watersheds with funding from the Kickapoo Valley Reforestation Fund and the National Science Foundation. Marissa Beaty, Maggie Fullmer, and Julia Meyer all received funding through the UW-Madison Center for the Humanities Undergraduate Exchange Program (HEX-U) to continue their public-facing research projects into flood-borne illness, mental health resources, and photo-based storytelling for the year beyond their initial course enrollment. A number of UW-La Crosse undergrads, too, were inspired to embrace career paths that would allow them to continue to listen to people's stories and advocate for vulnerable populations. In spring 2020, the Driftless Writing Center was awarded the Outstanding Community Partner Award from the Morgridge Center for their "demonstrated excellence in partnering with a university entity to provide opportunities for students to engage in and learn from the community."

Ultimately, in the spirit of dynamic reciprocity, we want to argue that rhetorically informed, community-based work—when practiced mindfully and tactically and built over time periods that exceed university semesters—can offer an important model for community-university collaboration to support community literacy efforts and student learning outcomes, while critiquing and potentially upending structural asymmetries. The success of the Stories from the Flood project and of our collaboration—"success" as a constellation of the ability to gather one hundred oral history narratives about local flooding; to meet community-identified goals and student learning outcomes; to extend, deepen, and refine the relationship over multiple semesters and now years; and to generate significant media attention, political attention, and university and external funding—came largely as the result of our explicit decision to resist an academic impulse towards "data collection," a move that challenged academic structures that demand rapid productivity and continued enrollment in the research-making enterprise. Mindful of cautions from Linda Tuhiwai Smith and Eve Tuck and K. Wayne Yang that researchers should acknowledge and mitigate harms of potential community-based collaborations, remain accountable to community partners, and avoid research meant only to legitimize predetermined outcomes through the voices of community members, our collaboration turned the academic imperative on its head: slowing the process of collaboration; amplifying marginalized community voices; and channeling university resources towards community-identified needs. The primary goal of Stories from the Flood, after all, was to help flood-affected residents process their individual and collective trauma, and we kept that focus as our central imperative.

Only after story gathering was halted by the COVID-19 pandemic, and we had cultivated a long-term commitment to dynamic and reciprocal collaboration—through many hours spent together in these rural watersheds and not on campus, through simple favors and acts of support, through advocacy for increased mental health resources in the area, through the securing of lots of little and big piles of university funding for the project—did we begin to turn towards something that might more properly fall under the orbit of "research." And even then, this was only because this research emerged organically and in concert with the secondary goal of the project: to create a historical record to inform future planning and support community healing. Local efforts to create a watershed-wide flood resilience plan seemed to demand this turn from trauma to recovery, and Stories from the Flood is beginning to serve as a touchpoint for conversations about flood resilience and as support for proposals seeking funding to make those important interventions. These flood stories address the rooted experiences, knowledges, and approaches to sudden, repeated, and ever-worsening floods among frontline communities, identifying everyday threats such as transportation access, food insecurity, and housing shortages. In this evolving context, the Stories from the Flood archive is becoming an invaluable resource for amplifying marginalized voices and fine-scale community stories that would not otherwise be included in formalized, science-based watershed planning processes.

Our hope is that this work offers a vision for the sorts of tactical projects proposed by Paula Mathieu in the context of community-based writing, working to create community-based partnerships that resist institutionalized, inflexible, and non-reciprocal approaches. Meanwhile, we want to argue that this work offers ways forward for engaged scholarship in rhetorical studies, composition, and technical communication centrally focused on social justice, as articulated by scholars like Natasha Jones, Rebecca Walton, and Kristen R. Moore ("The Technical Communicator as Advocate"; *Technical Communication After the Social Justice Turn*). One that takes seriously the idea that research—or at least a model of academic research as extraction of data, of networks, of knowledge—is not the way forward. In fact, much of the amazingness that has unfolded from the Stories from the Flood collaboration has come from resisting the impulse to research. Instead, we focused on reciprocity by creating opportunities for collaboration, inspiration, and engagement; crafting grant proposals around community-identified needs; and generally working to create an infrastructure based on the idea of doing whatever Stories from the Flood and the wider watershed community needed at any given moment. That work is often chaotic, but it is also magical.

Our shared labor towards dynamic reciprocity enabled the project's central goal: to create a means for flood-affected residents to respond, in community, to disaster by re-narrating their stories and transforming together through that process. As Robin Wall Kimmerer has argued: "Stories are among our most potent tools for restoring the land as well as our relationship to land. We need to unearth the old stories that live in a place and begin to create new ones, for we are storymakers, not just storytellers. All stories are connected, new ones woven from the threads of the old" (341). By sitting down, truly listening, and truly being heard, Stories from the Flood positioned community members, students, and faculty to create new stories together out of the old: about flooding, resilience, resistance, and university intervention. We came together to see ourselves—all of us—as "community members invested in making structural asymmetries legible and open to deep revision" (Bernardo and Guinsatao Monberg 85). And we recognize that this is ongoing work. As the CLEAR lab, directed by Max Liboiron, has insisted, "Collectivities are made, remade, and maintained—they are not born ready-made, and their continuity is a result of ongoing gratitude and reciprocity" (18). The continuity of the collectivity we call Stories from the Flood continues to depend on the shared labor that drives active, continued, ongoing gratitude and reciprocity. Together—over time, slowly, repeatedly, we hope, in community, and with an eye towards equity—we continue to explore how storymaking can move us forward together.

Works Cited

Bernardo, Shane, and Terese Guinsatao Monberg. "Resituating Reciprocity within Longer Legacies of Colonization: A Conversation." *Community Literacy Journal*, vol. 14, no. 1, 2019, pp. 83-93. doi:10.25148/clj.14.1.009058.

Carlson, Erin Brock. "Embracing a Metic Lens for Community-Based Participatory Research in Technical Communication." *Technical Communication Quarterly*, vol. 29, no. 4, 2020, pp. 392–410. doi:10.1080/10572252.2020.1789745.

CLEAR. *CLEAR Lab Book: A Living Manual of Our Values, Guidelines, and Protocols, V.03*. Civic Laboratory for Environmental Action Research, Memorial University of Newfoundland and Labrador, 2021.

Cruz, Evelyn, and Lori Bakken. "Community Guidelines for Engaging with Research and Evaluators: A Toolkit For Community Agencies, Organizations And Coalitions." 2020. https://ictr.wisc.edu/documents/community-guidelines-for-engaging-with-researchers-and-evaluators/.

Cushman, Ellen, et al. "Response to 'Accepting the Roles Created for Us: The Ethics of Reciprocity.'" *College Composition and Communication*, vol. 56, no. 1, 2004, pp. 150–156. doi:10.2307/4140685.

DeSalvo, Louise A. *Writing as a Way of Healing: How Telling Our Stories Transforms Our Lives*. Beacon Press, 2000.

DeWolfe, Deborah J. *Training Manual for Mental Health and Human Service Workers in Major Disasters*. US Department of Health and Human Services, Substance Abuse and Mental Health Services Administration, Center for Mental Health Services, 2000.

Diver, Sibyl Wentz, and Margot Natalie Higgins. "Giving Back Through Collaborative Research: Towards a Practice of Dynamic Reciprocity." *Journal of Research Practice*, vol. 10, no. 2, 2014, M9.

Jones, Natasha N. "The Technical Communicator as Advocate: Integrating a Social Justice Approach in Technical Communication." *Journal of Technical Writing and Communication*, vol. 46, no. 3, 2016, pp. 342–361. doi:10.1177/0047281616639472.

Kimmerer, Robin Wall. *Braiding Sweetgrass: Indigenous Wisdom, Scientific Knowledge and the Teachings of Plants*. Milkweed Editions, 2013.

Ladson-Billings, Gloria. "Toward a Theory of Culturally Relevant Pedagogy." *American Educational Research Journal*, vol. 32, no. 3, 1995, pp. 465–491.

Lemley, Christine K. *Practicing Critical Oral History: Connecting School and Community*. Routledge, 2017.

Lu, Jennifer. "Kickapoo Valley Faces Long, Winding Road to Flood Recovery." *La Crosse Tribune*, 29 Aug. 2019.

Mathieu, Paula. *Tactics of Hope: The Public Turn in English Composition*. Boynton/Cook Publishers, 2005.

Miller, Elisabeth, et al. "Keywords: Reciprocity." *Community Literacy Journal*, vol. 5, no. 2, 2011, pp. 171–178.

Morgridge Center for Public Service. University of Wisconsin-Madison, https://morgridge.wisc.edu/.

Opel, Dawn S., and Donnie Johnson Sackey. "Reciprocity in Community-engaged Food and Environmental Justice Scholarship." *Community Literacy Journal*, vol. 14, no. 1, 2019, pp. 1–6. doi:10.25148/clj.14.1.009052.

Pennebaker, James W., and Joshua M. Smyth. *Opening Up by Writing it Down: How Expressive Writing Improves Health and Eases Emotional Pain*. Guilford Publications, 2016.

Powell, Katrina M., and Pamela Takayoshi. "Accepting Roles Created for Us: The Ethics of Reciprocity." *College Composition and Communication*, vol. 54, no. 3, 2003, pp. 394–422. doi: 10.2307/3594171.

"The Power of Experience (With Caroline Gottschalk Druschke)." *Human Powered* from the Wisconsin Humanities Council, 2021, https://wisconsinhumanities.org/episode-2/.

Rush, Elizabeth. *Rising: Dispatches from the New American Shore*. Milkweed Editions, 2019.

Smith, Linda Tuhiwai. *Decolonizing Methodologies: Research and Indigenous Peoples*. Zed Books Ltd., 2012.

Tuck, Eve, and K. Wayne Yang. "R-words: Refusing Research." *Humanizing Research: Decolonizing Qualitative Inquiry with Youth and Communities*, edited by Django Paris and Maisha T. Winn, Sage Publications, 2013, pp. 223–247.

U.S. Census Bureau. "Vernon County, Wisconsin; Wisconsin; United States (V2019)." Quick Facts, 28 May 2021, www.census.gov/quickfacts/fact/table/vernoncountywisconsin,US/PST045219.

Walton, Rebeca, et al. *Technical Communication After the Social Justice Turn: Building Coalitions for Action*. Routledge, 2019.

Weir, Jessica K., et al. "Investigating Best Practice: Doctoral Fieldwork Experiences With and Without Indigenous Communities in Settler-colonial Societies." *ACME: An International Journal for Critical Geographies*, vol. 18, no. 6, 2019, pp. 1300–1320, https://acme-ojs-test.unbc.ca/index.php/acme/article/view/1751.

Wilson, Richelle. "Living with Floods: A Conversation with Caroline Gottschalk Druschke." *Edge Effects* from Center for Culture, History, and Environment within the Nelson Institute for Environmental Studies at the University of Wisconsin-Madison, 2021, https://edgeeffects.net/caroline-gottschalk-druschke.

Author Bios

Caroline Gottschalk Druschke is a professor of rhetoric and composition in The Department of English at the University of Wisconsin-Madison where her research and teaching focus on community-based learning, public engagement, and freshwater science.

Tamara Dean is a widely published writer of fiction and nonfiction, including a book about sustainable living, *The Human-Powered Home*. She has served on the boards of various arts and environmental organizations and teaches writing workshops independently and through The Loft in Minneapolis.

Margot Higgins is an Associate Teaching Professor in The Environmental Studies Program at the University of Wisconsin-La Crosse, who conducted several interviews for Stories from the Flood (SFTF). She teaches a seminar on the Driftless region and has engaged students in SFTF by instructing them to conduct interviews, listen to and index transcripts for The Oral History Program at UW-L.

Marissa Beaty is the Program Coordinator for The South Asia Summer Language Institute at the University of Wisconsin-Madison. She continues to participate in environmental research on her own time and has hopes to pursue further graduate work on environmental policy and protection.

Lisa Henner holds a BA from Washington University in St. Louis, and completed her graduate work at DePaul University, Chicago focused on the teaching of writing in a workshop setting. Lisa co-founded the Driftless Writing Center.

Robin Hosemann is a mental health counselor in Viroqua, Wisconsin. Prior to earning an MS in mental health counseling from Viterbo University, she was a classroom teacher and library media specialist in rural schools.

Julia Meyer is a middle school teacher in the Milwaukee Public Schools District. She is also a graduate student at Mount Mary University pursuing a Master of Arts in Education. Julia graduated from the University of Wisconsin-Madison with undergraduate degrees in Political Science and English Literature.

Ben Sellers is a researcher with the Townsend Lab and Headwaters Lab at the University of Wisconsin-Madison. He is interested in stream ecology and remote sensing and uses drones to provide insights for natural resource management.

Sydney Widell is a master's student in Freshwater and Marine Sciences at University of Wisconsin-Madison. Her work is centered on flooding and community impacts.

Tenzin Woser is a User Experience Designer at Gigasearch. A graduate from the University of Wisconsin-Madison in Journalism and Sociology, he leverages an understanding of and empathy for people to design products that help them accomplish their goals.

Write Your Roots Disrupted: Community Writing in Performance in the Time of COVID

Sarah Moon

Abstract

This article presents a profile of the community writing and performance project Write Your Roots, organized by the author, which was disrupted by the impact of COVID-19 in early 2020. The project narrative is framed by the theoretical basis for the project, rooted in the concept of "making space," which borrows from Michel de Certeau's concepts of space and Sidney Dobrin's definition of "occupation." The article then offers a narrative of the Write Your Roots project in Providence, RI in 2020 leading up to and beyond the effects of COVID-19. Following the narrative, the author reflects on the project, reading its disruption through its theoretical framework to draw conclusions about the importance of liveness and publicness toward the project goals of "making space."

Keywords

performance, COVID-19, ecocomposition, public

The Write Your Roots project invites community members to volunteer to write and perform a monologue about a facet of their relationship with food that they feel inspired to share. The project's concrete goals are to build community among people who share a love of food and to spread awareness about progressive food efforts in the local area where the project occurs. At an in person kick-off meeting, writers share ideas and meet trained writing coaches with whom they'll be working to develop their monologues. After this meeting, writers can opt to meet in person or virtually with their writing coach weekly for four weeks to receive feedback on their developing monologues. With monologue drafts in hand, writers begin rehearsing their pieces as theatrical performances. The project culminates in a live performance of the monologues followed by a talkback where community food leaders join the performers on stage and a broader conversation about food in the community can take place.

The first Write Your Roots began in the fall of 2016 and became the focal point of my dissertation. CLiCK, a nonprofit organization in Willimantic, Connecticut that provides commercially licensed kitchen space to small scale food producers, served as our organizational partner, providing community contacts, promotion for the event, and rehearsal and performance space. We also partnered with GROW Windham, a local nonprofit whose mission is to build a stronger community and local food system, for the talkback after the performance. One participant wrote about eating free and inexpensive foods like passionfruit, eggs, rice and beans growing up in Puerto

Rico. Another wrote about "eating [his] way around town" as a child in Coaldale, Pennsylvania, and another about teaching nutrition in the public schools. And the youngest participant, a high school junior, wrote about serving meals to Willimantic's homeless population. The project successfully attracted diverse audiences from the community, producing lively talkback sessions and instigating subsequent community collaborations; I knew that I would want to carry it out again.

In 2019, I moved to another former mill town, Pawtucket, Rhode Island, to be closer to my new job. I didn't know anybody in this new place, but I was eager to test Write Your Roots' transferability in Pawtucket. I wondered though about Eli Goldblatt's emphasis in *Because We Live Here* on relationship building as a precursor to community writing work. Did I need to build relationships in this new place before I could launch a community writing project?

Though I recognized the sensitivity of entering into a new community as an outsider and guiding a project that would in some way reflect the community, I knew that given the nature of Write Your Roots, it would be the participating residents who would craft the messages of our performance. Other than the focusing theme of one's personal relationship with food, there were no bounds on the types of stories that could be written. I felt empowered to launch the project also in part because of what LeCluyse, Onwuzuruoha, and Wilde write in "Write Here, Right Now: Shifting a Community Writing Center from a Place to a Practice," that Write Your Roots, like their project, "maintains its identity not by where it operates but by what it does and who does it" (114). In the case of Write Your Roots, the *what* was a standard sequence of literate and performance rehearsal practices and the *who* a diverse array of volunteer community members who share a common interest around food. In this new place, I could test the validity of this aspiration on a second run of the project with the constant of myself as project facilitator.

Space, Place and Stage

As a community writing and performance project, Write Your Roots opens space for people to think about food from the perspective of *we the eaters*. Write Your Roots can claim the 2011 activist uprising Occupy Wall Street as an ideological progenitor. Like the organizers of Occupy, I was interested in a project that formed resistance to the societal domination of corporate forces and monocultures, particularly in defining the places where we live and eat. This project was born, in part, out of my desire to *make* space *in* place against the chilling effect of forces that have foreclosed the opportunity for what I call *ground-motion*, the activity of individuals and groups of people in the places where they live. The ultimate goal of the kind of space-making I hope Write Your Roots can achieve is the production of locality, a sense of place that is constructed and maintained by the creative—in the broadest possible scope of that word—activity of the people who live there.

In *The Practice of Everyday Life*, Michel de Certeau identifies cooking as one of the activities that affords opportunities to consumers who have been rendered "immigrants in a system too vast to be their own" (xx) to adapt "the dominant cultural economy...to their own interests and their own rules" (xiv). To put de Certeau's insights into perspective, ways of thinking about food are dominated by media messages received through television, radio and the internet, fad diets, social media trends and place-dominating corporate presences like fast food dining franchises and grocery stores chains. Yet, we all have personal food histories that help define us; we all experience an ongoing struggle to balance our income, our cooking skills, our food access, our health and our hunger. In short, food can be an extremely place-rooting—eating locally—and place-creating—cooking locally—force. Thus, I see the food-themed public storytelling of Write Your Roots as a way of wresting space from corporate forces and monocultures both tangible and residual.

Live performance on stage is a key component of Write Your Roots because it makes the project public and, thus, part of the many things that happen in and help define a place. A stage is never a definite place, but always a space waiting to be defined through performance, design and the audience's imagination. Stages defy the imposition of societal norms and monocultural or corporate forces to insert fresh creative activity into a community's collective perception of its home place. In studying the potential of embodied performance to directly impact communities, I was inspired by concepts of place and space in the work of Sidney Dobrin and Michel De Certeau. Both authors emphasize the *writability* of space as opposed to place. Space, Dobrin writes in "Occupying Composition," can be thought of as free and open to movement, while place is stable, fixed, and defined. "Space," Dobrin writes, "is yet to be written. It is potential; it is imagination" (17). Space, by this definition, is open to anyone who is present at a given time to fill and define.

On the stage, the fixed perceptions of a given place cannot foreclose the possibilities of what may happen there. Similarly, many towns and smaller communities across the country suffer under negative labels of "dangerous," having "poor schools," or being "dead," leaving some residents to limit their conception of what is possible there, thereby opening the door for corporate forces to step into the vacuum. These are the types of places where a project like Write Your Roots may most meaningfully contribute to local revitalization. For example, the first community context for Write Your Roots, Willimantic, CT, a former mill town near to UConn where I was a graduate student, had long been negatively branded with the moniker of "Heroin Town" given to it by a *60 Minutes* TV news segment in 2003. In a 2019 news story about a proposal to demolish two vacant former hotels in Willimantic, state representative Susan Johnson commented on the *60 Minutes* piece, "'We had a place here for people with addictions. We had been dealing with addictive problems for years and years and years...the ["Heroin Town" coverage] did nothing but help ruin the town'" (Bassler).

The heavy baggage of that negative identity could be shed for the community-built Write Your Roots performance. For this rewriting of collective perceptions of place, Dobrin provides inspiration, "Space is yet to be written because space has not (yet) been given meaning; it awaits occupation. Space itself does not then occupy a different location than place, but the same locations, only as locations yet to be written, yet to be produced" (17-18). Adapting this idea to my intentions for Write Your Roots, I embraced the potential it suggests for making existing community locations, whether saddled with negative reputations or overtaken by corporate dominance, into *spaces* and encouraging community members' creativity to define them anew. Write Your Roots, just like street theater or a movement like Occupy Wall Street, is an effort to write and produce space collaboratively by *the people* in ways that contribute to a longer term, locally-driven revitalization of place.

Project in Motion

While the *ground-motion* I imagined facilitating through Write Your Roots involved community members, the initial motion of the project rested solely on me beginning to form community contacts. Bringing Write Your Roots to Pawtucket/Providence began with a process of developing relationships with local organizations. My first move was to contact Farm Fresh Rhode Island (FFRI), a statewide nonprofit that runs several farmers' markets in Rhode Island, about sponsoring the project. They agreed to help publicize the project and bring representatives to the performance talkback. This gave me enough of a sense of support to create a Call for Participants flyer that was distributed in November 2019 at the Providence Winter Market held in Pawtucket's Hope Artiste Village, through social media accounts managed by FFRI and posted at local cafes and stores.

To find our writing coaches, I reached out through existing and new contacts at University of Rhode Island (URI) and Brown University. Jeremiah Dyehouse at URI shared the call with his network of Rhode Island contacts and two adjunct writing instructors, Genette Merin and Kristen Falso, responded to his call with interest. Another writing coach, Kate Niles, came to me through a contact I met when presenting on Write Your Roots as part of the "Almanac of Garden-Based Writing" workshop at the 2019 Community Writing Conference in Philadelphia. A novelist and therapist, she had just moved to Providence from New Mexico and was looking to connect with others interested in community writing. The last coach, Kendall Morris, an MFA poetry student and graduate writing instructor, responded to the call I put out to the creative writing graduate program at Brown. Having successfully put together a local team, I finally felt as though the project was truly in motion.

With our four writing coaches secured, the next piece to coordinate was our performance location. Coincidentally, there was a small, local theater called Etnias Global in Hope Artiste Village where FFRI ran their Providence Winter Farmers Market, tucked between a produce stand and a cheese kiosk. Etnias Global produces Spanish-speaking plays and the annual Festival Internacional de Teatro Hispanoamericano de Rhode Island. I met with its artistic director, Elvys Ruiz, in December 2019 and he generously agreed to provide our performance space for no cost on the basis of his own commitment to serve the local community by providing an outlet for its creative expression. The final step for setting the project in motion would be identifying our participants. Ultimately, eight people responded to the call with the desire to take part in the project. Most of them, in addition to the four writing coaches, were able to attend our first meeting at Etnias Global on Saturday, January 4, 2020.

At that first meeting, each writer/performer and writing coach introduced themselves. The participants were Jess, Robin, Nicholas, Jonathan, Cindy, Kunal, Peter and Karla. After introductions, the writers shared their tentative ideas for monologues, which included Jonathan's idea to write about what cooking for a beloved person means, Karla's plan to write about caring for animals on a farm where they are raised for meat and dairy, Kunal's idea to write about integrating cooking influences from India, the American South and Pacific Northwest, and Cindy's plan to write about being a professional beekeeper. At this meeting, writers were also matched with writing coaches based on their mutual availability and scheduled their first meeting.

After the project kickoff meeting each writer met one-on-one with their writing coach three to four times over the next four weeks. Most of these meetings took place over Zoom. Coaches' early feedback on drafts came mostly in the form of questions that prompted writers to elaborate further on certain aspects of their monologues. This work was similar to a writing center consultation, where coaches focused on organization, areas for elaboration or trimming, tone and then sentence-level refinements. I worked with Cindy, the beekeeper, and much of my feedback was geared toward encouraging more description of her personal experience of the events she relayed. By the final session, each writer had a completed draft ready on which they received final, fine-tuning comments.

In early February, a little over a month after our first meeting, I invited the writers and writing coaches to my new home in Pawtucket for a read-through of the fresh drafts of our eight food monologues. Our family, having first rented an apartment in Pawtucket, had just moved to our new house two weeks prior. At that point, it was very much a blank space to us, "yet to be written" as Dobrin writes. Having this gathering at that early stage of living in our home, at our big, new dining table, contributed significantly to defining the new space. More than paint color, wall décor or furniture, the activity of that read-through contributed to our perception of our new home. It lent the sense that our home was a welcoming space that invited the personality, creativity and insights of those outside our immediate family to inter-weave with our own energies. Culturally, we have come to accept fixed, dictated ideas of places and this includes our homes where we obsess over design features that we feel will project what we want our home to be. Michel de Certeau, however, calls attention to the historically obscured role of activity, or what I call *ground-motion*, in forming our conception of places. De Certeau asserts that maps— such as a floorplan of a new home, for example—represent fixed conceptions of *places* devoid of activity. Stories, in contrast to maps, he writes, can be a means of animating places, returning them to the status of spaces. He writes, "everyday stories tell us what one can do in [a place] and make out of it. They are treatments of space" (122). He writes that a story "founds spaces" (123) and "opens a legitimate *theater* for practical *actions*" (125).

It is interesting to consider this theoretical perspective in light of private spaces like one's home. While a sense of one's private home can become quite fixed, defined by the habitual activity and interactions of the people living within it, that sense can be disrupted and revised through the activity of outsiders within its walls. I have always found that any social gathering, from a dinner with friends to a big holiday party, brings new energy into my home. It also disrupts fixed patterns by necessitating intensive cleaning, de-cluttering and the movement of furniture. Consistently, I feel *better* in my home space the morning after hosting a social event. The fresh activity shakes up the dull grooves of a home's inhabitants' use of it and opens up a new sense of possibility, a new sense of space. This is De Certeau's and Dobrin's theories of space-making confirmed within the narrow, controllable boundaries of the home. Can we extrapolate this experience to apply similarly to our larger, shared home spaces in the neighborhoods and towns where we live? Write Your Roots rests on the belief that we can.

The next step of our Write Your Roots process, beginning rehearsals, began to open the space-making activity I'd experienced in my home to more public spaces: Urban Greens Co-op in downtown Providence and the Etnias Global theatre in Pawtucket. Our work at Urban Greens was a fulfillment of one part of the Co-op's Mission Statement "to create a space for collaboration and cross-pollination among multiple organizations, cultures, and communities…" ("Mission"). To this end, the community room where we rehearsed, with glass walls on one side, allowed workers and customers to see the ways in which Write Your Roots was coming together. At Etnias Global, our rehearsals were not observed but our work was a precursor for public performance. By rehearsing in the space, we began claiming it and bringing it to life with our vision. The next step would make our activity fully public. We were set to perform our show, followed by an audience talkback with the writer-performers and Farm Fresh Rhode Island, at Etnias Global Theater on Saturday, March 14, 2020.

Disruption: COVID-19

This is where the story shifts from what might have been a community writing project success story to a story of a project disrupted and diverted. The pandemic challenged our notions of space-making by first separating us in space, inserting imaginary dividing lines, then separating us even more severely. Just as I was taking orders for pizza toppings to feed people during our dress rehearsal, the first COVID-19 diagnosis was announced in New England. I quickly sent an email to the group stating that the stage could hold only one performer at a time so that we would be following public health directives to socially distance. This meant that we wouldn't be able to do our planned closing moment sitting around the table together reading Joy Harjo's poem "Perhaps the World Ends Here" and would have to come up with an alternative conclusion. We considered needing to limit the audience and leave seats empty between audience members. Throughout this time of trying to adapt to early COVID-19 precautions, my sole goal was to ensure that all the work that we had put into Write Your Roots up to that point would not be lost.

But the week we were supposed to perform, the response to the COVID pandemic brought more disruption. Schools closed and a stay-at-home order was put in place. Fear rose. Farm Fresh Rhode Island would still hold their winter farmers market for shoppers but would allow no form of social gathering at the market. By

Wednesday of that week, there didn't seem to be a choice left to be made. We canceled our March performance.

Though canceling our performance was a loss, each participant was also going through their own set of private losses at this time, their own unique psychological response to those losses and to the new, extreme uncertainty and isolation we all faced. The wisest move seemed to be to put the project on hold and wait the pandemic out, a plan that seemed reasonable at the time. When we canceled the performance, some of the participants let me know that they wouldn't be able to go forward with the project. I tried not to grieve that, but to focus on what was still possible. On March 12, I wrote to the group that I was thinking about June 6 or 7 for the new performance date with pick-up rehearsals starting two weeks before. I told everyone I would check in at the beginning of May.

But by late May of 2020, large groups of people gathering indoors was still not possible. There were no indoor theater productions happening anywhere in our area, including at the Etnias Global theater. We postponed again, in hopes that we could perform in September. Looking back on this series of pushed back dates, my hope seems foolish, like chasing a receding wave out to sea. But we, or at least I, didn't want to believe in the worst-case scenario, and it was probably best for our morale if we thought we might soon see light at the end of the pandemic tunnel. As I stated earlier, what follows then is not a success story, but a story about what we do as community writing practitioners when our best laid plans are thwarted by forces beyond our control.

How Much Does "Live" Matter?

Although it seemed like the whole world was migrating to Zoom, I resisted the idea of pivoting away from a live, in-person performance. Toward the end of July, I put the question out to the group about whether they felt comfortable with mounting a September production. One person did, one person was ambivalent, and two were not really comfortable with it. It was clear from their responses that if we wanted to present our work, I would have to let go of my attachment to an in-person production. I chafed at the idea. Write Your Roots, for me, was defined by community members claiming actual space for themselves and a wider community in front of a live audience.

At this point in the story, I could go in the direction of saying that we produced a digital version of Write Your Roots and realized the fluidity of the project model or realized that digital was actually a superior medium because it can reach so many more people. Another person might have felt that way, for good reason, but I didn't. Rather, I want to explain why pivoting to a digital format helped affirm my commitment to live, in-person performance.

Live, in-person performance retains a unique power and cultural significance even in these times of highly accessible, digital content and communication. This is not to make the argument that it is superior. In *Liveness: Performance in a Mediatized Culture*, Philip Auslander challenges the perspective that puts live, in-person performance into a binary with video-recorded or streaming performance. Auslander writes that some theorists seem to approach live performance as a kind of *pure* medium that exists before and apart from video performance. But Auslander argues that these thinkers operate under a false premise that such purity is actually possible. He writes, "All too often, such analyses take on the air of a melodrama in which virtuous live performance is threatened…by its insidious Other, with which it is locked in a life-and-death struggle. From this point of view, once live performance succumbs to mediatization, it loses its ontological integrity" (46). Auslander counters that live and mediatized performance are not in opposition with one another, but instead have a relation of "dependence and imbrications" (56). As an example, he offers the Walt Disney Company's division specifically devoted to repurposing its films into live performances. "The fact of the eventual live performance," writes Auslander, "makes the television program more compelling, independent of the theatrical production's quality or reception" (29). Although we exist in an era where digital performance is ubiquitous, and digital performance can carry so much of what live performance offers, it cannot carry all of it. Live performance still maintains a unique power. And one of those powers is to make space and redefine our sense of place.

I share Philip Auslander's work as a way of responding to those who might ask of the Write Your Roots project, "Why insist on live performance today given the incredible digital tools accessible to us?" First, I agree with Auslander that live performance is not an underdog on the brink of relevance but rather exists and will always exist in relationship with mediatized culture. As Auslander points out, even the corporate entertainment giants acknowledge there is still a sociocultural value attached to live, in-person events that spurs media attention that might not be given to a solely mediatized event. If corporate giant Disney recognizes this, why wouldn't we, who are already on the ground, recognize this and take advantage of our authentic community networks to bring live performance to life in our communities?

I am insistent on live performance of community writing because of my interest in how we *make* space *in* place against corporate, monocultural and extractive forces that diminish it. In Write Your Roots, the writer-performers make space by telling their stories related to their experiences with food, inviting the audience to connect with those stories by responding with their own stories or asking questions. After the performance is over, a community of people now understands themselves as connected to each of those whose stories they've just watched and heard live and in-person. Their sense of the place they live is now, to some degree, enlarged or even rewritten by the community members' stories they've heard. In a live performance, we would have been able to look at each other's faces. We would have been able to field questions from the audience and even form connections that might live beyond the life of the performance.

The conditions of the pandemic were such that there was no realistic path to a live performance of the monologues. I couldn't ask participants to do something they weren't comfortable with or ask an audience to be enthusiastic about being around other people. Once I finally accepted this, it was definitely painful, especially when so many of us could feel the need, that had only increased since the arrival of

COVID-19, for people to come together in community to heal wounds of division, to build hope through mutual support, to co-imagine our future.

In the end, we produced a video that included four of the original eight participants' monologues and a Zoom group reading of Harjo's poem. FFRI shared the video, participants shared it through our personal social media and email contacts, and I shared it with Write Your Roots contacts. But other than words of congratulations, there was no engagement with viewers about what they saw or how they connected with it. The video performance couldn't produce the same sense of space creation that the live event could. One thing the video did give us, though, was a way to demonstrate the work to potential partners and participants, which will be valuable in the future. Despite everything, it still felt good to see the work through in some form, to produce something we could show people. It felt like an expression of courage in the face of the overwhelming circumstances we had been dealing with since March 2020, and an affirmation of what had brought us together in the first place. And it had made a difference in the lives of those who participated. One participant wrote to me in a notecard just recently, "Being part of Write Your Roots was one of the best things I've done for myself in recent years." If nothing else, the video we made was a partial record of the work we had done and the hope we had had for a live performance amongst our local community, a marker that our spirits were still willing and that we would be back, one day.

Conclusion

What do we take away from this disrupted Write Your Roots? The first take-away is that, as a community writing and performance project, Write Your Roots is a model that is definitely adaptable to different places and participants. If you're entering that place with a humble, open stance and a willingness to learn and to pivot, you have every right to go ahead. In part, this is because while there is a certain theoretical drive for the project, its concrete goals are open to being defined by the individuals who volunteer to participate. In *Rhetoric of Respect*, Tiffany Rousculp makes a powerful case for community writing project planners to *always* put individuals first, honoring the context in which those individuals live their daily lives and the personal motivation they bring to writing over the political goals of a given project, noting that "when space [is] made for them to speak/write what they [choose], change [can] happen in ways we might not have anticipated" (111). In the future, I would enhance this aspect of the project by asking at our first meeting what personal goals participants have for the project and, if any, what community-oriented goals they would like to set for the project.

Secondly, on a personal level, I experienced how community writing projects can be lifelines in difficult times. Through them, we form relationships of mutual feeling, admiration and honesty. These kinds of connections serve us well when tough times hit. We can lean on these connections; we can help each other make it through. At the same time, some challenges mean that a person may not have the space for extracurriculars for the time being. In addition to being able to pivot ourselves, we have to make space for participants to pivot as their life circumstances change, while communicating that their work was valued.

Thirdly, though our project didn't ultimately appear before an audience on a stage, we still experienced some of the space-making power of the work, whether in the reading at my new home, in the community room at Urban Greens Co-op or in rehearsal at Etnias Global. Relationships were formed that have continued beyond the life of the project and certainly, for me, become an important facet of this new place where I live. The people of Write Your Roots and the relationships I formed with them helped define this place, Pawtucket, my new home, to me as friendly and supportive.

Finally, for all of us participants of the 2020 Write Your Roots, our collective perceptions of food were expanded, nuanced and enriched. I will never forget the dedication Jonathan, a religion professor at Wheaton, showed in explaining what it meant to him to make Mary Berry's strawberry cake for his wife. I will never forget learning from Jess's journey as a lifelong food-lover to always be thankful for *hunger*. I will never forget the way Karla enacted helping a cow give birth to a calf on her farm. And I will never forget Nicholas tenderly recounting how his mother patiently taught him how to cook, down to his *mise en place*. Though remembering the impact of these stories brings up the grief that they didn't reach a live audience, it also reminds me of the power of this project to help us reconceptualize and reclaim control of our relationship to food.

I feel that when Write Your Roots happens again, the togetherness the new group shares will be marked by all the togetherness we missed during the time of COVID. COVID-19 and the overlapping crisis of the George Floyd murder and ensuing surge of the Black Lives Matter movement made many of us more keenly aware of the community bonds we have sacrificed or never formed as a result of societal divisions and economic forces that delimit our personal time. In the absence of these bonds that help generate a people-centric locality in the places where we live and eat, entropic and/or corporate forces have taken greater hold in many places than they had before 2020. Given this, it may be, now that many of the limits of COVID-19 have lifted, we will feel even more inspired to courageously make space for a plurality of voices in the places where we live. Write Your Roots is one attempt at this.

Works Cited

Auslander, Philip. *Liveness: Performance in a Mediatized Culture*. Routledge, 2011.

Bassler, Cassandra. "Historic Willimantic, Connecticut to Demolish Rough Reputation." *NENC*, 12 Mar. 2019, https://nenc.news/historic-willimantic-connecticut-to-demolish-rough-reputation/.

De Certeau, Michel. *The Practice of Everyday Life*. Trans. Steven F. Rendall. U of California P, 1984.

Dobrin, Sidney. "Occupying Composition." *Locations of Composition*, edited by ChristopherKeller and Christian R. Weisser, State U of New York P, 2007.

Goldblatt, Eli. *Because We Live Here: Sponsoring Literacy beyond the College Curriculum*. Hampton, 2007.

Harjo, Joy. "Perhaps the World Ends Here by Joy Harjo." *Poetry Foundation*, Poetry Foundation, https:/-www.poetryfoundation.org/poems/49622/perhaps-the-world-ends-here.

LeCluyse, Christopher, et al. "Write Here, Right Now: Shifting a Community Writing Center from a Place to a Practice." *Community Literacy Journal*, vol. 15, no. 1, 2021, pp. 112–20, doi:10.25148/clj.15.1.009368.

"Mission." *Urban Greens Co-Op Market*, 31 Oct. 2021, https://urbangreens.com/about/#mission.

Rousculp, Tiffany. *Rhetoric of Respect: Recognizing Change at a Community Writing Center*. NCTE, 2014.

Author Bio

Dr. Sarah Moon is an Assistant Professor of Humanities at Massachusetts Maritime Academy. Her work has been published in *Community Literacy Journal, Literacy in Composition Studies, H-Net Nutrition, The Journal of Multimodal Rhetorics,* and *Center for Sustainable Practices in the Arts*. Her essay "The Room Where It Happen(ed)" is forthcoming in the book *The Art of Touch: A Collection of Prose and Poetry from the Pandemic and Beyond* from University of Georgia press. She is the founder and director of community writing and performance project Write Your Roots as well as the Composition pedagogy collective Teaching Democracy.

Bilingual Comics on the Border as Graphic Medicine: Journaling and Doodling for Dementia Caregiving during the COVID-19 Pandemic

Elvira Carrizal-Dukes, Maria Isela Maier, Sarah Y. Jimenez, Jacob Martinez, David Hernandez, and Ronnie Dukes

Abstract

The use of comics can be a powerful tool to expand educational outreach efforts for improving the health and well-being of people everywhere. Dr. Ian Williams coined the term "graphic medicine" to denote the use of comics in medical education and patient care ("Graphic Medicine"). Alzheimer's disease affects approximately five million Americans and is expected to triple to 13.8 million by 2050. Hispanics and Blacks are disproportionately affected at a higher rate than other groups ("Facts and Figures"). There is a lack of culturally relevant educational materials available for these populations. To address this disparity, an interdisciplinary community engaged collaboration was initiated with the Alzheimer's Association West Texas Chapter, The University of Texas at El Paso (UTEP), and Dukes Comics to produce a series of virtual workshops entitled, "Journaling and Doodling for Stress Reduction and Relaxation" for caregivers of people living with Alzheimer's and other dementias. These sessions were live-streamed and began during the COVID-19 pandemic. Spanish sessions have also been provided to the public. Health information about the disease process and common caregiver challenges are provided in each session. A guided journaling and doodling activity are also included. Journaling has been shown to be an effective and easy tool to use for stress management (Scott). The impetus behind this project was to address the dire need for increasing access to Alzheimer's disease education and resources in El Paso, Texas, a border community that is also home to Fort Bliss Army base. Hispanics comprise approximately 82% of the population and include a large Spanish-speaking segment. Language is often a barrier to health care access and education. To meet the aim of increasing accessibility, the workshops and comics are available in both English and Spanish and soon in-person. This project received a 2022 joint seed grant from Texas Tech University Health Sciences Center El Paso and UTEP to conduct research and examine data from these workshops that will be provided in-person in marginalized and multilingual Latina communities surrounding El Paso starting in the fall.

Keywords

graphic medicine, comics, bilingual, Alzheimer's, dementia, caregiving, U.S.-Mexico border, interdisciplinary, community engaged, journaling, doodling

Imagine a seven-year-old Latina girl tugging at her mother's apron asking, "What is wrong with abuelita? She doesn't remember how to make tortillas." The mother struggles with how to explain to her young daughter that abuelita is suffering from Alzheimer's disease. The family struggles with how to deal with abuelita who sometimes shows aggression and suspicion, especially when she is feeling confused and forgetful. This is a scenario that one might find here in El Paso, Texas, where the community is primarily Hispanic and where the literacy project discussed in this article is based.

Accessibility to resources that are culturally and linguistically representative of families' lived experiences is needed now more than ever as Alzheimer's is rising and has a high impact on Hispanics and Blacks, compared to other races ("Facts and Figures"). Considering this data, and the increasing complexity of problems that affect global health, creating innovative strategies to educate individuals and communities to manage these challenges is pivotal. Therefore, working collaboratively with faculty from The University of Texas at El Paso (UTEP) and partnering with community graphic novel artists and the Alzheimer's Association – West Texas Chapter, a community-based literacy project was designed to address the need for health information that supports families from diverse backgrounds who are dealing with life-altering diseases such as Alzheimer's and other dementias. Collective efforts led to the creation of a series of virtual workshops that began during the COVID-19 pandemic titled, "Journal Writing and Doodling for Stress Reduction and Relaxation" targeted in general at caregivers of Alzheimer's patients. The workshops and comics are offered bilingually in English and Spanish language virtually to provide culturally relevant materials for marginalized and multilingual populations.

Currently, there is a lack of health literacies addressing Alzheimer's and other dementias available in languages other than English. In fact, language has been identified as a social determinant that has a major influence on healthcare access and delivery (Fiscella et al. 56; Mariñez-Lora et al. 118; Sentell et al. 290-291). Local initiatives require the help of local stakeholders who clearly understand the community, Alzheimer's diseases, and innovative approaches to reach specific audiences. Initially, the workshops featured sessions in the English language and were virtual during the quarantine in 2020. Later in this article, we provide links to the online videos. Understanding the digital divide in underserved communities, these workshops will soon be offered in person.

The Setting

Alzheimer's disease and other dementias is a growing global crisis requiring creative approaches to health literacies. According to the Alzheimer's Association, this disease affects approximately 6.5 million Americans and is expected to more than double to 13.8 million by 2050. In El Paso and Hudspeth counties, 107,459 people are aged 65 and over. After analyzing data trends, 12% of Texans aged 65+ are living with Alzheimer's or another dementia ("Facts and Figures"). When applied to the counties of El Paso and Hudspeth, it is estimated that approximately 12,895 people are affected by this disease ("Facts and Figures"). This data indicates that the disease will impact everyone living in these communities in one way or another. Communities with marginalized populations such as El Paso are especially impacted.

Situated along the U.S.-Mexico border, El Paso is one of the world's largest bi-national and bilingual metropolitan areas. Hispanics comprise approximately 82% of the population and include a large Spanish-speaking segment; in fact, two-thirds of El Paso households identify as Spanish speakers ("American Community Survey"). Language may often be a barrier to health care access and education. To meet the aim of increasing accessibility to Spanish language speakers, virtual workshops and comics in Spanish were provided. El Paso is also home to the U.S. Army's Fort Bliss post which adds to the diversity of the city. Fort Bliss documents their own population apart from the city of El Paso reporting a population with 16.7% Black and 26.6% Latino individuals ("QuickFacts"). It is evident that El Paso, coupled with Fort Bliss, is home to the populations most affected by this disease.

Members of diverse communities are more likely to endure poverty and have less access to quality health care; as a result, they are more likely to develop risk factors for Alzheimer's and other dementia such as cardiovascular disease and diabetes. Compared to Whites, studies show that Blacks are twice as likely, and Hispanics are 1.5 times more likely to develop Alzheimer's (Facts and Figures"). For these reasons, developing health literacy resources for diverse populations that address cultural, linguistic, and geopolitical factors should be considered.

Comics as Health Narratives

The use of health narratives illustrated via comics expand the accessibility of these efforts and can be a powerful tool in improving the health and wellbeing of citizens everywhere. Williams, a comics artist, physician, and founder of the Graphic Medicine website, coined the term "graphic medicine" to denote the use of comics in medical education and patient care ("Graphic Medicine"). Graphic medicine has shown to be an excellent visual health literacy resource that can provide "new insights into the personal experience of illness" (Green and Myers 574). The comics in our workshops are designed to increase the caregivers' understanding of their experience to adopt a "more considerate and enlightened attitude" when dealing with individuals living with Alzheimer's and other dementias (Williams 26). Oftentimes caregivers may not be medical professionals, and they may benefit from examples of common stressful situations, so that caregivers may understand their own emotions and learn coping strategies. According to Squier, "graphic narrative has the capacity to articulate aspects of social experience that escape both the normal realms of medicine and the comforts of canonical literature" (130). Illustrated health narratives may provide a less intimidating source of information supplementing text-based materials.

The Origin Story —Así empezó la historia

Understanding the statistics where 59% of family caregivers of people with dementia rate their emotional stress as high or very high vs. 41% of other caregivers, Alzheimer's Association – West Texas Chapter executive director David Hernandez, MA and Sarah Jimenez, PhD, RN, a volunteer support group facilitator, and Assistant Professor of Nursing at the UTEP, began conversations around expanding activities for support groups. Having prior experience with reflection journaling, Dr. Jimenez proposed the idea of expanding activities for caregivers and family members to reduce stress as a self-care intervention. Mr. Hernandez, with a background in art education and experience in early-stage social engagement Alzheimer's programming, reached out to local comic book artists Elvira Carrizal-Dukes, PhD, MFA, Chicano Studies Assistant Professor of Instruction, UTEP, and artist Ronnie Dukes to assist with this endeavor. Comic book author Dr. Carrizal-Dukes led the journaling segment, while artist Mr. Dukes conducted the doodling activity. Caregivers of people with dementia are more likely than other caregivers to help with emotional or mental health problems (41% vs. 16%) and behavioral issues (15% vs. 4%) ("Facts and Figures"). Therefore, expanding support groups from only providing a forum for discussion, the activity of journaling and doodling was introduced as an additional approach to reduce stress using a series of workshops. Reflection journaling provides an outlet for participants to focus on their own personal experiences.

During the workshops, a facilitator guides participants to journal and doodle. We introduce the journaling practice and explain that journaling, or expressive writing, is a process by which one writes down thoughts and feelings. The activities of journaling enhance self-exploration and emotional processing, reduce stress, and promote relaxation (Scott). As a result, the workshops were designed and promoted to address stress relief and relaxation for caregivers. Journaling and doodling combine writing, drawing, and relaxation, exercising body and mind. It can be used as a form of therapy and can be useful during challenging times. It can be a positive distraction, an unconscious engagement with a creative activity, and a form of self-care.

The Workshops

The initial workshops consisted of one-hour sessions with a theme of common behaviors exhibited by patients with Alzheimer's such as repetition, anxiety and agitation, aggression, and suspicion, wandering and confusion. The themes are illustrated through four-panel comics, which are called the Comic of the Day. To begin the session, the facilitator explains what journaling and doodling is, followed by a list of materials needed, such as paper and pen or pencil. Before beginning the activity, the facilitator stresses the health benefits of participation. A Comic of the Day is then introduced to illustrate common stressful situations a caregiver may find themselves in when caring for an individual living with Alzheimer's disease. By highlighting these scenarios, participants may become aware of their feelings or emotions.

As the workshops were deployed, it became evident that the workshops were not reaching the Spanish-speaking segment of the local population as the workshops were being offered in English only. To expand the reach of the workshops to include Spanish speakers, the team also grew with the addition of three members: Maria Isela Maier, PhD, Assistant Professor of Instruction, Rhetoric and Writing Studies, UTEP; Jacob Martinez, PhD, RN, Assistant Professor of Nursing, UTEP; and Maria Llamas, MPA, Director of Programs, Alzheimer's Association – West Texas Chapter. The following section presents the four-panel comics and video links associated with this community literacy project. A four-panel comic is sequential art in four frames. For the purposes of this article, we are including one English language and one Spanish language four-panel comic.

The Comics

The Comic of the Day is written by comic author Dr. Carrizal-Dukes and illustrated by Mr. Dukes. The comics are hand drawn, inked, colored, and lettered by Mr. Dukes of DUKEScomics.com. They used characters from their graphic novel *A.W.O.L.* and placed them in scenes showing Cruz, the daughter, caregiving for her dad, Mr. Ochoa whom she calls Apá, a term of endearment used in some Latino households. In *A.W.O.L.*, Cruz is an Army soldier who leaves the military briefly without permission to find her younger brother who has been kidnapped. Mr. Ochoa is a retired United States Marine soldier who has diabetes and prosthetic legs. In the graphic novel, we also see Cruz administering his insulin for his diabetes. It's implied in the story that Mr. Ochoa has Alzheimer's or another dementia. Placing Cruz and Mr. Ochoa in these Alzheimer's scenarios felt like a natural fit.

In preparation for writing the four-panel comic strips, Dr. Carrizal-Dukes researched educational material from the Alzheimer's Association. For these comics, she focused on the common behaviors exhibited by individuals living with Alzheimer's or other dementia and reviewed strategies for caregivers on how to navigate these challenges. The behaviors presented in our workshops included anger and aggression, anxiety or agitation, forgetfulness and confusion, repetition, suspicion, and wandering. Dr. Carrizal-Dukes wrote five short scripts before the COVID-19 pandemic. Once quarantine began and as a response to heightened stress experienced by caregivers, she revised the dialogue to center on unique caregiving challenges resulting from COVID-19 restrictions.

Figure 1. Comic #1.

In this first four-panel comic labeled as Figure 1, the theme is repetition, and the script for this scenario was written before the COVID-19 pandemic. In panel one, Cruz and Mr. Ochoa are sitting at the kitchen table. They are drinking coffee. The morning sun streams through the kitchen window above the sink. Mr. Ochoa asks his daughter Cruz if his son is home, "Is Esteban home, yet?" Cruz responds, "Not yet, Apá."

In panel two, it's later in the day, and Mr. Ochoa is having lunch at the kitchen table. There is a glass of lemonade and a plate of enchiladas with rice and beans. Cruz is in the background walking toward her dad with a plate in her hands. Mr. Ochoa speaks first, repeating the same question. He asks Cruz, "Is Esteban home, yet?" Cruz responds, "Let's shine your shoes before he gets home." Dad responds, "Okay, that's a good idea."

In panel three, Cruz and her dad are now sitting in the living room shining shoes. Mr. Ochoa sits in a green comfy chair and Cruz sits on the floor by his feet. The dad says, "My mother would write to me when I was in the service." Cruz responds, "That's great, Apá. What did she write about?"

In panel four, the last panel, Cruz is alone writing in her journal at her desk. It's the end of the day. We can assume her dad has gone to bed. There is a cup of hot tea on the table next to Cruz' journal. She has a pencil in her hand. We see handwriting on the open page in her journal. As if reading Cruz' thoughts, the text above her head reads "Dear Journal, When IS Esteban getting home?"

After Dr. Carrizal-Dukes reads the dialogue, Dr. Jimenez then discusses the Alzheimer's Association four-step process to follow and apply to any behavior. In Comic of the Day, Figure 1, this is how Cruz addresses repetition with her dad, Mr. Ochoa, in this four-panel comic.

1. Who was present when repetition happened?

In this case, only Cruz and her dad are present. The son Esteban is missing, which is what is triggering her dad.

2. What happened just before and after the behavior happened?

This is a routine Cruz experiences with her dad in the morning at breakfast whenever her brother Esteban is out of town working. After the behavior happened, Cruz stayed calm. She answered her dad's repeated question. She stays with him in his reality. Cruz distracts her dad by offering a soothing activity for her dad. Cruz participates in shoe shining with her dad. She reminds him he's not alone. Cruz engages in conversation that is a positive trigger for her dad. This leads to him having positive feelings and memories.

3. Where did the behavior take place?

The behavior took place in the kitchen where the family usually sits together to eat breakfast. Seeing Esteban's empty chair at the table could be triggering Cruz' dad. Cruz moved her dad to a different room to shine shoes.

4. When does the behavior tend to occur?

It usually happens in the morning during breakfast.

5. How did Cruz react?

Cruz is patient and has gotten used to her dad asking for Esteban when he's not home. Sometimes she'll call Esteban on the phone before breakfast, so her dad hears Esteban's voice. After discussing these strategies with caregivers in our workshops, Dr. Carrizal-Dukes commences the journaling exercise. She begins by bringing awareness to breathing. She guides the caregivers to take three deep breaths saying, "Inhale deeply through your nose and exhale out through your mouth." After doing this, she asks questions for the caregivers to reflect on. For example, what is your story with repetition and the one you're caring for? How did you react? These questions prompt the caregiver to think about his/her own experiences dealing with repetition. The question also asks caregivers to reflect on their own actions in the real-life situation.

After a few minutes of writing, Dr. Carrizal-Dukes then prompts the caregivers to write down the opposite of what the caregiver sees, hears, or feels. The caregivers write for about five minutes, and they are instructed to write nonstop and not edit their work. Caregivers are reminded to let their hand and writing tool (pen/pencil) flow nonstop. They are told that there is no right or wrong answer. They are instructed to write honestly and from the heart and to write their own story.

Once the journaling exercise is completed, Mr. Dukes introduces the doodling exercise for caregivers and incorporates the theme of repetition during the facilitation. Like the journaling exercise, he begins with deep breathing. For this sketch diary, Mr. Dukes guides the caregiver as they begin to doodle. He starts by asking them to repeat the same drawing motion. The drawing can be a shape or an abstract idea. Caregivers can even look away from the paper or close their eyes and just do the motion repeatedly. Mr. Dukes instructs participants to always doodle lightly. When they finish, he asks them to examine what they have on the paper and make something out of it or elaborate on things that they see within the doodle. He sets a timer for five minutes and suggests to participants to doodle lightly and nonstop.

Mr. Dukes concludes the doodling segment by recommending participants to keep a daily journal and sketch diary to describe their experiences and feelings that relate to caregiving. Writing and sketching emotions can help individuals heal during stressful times. At the end of the workshop, participants are invited to share their work with other participants or on social media using the hashtags #journalingforalzheimers, #doodlingforalzheimers and #endalz. Following is a Comic of the Day written in Spanish including the script but omitting the four-step process that was already provided in English.

Figure 2. Comic #2, in Spanish

El tema de este cómic del cuidador de alzheimer, es repetición durante el tiempo de COVID-19.

Este es un cómic de cuatro paneles que presenta a una hija que cuida a su papá que tiene demencia. El papá repite la misma pregunta porque olvida que ya la hizo. En el primer panel, los dos están bebiendo café en la cocina. Apá pregunta, ¿Ya terminó COVID? Cruz le responde, "Todavía no, Apá."

En el segundo panel, están almorzando. Y Apá repite la pregunta, "¿Ya terminó COVID?" Cruz responde, "Ahora hay una vacuna contra el COVID-19, Apá." El Apá agrega, "No, esa es una mala idea."

En el tercer panel, están sentados en la sala mientras el padre brilla sus zapatos, y parece que cambia de opinión sobre la vacuna. Apá comenta, "Quiero que se acabe COVID. Quiero ver a mi hijo, ir a la tienda. Creo que iré a ponerme la vacuna, Cruzita." Cruz añade, "Yo también me voy a poner la vacuna contra COVID-19, Apá. Lo hago para protegernos."

En el cuarto panel, la hija toma té y está sola escribiendo en su diario. Escribe, "Estimado diario: ¿Cuándo terminará esta pandemia?"

It is important to note that during the workshops, along with reading the comic, we do provide strategies for caregivers to navigate these sensitive situations. However, for the purposes of this article, we have not included the discussion of the strategies in Spanish.

These bilingual Comic of the Day examples illustrate the common behaviors experienced by caregivers of individuals living with Alzheimer's or other dementias. The comics feature individuals that are representative of the diverse population of the El Paso region. Additionally, the comics target the demographics that are most affected by Alzheimer's and other dementias. This ongoing community literacy project was aimed at the public, but specifically for caregivers. The goals addressed were: 1) To raise awareness about Alzheimer's and dementias' impact on the community. 2) To provide journaling and doodling workshops for stress reduction and relaxation 3) To introduce bilingual comics as graphic medicine for caregivers promoting awareness and education and, 4) To promote journaling and doodling for relaxation and stress reduction.

Moving Forward

As pandemic restrictions are lifted, the Alzheimer's "Journal Writing and Doodling for Stress Reduction and Relaxation" bilingual workshops will be offered both virtually and in-person throughout west Texas. Initially, we started this community literacy project in English. Considering multilingual audiences' culture and contexts in the El Paso region and addressing the need for supplementary Spanish language health literacies, the Spanish comics and Spanish language workshops were designed to help fill this void.

Disciplinarily, our goal is to create and share educational modules like the journaling and doodling workshops with educators and students to engage with their communities through health literacies, illustrated narratives, and bilingual content. Another goal is to engage students in cross-disciplinary collaborations in which they can use their collective talents to provide health education using digital platforms. Professionally, we are developing graphic medicine geared toward families with young children to help facilitate conversations about sensitive issues such as coping with loved ones living with Alzheimer's and other dementias. More importantly, projects like journaling and doodling workshops will help promote discourse about health literacy information aimed at bilingual and bicultural audiences. It is important to note that this innovative community literacy project was made possible with the collaboration among university faculty, nonprofit organization leaders, and community artists.

The Workshop Videos

The Alzheimer's comics and the recorded workshop series may be accessed through the DUKEScomics website https://www.dukescomics.com/workshops.

The two bilingual recorded workshops featured in this article, one conducted in Summer 2020 can be accessed here https://youtu.be/F7IV6dU9TFk , and the Spanish from Spring 2022 can be accessed here https://youtu.be/J34BB3_t1-4.

The Alzheimer's Association has a 24/7 Helpline number for caregivers: 1-800-272-3900 or visit their website alz.org. It can help to have a dementia-trained professional to talk with when you feel overwhelmed or at a loss for what to try next

Works Cited

"American Community Survey." *U.S. Census Bureau*. 2018.

Dukes, Ronnie. "Workshops" *DUKEScomics*, https://www.dukescomics.com/workshops.

"Facts and Figures" *Alzheimer's Association*. 2022, https://www.alz.org/alzheimers dementia/facts-figures.

Fiscella, Kevin, et al. "Disparities in Health Care by Race, Ethnicity, and Language among the Insured: Findings from a National Sample." *Medical Care*, vol. 40, no. 1, Jan. 2002, pp.14, 52–59. EBSCOhost, https://doi-org.utep.idm.oclc.org/10.1097/00005650-200201000- 00007.

Green, Michael J., and Kimberly R. Myers. "Graphic Medicine: Use of Comics in Medical Education and Patient Care." *Bmj*, 2010, p 340.

Maríñez-Lora, Ané M., et al. "A Framework for Translating an Evidence-Based Intervention from English to Spanish." *Hispanic Journal of Behavioral Sciences*, vol. 38, no. 1, Feb. 2016, pp. 117–33. EBSCOhost, https://doi org.utep.idm.oclc.org/10.1177/0739986315612769.

"QuickFacts: Fort Bliss CDP, Texas." *United States Census Bureau*, 2022, https://www.census.gov/quickfacts/fact/table/fortblisscdptexas/RHI225220#RHI225220.

Scott, Elizabeth. "The Benefits of Journaling for Stress Management." *Very Well Mind*, Dotdash Media, Inc., 2020, https://www.verywellmind.com/the-benefits-of-journaling-for-stress-management-3144611.

Sentell, Tetine, et al. "Access to Mental Health Treatment by English Language Proficiency and Race/Ethnicity." *Journal of General Internal Medicine*, vol. 22, no. Suppl 2, Nov. 2007, pp. 289–93. EBSCOhost, https://doi-org.utep.idm.oclc.org/10.1007/s11606-007-0345-7.

Squier, Susan M. "Literature and medicine, future tense: Making it graphic." *Literature and Medicine*, vol. 27, no. 2, 2008, pp 124-152. *The Penn State Research Database*, doi: DOI: 10.1353/lm.0.0031

Williams, Ian. "Graphic medicine: comics as medical narrative." *Graphic Medicine Manifesto*, edited by Susan Squier and Ian Williams, Penn State University Press, 2012, pp 21-27.

Williams, Ian. "What Is "Graphic Medicine"?" *Graphic Medicine*, Graphic Medicine International Collective, 2022, https://www.graphicmedicine.org/why-graphic-medicine/.

Author Bios

Elvira Carrizal-Dukes, Ph.D., M.F.A., is an Assistant Professor of Instruction of Chicana/o studies at the University of Texas at El Paso, where she teaches Chicana/o Cinema and Theatre, American Cinema of the US-Mexico Border, The Roots of Latina/o Hip Hop, and Chicano/Latino Music in the U.S. Her current teaching and scholarly projects center on Cholx consciousness, Visual Rhetoric, and Comics. To learn more, go to: www.DUKEScomics.com.

Maria Isela Maier, Ph.D., is Assistant Professor of Instruction at The University of Texas at El Paso where she teaches in the Rhetoric and Writing Studies Program in the English Department. Her teaching and scholarly projects center or language diversity, undergraduate research and community engagement in writing and pedagogy.

Sarah Yvonne Jimenez, Ph.D., RN, is an assistant professor of Nursing at the University of Texas at El Paso, El Paso, Texas where she teaches a nursing introductory course in the undergraduate nursing program. Her research focuses on stressors that affect the mental and physical health of individuals who care for family members living with Alzheimer's disease and other dementia along the U.S. Mexican border. Her scholarly projects focus on interventions that combine the arts with health education to improve health outcomes and quality of life for those living with dementia and their caregivers.

Jacob Martinez, Ph.D., RN, is a community health nurse who serves as an assistant professor at the University of Texas at El Paso School of Nursing. His research focuses on better understanding and addressing a cadre of health disparities affecting vulnerable US-Mexico Border Latinx populations.

David Andrew Hernandez, MA, serves as the Executive Director of the Alzheimer's Association West Texas Chapter. Through his leadership, he works with volunteers, staff, and supporters to further the mission across 80 counties of West Texas. The mission of the Alzheimer's Association is to lead the way to end Alzheimer's and all other dementia—by accelerating global research, driving risk reduction and early detection, and maximizing quality care and support.

Ronnie Dukes, A.A.S., was born on the south side of Chicago and is a comic book creator. He earned his degree in computer animation in Minneapolis before relocating to Harlem, Manhattan where he began to paint and exhibit work throughout the city. Currently based in New Mexico, Ronnie created his publishing company DUKEScomics.com with his wife, partner Elvira Carrizal-Dukes, featuring their first major print project A.W.O.L., a full-color graphic novel available in English, Japanese and Spanish.

Book and New Media Reviews

From the Book and New Media Review Editor's Desk

Jessica Shumake, Editor
University of Notre Dame

For readers who are looking for great books to read this summer, these reviewers offer thoughtful recommendations. I wish to thank Michael J. Benjamin, Jennifer Smith Daniel, Meng-Hsien (Neal) Liu, Angela F. Jacobs, and Erin Schaefer for accompanying me on a "long journey" to see these reviews in print. The documentary filmmaker Albert Maysles, says that a "long journey" implies movement away from one's initial starting place—to a new location—where better questions can be asked, new perspectives appreciated, and the audience carried further "spiritually, aesthetically, ethically, or whatever" (Maysles and Pryluck 9). In terms of the reviewers whose work is featured here, I'm grateful we've taken *ourselves* on a long journey and I'm hopeful *CLJ* readers will enjoy the ride.

Works Cited

Maysles, Albert, and Calvin Pryluck. "Seeking to Take the Longest Journey: A Conversation with Albert Maysles." *Journal of the University Film Association* 28.2 (1976): 9–16.

Linguistic Justice: Black Language, Literacy, Identity, and Pedagogy

April Baker-Bell
NCTE-Routledge, 2020, pp. 128

Reviewed by Michael J. Benjamin
University of Louisville

April Baker-Bell done known what she did with *Linguistic Justice: Black Language, Literacy, Identity, and Pedagogy* when she titled her first chapter "Black Language is Good on Any MLK Boulevard."

I knew what she did, too, as The Carters' "Black Effect" played in my head as I read the title. A masterful reference provided Baker-Bell's, and *Linguistic Justice*'s, relationship to Geneva Smitherman. Smitherman, aka Dr. G, aka the Jay-Z of Academics, states in the foreword "mos def, this is the book we have been waiting for" (xvi). She ain't wrong. The book is so good I had to read it twice to even begin to think about critiquing it as it intricately weaves together theory and practice. A self-admitted part manifesto, part theory reader, and part critical praxis collection, *Linguistic Justice* almost effortlessly glides from the NCTE/CCCC's 1974 Students' Right to Their Own Language (SRTOL) resolution to the Black Lives Matter's mission statement. The book is a call to action, to "radically imagine and create a world free of anti-blackness" and a larger education system that values Black students' language and literacies (3). The tie between valuing Black Language and striving towards a world rid of anti-black racism is demonstrated viscerally in the death of Eric Garner. Baker-Bell cites the death of Garner a couple different times in the book, highlighting his use of White Mainstream English ("I cannot breathe") as a police officer choked him to death. Baker-Bell could not have known that her book would be published amidst the COVID-19 pandemic which disproportionately wreaked havoc on minorities and just weeks before the murder of George Floyd, the life choked out of him by a police officer. Yet, the context into which *Linguistic Justice* was published is the point: the oppression and dehumanization of Black folx is omnipresent and radiates from the classroom into the community. From within the classroom, we ought to dismantle Anti-Black Linguistic Racism and destabilize white linguistic hegemony.

A "Black Language Theoreticum" or theory meets practicum book, *Linguistic Justice* argues for an Antiracist Black Language Pedagogy, enacted by Baker-Bell at Detroit's Leadership Academy, a public charter school on the Westside of the city where ninety-nine percent of the student body is Black-American (8). A "teacher-scholar-activist project [done] with young people in Detroit," Baker-Bell's book highlights the way Anti-Black Linguistic Racism has oppressed and permeated Black students and Black Language-speakers, ultimately damaging their sense of self and identity (8). In its advocacy for Antiracist Black Language Pedagogy, *Linguistic Justice* offers seven critical inquiry-based learning experiences that offer Black students the opportunity to learn through and about Black Language. Baker-Bell offers a collection of images, dialogues, charts, graphs, instructional maps, artwork, stories, and weblinks in order to both show the dynamism of Black Language and how she understands and interacts with Black Language daily. Tying together Black death and Anti-Black Linguistic Racism, Baker-Bell argues for demolishing linguistic hierarchies for the sake of demolishing racial ones.

In chapter one, "Black Language is Good on Any MLK Boulevard," which doubles as the introduction, Baker-Bell interrogates the bonds between race, culture, and language. Cementing herself in the tradition of Smitherman, Elaine Richardson (lovingly referred to as Docta E), Valerie Kinloch, Carmen Kynard, and many more invested in Black rhetorics, Baker-Bell begins by establishing her connection to Detroit and Michigan at large. An important note, as she points out, provided the state's deeply entrenched position in the language wars. Owning up to her former naivete, Baker-Bell indicates the desire to create a book that enacts bell hooks' "revolutionary pedagogy of resistance," especially given the history of Black Language research "in the D" and the landmark 1977 Ann Arbor Black English case (4). *Linguistic Justice* is personal, with further impetus for the project stemming from a presentation at the 2017 National Council of Teachers of English annual convention where teachers advocated for code-switching as a means to dismantle white supremacy. The remark, Baker-Bell notes, came from a young Black teacher and fails to "realize that standard English is a byproduct of white supremacy" (6). Discomforted by the way the comment fostered a sense of relief for the white teachers in the room, Baker-Bell argues for "the need for *Black Linguistic Consciousness*" to prevent such anti-Black statements to serve as further justification for "racist language policies, practices, pedagogies, and classrooms" (7).

Vital to chapter one also is the definition of key terms and Baker-Bell's linguistic choices throughout the book. She intentionally uses Smitherman's Black Language instead of African American Language or African American Vernacular English to both demonstrate Black Language's standing as its own language that includes features of West African Languages in an American context and align her work with the mission of Black Liberation movements. Likewise, she uses Alim and Smitherman's White Mainstream English instead of Dominant American English, standard English, or academic English to make visible the racial component to language and destabilize this concept that this iteration of English is more important than Black Language. It is these moments of definition-setting that Baker-Bell makes her theoretical imprint and unites her audiences, demonstrating the importance of our rhetorical choices in scholarship and in the world at-large.

In chapter two, "What's Anti-Blackness Got To Do Wit It?," Baker-Bell describes Anti-Black Linguistic Racism and its quotidian persecution and dehumanization of Black Language-speakers and its relationship to the marginalization, colonization, and policing of black bodies. Positioning this type of linguistic oppression as unique, Baker-Bell highlights how Anti-Black Linguistic Racism is routinely evident in our "research, disciplinary discourses, curricular choices, pedagogical practices, and teacher attitudes" (12). It is here that Baker-Bell provides the theoretical backbone to *Linguistic Justice*, weaving together Critical Race Theory, sociolinguistics, and pedagogy. These theoretical underpinnings ultimately scaffold into three approaches to language pedagogy: eradicationist language pedagogy, respectability language pedagogy, and antiracist Black Language pedagogy. Labeling the first as a lack of acknowledgment of Black Language and the second as a "surrender to whiteness," Baker-Bell defines the third as centering Black Language (28). She envisions an approach that destabilizes white linguistic hegemony and undoes Anti-Black Linguistic Racism and the internalization of it by students.

Chapter two, in its conclusion, also finds Baker-Bell providing ten framing ideas for an Antiracist Black Language Education and Pedagogy. She argues that it is vital that the ideas be "embodied in any transformative approach that seeks to dismantle Anti-Black Linguistic Racism and student's internalization of it" (34). At their core, the ideas all "(1) center blackness; (2) confront white linguistic and cultural hegemony; and (3) contest antiblackness" (32). It is here where Baker-Bell makes highly explicit the harms of code-switching and other appeasement and respectability language education policies. It is also here where Baker-Bell provides the seven critical inquiry-based Black Language artifacts, such as Black Language & Identity and Study of the Grammatical and Rhetorical Features of Black Language. These artifacts inform the practical application component of the book, powering the lesson plans Baker-Bell describes throughout the remaining chapters with each artifact coming with a student learning outcome.

In chapter three, "Killing Them Softly," Baker-Bell starts with a "Detroit literacy practice," as the students at Leadership Academy "ask a series of questions that help them place each other on a map and/or distinguish *the real* (those who lived/lived in Detroit) from *the fake* (those who claim Detroit but have never lived there or did not live there pregentrification)" (42). A native New Yorker, this literacy practice warmed my heart as we use a very similar test to figure out the very same thing. Baker-Bell narrativizes the beginning of her work at the Leadership Academy, demonstrating that she is not, indeed, one of those "'hit it and quit it' researchers that enter into schools and classrooms, collect data, and bounce" (41). She argues for educators to listen to the voices of Black Language speakers and proceeds to center the voices of her students through composite character counterstorying, which she defines as "a critical race methodological tool that allows researchers to merge data analysis with creative writing to expose patterns of racialized inequality and deepen our understanding of the ways race and racism affect the lives and lived experiences of people of color as individuals and as groups in schools" (44). Through these counterstories, Baker-Bell demonstrates the unaccounted effects of eradicationist and respectability language pedagogy, namely Anti-Black Linguistic Racism and linguistic double consciousness and the need for a revised literacy and language education.

In chapter four, "Scoff No More," Baker-Bell illuminates how theory, research, and practice can enhance each other to pursue linguistic and racial justice while simultaneously providing "ethnographic snapshots" of how students at Leadership Academy reacted to the Black Language Artifacts (64). Structured around each artifact and also a direct response to Carter G. Woodson's point about Black students learning to hate their own language instead of learning about it, this chapter is perhaps the crown jewel of the book. Replete with activities, worksheets, and lessons about the syntax, semantics, pronunciation, and rhetorical features of Black Language, chapter four is Antiracist Black Language Pedagogy in its full praxis glory. I found myself personally taken by Baker-Bell's discussion of Black Language Artifact 3: Study of Grammatical and Rhetorical Features of Black Language. Employing an approach to grammar that asked students to observe, explore, and describe the literacies of their "native" language, Baker-Bell avoids simply explaining how the Black Language works (76). Instead, she provides highlights on the syntax, semantics, slang, and phonology of Black Language as on display by the students at Leadership Academy, as well as the rhetorical features such as signifyin', playing the dozens, and linguistic inventiveness. Baker-Bell highlights how many aspects of Black Language do not translate into White Mainstream English, even if portions of Black Language are co-opted into the broader English language.

Linguistic Justice's main weakness is evident in the disparity between chapters three and four. Chapter three, while certainly important due to its role in setting the scene of Leadership Academy, Baker-Bell's place as a researcher, and outlining the book's methodology, does not go into the same depth in its discussion of the Black Language artifacts as chapter four. Going into just two of the artifacts—compared to the five parsed in chapter four—these two chapters feel disproportionate in their delivering of the book's overall content. This may be on purpose and understood as a strength rather than a weakness: *Linguistic Justice* is mean to be read as a book and each chapter should not be separated from the rest. However, as ideas from each chapter bleed into each other and lead to some repetition, it can begin to feel as if the takeaways from chapter four dwarf the ones in chapter three, even given the power of the counterstories in the third chapter.

In chapter five, "Black Linguistic Consciousness," Baker-Bell continues the use of counterstory, this time focusing much further on the results of her work at Leadership Academy. While Baker-Bell highlights a shift in much of the students' thinking around Black Language, the counterstories also show that "an Antiracist Black Language Pedagogy alone cannot solve Anti-Black Racism and white linguistic hegemony" (97). Not solely triumphant, Baker-Bell clarifies the purpose of the book: "to give Black students the tools to liberate themselves from oppression" (100). Cementing that Antiracist Black Language Pedagogy supplied her students with the ability to name their experiences with linguistic racism, the ability to interrogate linguistic oppression, and a language and literacy education that values their backgrounds and selves, Baker-Bell concludes by directly addressing the reader, "I encourage language and literacy educators to position themselves as learners and allow your students to do their part by teaching you" (101).

In chapter six, "'THUG LIFE': Bonus Chapter: Five Years After Leadership Academy," Baker-Bell blends the theories of Tupac Shakur with Angie Thomas' 2017 novel, *The Hate U Give* as a critique of the white supremacist capitalist system. This bonus chapter is fully practical, going through each of the seven artifacts with a lesson plan, while also adding an eighth bonus artifact. A project born from her English Teacher Education courses, Baker-Bell supplies a thoughtful follow-up on her work at Leadership Academy and the most explicitly sketched out implementation of Antiracist Black Language Pedagogy.

I cannot lavish enough praise on *Linguistic Justice*. As a graduate student in his last semester of coursework, Baker-Bell's book has served as a crucial tying together of the numerous threads in the field of rhetoric and composition. With its eye towards theory and practice, the scholarly and the activist, Baker-Bell's book provides a trusty guide to critical teaching, demonstrating how to blend theory with practice. The book is at its strongest in the sections that weave together the counterstories of students with theory. My deepest critique is the way the book carries from chapter-to-chapter, without the clear delineation seen in other books of its ilk. That said, *Linguistic Justice: Black Language, Literacy, Identity, and Pedagogy* has helped crystallize my understanding of the relationship between what we do in the classroom and how it reverberates in the larger community. I urge you to read it, fully expecting it to have the same effect.

On Teacher Neutrality: Politics, Praxis, and Performativity

Edited by Daniel P. Richards
Utah State UP, 2020, 291 pp.

Reviewed by Jennifer Smith Daniel
Queens University of Charlotte

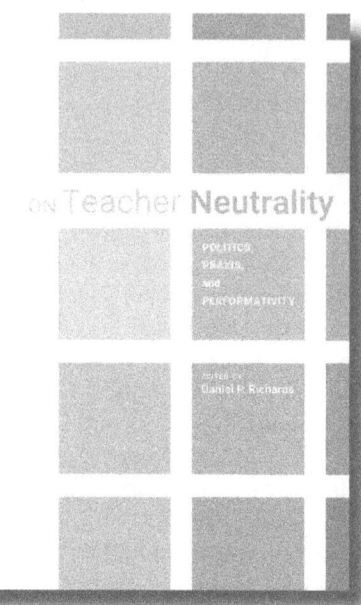

While teacher neutrality is a contested concept within the field of rhetoric and composition, the public often expects a teacher's neutral position. Daniel P. Richard's collection of essays grapples with this disconnect in *On Teacher Neutrality: Politics, Praxis, and Performativity*. The collection's purpose is three-fold: to complicate in order to clarify the term *neutrality*; to bring "depth to how neutrality operates differently in various institutional settings"; and to "nuance" ways neutrality may or may not be applied in those settings (14). Richards opens the collection by framing our current political discourses about education pointing to external pressures from advocacy groups such as Turning Point USA and internal pressures from neoliberal institutions. This edited collection challenges "teachers of writing to explore further and more fully and honestly the ramifications of a ubiquitous position of non-neutrality [...] against a larger social scene that still believes in and expects neutrality in education" (13). His caution is not wrong—particularly in pointing out that while our field may understand that teaching is a political endeavor, the discourses through which our students are reading us tell another story. Readers will appreciate the ways the collection works towards theorizing the phenomenon of teacher neutrality and how the public's static perception may be complicated. To more deeply engage the theories, readers may wish to read Karen Kopelson's "Rhetoric on the Edge of Cunning; or, The Performance of Neutrality" as the essay is a prominent support or counter for most of the collection's essays. Using a variety of methodologies, Richards and the other contributors test the ways neutrality and non-neutrality either serve our goals as teachers of writing or hinder them.

Meaghan Brewer's essay "The Limits of Neutrality" opens up part one of the book with this anchoring idea: "The idea of the teacher as politically neutral appears to be a cultural commonplace" (27). Brewer's research suggests that the graduate teachers from her study had a couple of approaches for neutrality as they negotiated the politically informed curriculum they were assigned; a performance which centered on keeping the student focus at the level of the text. She notes that many graduate instructors seemed unaware of their neutral stance, which "were [...] influenced by interactions with past professors and other literacy sponsors, as well as cultural prototypes for the 'ideal professor'" (Brewer 32). These differing accounts of how to perform neutrality illustrate Brewer's assertion that "different institutional settings demand different degrees of neutrality"—a point taken up more thoroughly and explicitly with the lenses of praxis and performativity later in the book. Brewer makes visible an essential need to train new graduate instructors to "operate as teacher-rhetors, recognizing the classroom as a rhetorical space for accomplishing the work of education" (39).

Chapter two by Jason C. Evans, "Living in Contradiction: Translingual Writing Pedagogies and the Two-Year College" asks a germane question for instructors of writing: "What are we doing, really?" Evans bids readers to consider how instructors (particularly at two-year-colleges) sit at "nexus of contradictions" and how "composition's dominant attitudes about language position [it] in relation to [...] students" (41). He reminds readers that students come to our courses with their own agendas and goals that may lay in more practical pathways than our democratic ones. Evans interrogates the theories of linguistic capital, capitalism, and social-class in the chapter not to deflate the field's idealistic aims but to remind us that those aims are always contingent. Evans notes in his conclusion that "students' instrumental understanding of college" may cause tension between the goals of translingual writing pedagogies and students' instrumental goals, but concentrating that tension mostly at the level of the student seems to miss the opportunity to acknowledge how systems of power co-opt language and invite students into a conversation that addresses language as a tool for both access and exclusion (53).

Jessica Clements' tidy chapter "Walking the Narrow Ridge: When Performing Neutrality Isn't an Option in the Vocation of the Christian Professor" shares her practical approach of utilizing *métis* within the context of an institution openly aligned with a Christian ethos. Clements posits that when the non-neutral position of the institution extends to the classroom, the institutions "should be willing to reward their instructors for subversive performance of neutrality as purposeful pedagogical *métis*" (Clements 55, emphasis original). During an invention exercise with the students, Clements adds words that may counter, or at least muddle, those initial student responses so that eventually her "covert stratagem" produced "critical dividends in the students' reflections" she shares as part of her research (62). What Clements seems to do is give the students the rhetorical space to think deeply about their projects through her use of *métis* to counter their preconceived expectations about assignment goals and their instructor's suspected alignment with the institution's Christian character.

The nexus of teacher neutrality and the precariousness of contingent faculty is the subject matter for Robert Samuels' essay "Contingent Faculty, Student Evaluation, and Pedagogical Neutrality." Samuels claims "that we can use the principles of the scientific method to posit that instruction should also be based on the ideals of neutrality, objectivity, empiricism, and universality" (72). His point is that even if teachers cannot be neutral, they should still aim for it. Framing his argument on the ideas of Descartes and Freud, Samuels echoes other contributors in the collection regarding the value of developing students' rhetorical agility to recognize how form and content operate together and that contexts drive what is rhetorically appropriate. Samuels draws a new understanding of neutrality as "a dialectical relationship between the modern quest for universality and the postmodern emphasis on cultural and historical differences" in which that universality is not reduced to an essential singularity but rather "expanded by the inclusion of new protected categories [. . .] fueled by postmodern minority-based social movements" (79).

The inter-chapter between Richards and John Timbur provides a fulcrum for the entire collection—particularly in light of Timbur's influence in our field, which is shaped by Freirean notions of education as a means of liberation. Timbur posits that students come with their expectations of teacher neutrality because of science: ". . . the ideas of neutrality and objectivity are interrelated historically in the formation of modern science" (85). Bias alters facts, and science addresses bias through "methodology"—the scientific method. Timbur suggests that despite their understanding that "scientific knowledge" is subject to the same pressures that rhetoric enacts on any phenomenon, scientists "also see politics, emotion, personality, as contaminating. And, science has sold that methodology, and established that authority in the production of knowledge" (86). Timbur suggests that we can reframe the idea of teacher neutrality in programming that is designed through interdisciplinarity such as WAC programs because these require faculty to work across disciplines to consider how knowledge is produced and legitimized (86). Timbur reminds readers—by paraphrasing Ken Bruffee—that "'how we teach is what we teach,'" which becomes significant to the ways teachers may perform neutrality in the classroom (89). For Timbur, the conversation around teacher neutrality "is a matter of working out what the authority of the teacher is. And I think bouncing off of the complexity that emerges when you start to talk about neutrality, and to see both what it screens and hides and what it authorizes" (94). What follows in Parts II and III of the collection addresses directly how neutrality can either obscure or legitimize. If politics end up being about people, then responding to the politics of teacher neutrality means factoring in the human contingencies in all their messiness. Part II of the book shifts from exploring the strategy of neutrality towards tactics for that strategy.

Kelly Blewett's chapter, "Strangers on Their Own Campus: Listening across Difference in Qualitative Research," invites a student's voice into the discussion. She suggests that despite the feeling of alienation that teachers—and likely students—feel when we engage a person with opposing values, we should consider simply pursuing a space of "mutual common ground, [decreased] fear, and [an increased . . .] sense of connectedness between students and teachers" (99). Over the course of interviews focusing on first-year writers, Blewett and her student shared what Lad Tobin calls "'purposeful self-disclosures'" (Tobin, as quoted in Blewett 102). These disclosures when read as neutrality can be experienced as "an openness to listening, to making a space for the student to explore their own" thoughts, which can be a "natural precursor to trust" (102). Blewett claims that her stance of neutrality was "not only a performance for students but also an orientation to students" (109). Blewett reminds readers that the discomfort about disclosing non-neutral positions is not just felt by instructors, but by students as well.

Christopher Michael Brown's chapter, "Believing Critically: Teaching Critical Thinking through the Conversion Narrative" also enacts an orientation towards neutrality in pragmatic ways for the classroom. Brown echoes the previous sentiments about the fraught nature of neutrality and invites readers to consider how "pedagogical approaches that seek to convert students along particular ideological lines may be less effective as a method of engaging students" in critical thinking processes (114). Instead he invites teachers to foster critical thinking through Burke's idea of *syllogistic progression form* (Brown 114, emphasis original). This tactic asks students to consider the how and why they came to have specific beliefs or values and to articulate that journey, which invites students into a naming process and makes visible to them the origins of their beliefs. Brown explains that routines of drafting and revision (by the student) and feedback (from the instructor) provides "students the analytical tools needed to recognize that the discourses that mediate their experience do not reflect timeless truths but emerge from—and are allied with—historically situated interests" (115). For Brown these tactics towards a neutrality, as a strategy, might work when the neutrality is about "enabling students to develop lines of inquiry on the basis of their own ideological commitments" in order to help students come to the understanding that "beliefs have a logical foundation" (118–119). Brown introduces the issue of student development and then posits that students are receptive to assignments they perceive "as akin to their own interests and commitments" (123).

The following chapter, "Ideology Through Process and Slow-Start Pedagogy: Co-Constructing the Path of Least Resistance in the Social Justice Writing Classroom" by Lauren F. Lichty and Karen Rosenberg also attend to the issue of how student development is a factor in resistance. They propose a slow-start pedagogy to minimize student resistance by "unmasking student assumptions about what a legitimate university classroom 'should' look like, de-centering professorial authority, legitimizing student experience as one form of valid evidence, providing productive outlets for student resistance, and enlisting students as active co-creators of the classroom learning community" (128–129). They argue for an "attention to process" so that "student resistance can be minimized by attending to developmental and contextual factors" in the "design [of] courses" (129). They emphasize further that "based on a read of our own institutional context [...] we argue that analyses of classroom practice are incomplete without the understanding of how classrooms are nested within particular institutional locations" (128). Indeed, the ecologies of higher education will come to factor into the tactics used by writers in later chapters. For Lichty and Rosenberg, sometimes student resistance is less about ideology and more about pedagogy.

Heather Fester extends these themes in chapter 9, entitled "Transparency as a Defense-less Act: Shining Light on Emerging Ideologies in an Activist Writing and Research Course." She contends that the tactic for occupying a non-neutral stance as an instructor must be the work of preparation around the classroom culture. Instructors should acknowledge the complexity of the non-neutral stance by "recognizing teacher positionality and the potential [for] student difference at the same time, in a way that doesn't dismiss possible tension in the space between" (147). Indeed, Hester asserts that "complexity recognizes that the instructor's beliefs are always already a visible part of [the] shared curricular ground" and as such "the space of the classroom needs to be *prepared*" (146, emphasis original). Fester suggests the tactics of co-creating a brave space with defined rules of engagement; student feedback loops that she creates through surveys and course design; and being transparent with students about choices for their shared learning. Fester prompts readers to consider that "our interpretation of cultural practices [are] powerful, influential, and mostly invisible" to students and that even "simple neutrality" performed in the classroom means that "the ideologies informing the curriculum as assignments can become invisible too" (157).

Mara Holt broadens the conversation by considering the impact of time and location as factors in the performance of teacher neutrality in her chapter "It Depends on the Context: Cultural Competencies in First-Year English." Holt takes readers to "three historical moments" in the early 90s, the early aughts, and just after the Presidential Election of 2016. She also relocates the conversation not just in terms of physical location, but also in terms of the curriculum as a site where the performance of teacher neutrality may or may not be a viable option. Holt reminds readers that "neutrality is a construction that assumes White is the only unbiased perspective" (163). Eventually, Holt realizes that the responsibility of curricular choices should not be driven by a fear of student resistance or teacher discomfort but by the kairotic moment being presented. At each moment in her timeline, Holt wants readers to understand that there was no one-size-fits-all answer to the situation she faced so she "responded to the context surrounding" her; "reflected on the possible [. . .] motives and the possible consequences"; "took a risk" because *any* choice she made—whether for a neutral or non-neutral stance—came with risks (174).

Tristan Abbott brings in the topic of assessment to the collection. He argues in "The *Mêtis* of Reliability: Using the *Framework for Success* to Aid the Performance of Neutrality Within Writing Assessment" that leveraging "objective-seeming and/or test-based assessment practices" might offer "a sort of distancing mechanism" to create a stance of neutrality for audiences beyond the academy (176). The assessment tool becomes the mediator between the material reality of non-neutrality for teachers and the need to "signal a disembodied objectivity" by the institution (177). Of particular use in the chapter is his discussion about the distance between validity and reliability and its impact on how institutions began to think about and measure writing abilities. He claims that the "embrace of validity over reliability has allowed for the development and implementation of assessment practices that, while imperfect, address many of the severe ethical and pedagogical concerns associated with a uniform or standardized approach to writing instruction" (181). Abbott draws our attention back to the idea of *mêtis* as posited by Kopelson and claims that there is a path to "appear less obviously subjective without substantially altering pedagogy" by using tools such as the *Framework for Success in Postsecondary Writing* (186). Abbott maintains that all assessment is imperfect, but intentional design can safeguard our pedagogical practices from the more draconian aspects of standardization.

The issues of design are salient for Adam Pacton's chapter that follows Abbott: "Massive Open Ideology: Ideological Neutrality in Arizona State's Composition MOOCs." Pacton sketches the design and implementation of two composition courses that complicate the ideas of teacher neutrality heretofore as a particularly American issue. He contends "that the multivalenced heterogeneity of [MOOCs] calls for a more nuanced stance on ideological commitment" (192). Pacton describes the process for designing these MOOC courses "began with the axiom that there is no view from nowhere" (194). The team used a process of *"theorizing"* ideological neutrality, which is "understood as a recursive, always-incomplete dialog between context, data, confirmation, prediction, and the epistemological scaffolding that undergirds them" (195, emphasis original). He states that they aimed for a *"direction* rather than a destination" to help refine their process (195, emphasis original). Pacton reaffirms the potential for the "broad outcomes" enumerated in position statements such as the *WPA Outcomes Statement for First-Year Composition* and *The Framework for Success in Postsecondary Writing* to become the tools for moving in the direction of ideological neutrality in both the course design and negotiating the "ideological commitments" found in LMSs (198). Pacton acknowledges that these types of tools are not fixed solutions for managing neutrality but merely one possibility for pursing "a kind of ideological equilibrium" (202).

If Part I is about the various theories possible in performing teacher neutrality and Part II is the pragmatic application of that performance, Part III is the reflection on the implications of that application. Romeo Garcia and Yndalecio Isaac Hinojosa offer a chapter meant to complicate the ideas present in Kopelson's original response of performative neutrality in reply to student resistance. Their initial move of contextualizing their own subject positions lends texture to their arguments for "unravel[ing] the term *resistance*" (207, emphasis original). In "Encounters with Friction: Engaging Resistance through Strategic Neutrality," their identities as a Mexican-American and Chicano from the southwest U.S. matters materially the moment they step into the classroom because they are "raced, gendered, and classed in various ways" (207). Garcia and Hinojosa draw on their lived experiences of learning "to listen [and] understand" in order "to respond to situations" (208). Here they are pointing to the difference between responding and reacting in a way that promotes the idea of *"friction as a nuance of resistance"* (208) in hopes of "shift[ing] away from resistance and from student-as-problem rationales" (208). For Garcia and Hinojosa, while the use of "strategic neutrality" can "mitigate resistance," student resistance was not something to be avoided so much as co-opted for the purpose of learning.

In "Turning Resistances into Engagement," Erika Johnson and Tawny LeBouef Tullia continue the promotion of resistance as a tactic ripe for creating meaningful learning. Johnson and Tullia explicitly address possible outcomes for teachers who are "authentically inhabiting [their] identities" in the classroom and how that has "proven to open more conversation than it closes" (222). They flatly state their unwillingness to perform neutrality as they feel it "robs [. . .] students of crucial and difficult conversations" (223). For Johnson and Tullia, as both "visibly and invisibly marked in how [they] identify," the idea of "cunning neutrality may prevent resistances from entering or impeding the writing classroom for some students, it may alienate or, even worse, fail to offer students who finally see themselves in us an opportunity to engage with their own identities" (223). Johnson and Tullia complicate the issue of power by asserting that within classrooms teachers are "both the powerful and the powerless" (226). Johnson and Tullia contend that resistance does not always stifle learning, but "that a pedagogy seated in the praxis of intersectionality and relationality" means that instructors also "engage" the process, which is "not fully possible from a positionality of neutrality" (231).

"Who is Afraid of Neutrality?: Performativity, Resignification, and the Jena Six in the Composition Classroom" by David Stubblefield and Chad Chisholm returns the conversation to arguing from the position "that neutrality is an indispensable concept for academic institutions [and] can produce unpredictable and desirable effects" (236). They contextualize their argument by providing a brief overview of the failed rise of the democratic classroom and the ramifications of the cultural reckoning of the 1960s, particularly as the composition classroom was affected by the theories of critical-pedagogy and expressivist scholars writing at the time. Stubblefield and Chisholm argue that a turn towards a "kind of oppositional pedagogy" became the tactic for bringing about the democratic classroom (240). Here they echo Kopelson's arguments for performing neutrality as a way to handle "today's hostile student audiences" (245). Providing an example from students at a "small historically Black college" regarding a student protest around the Jena Six, Chisholm suggests that he used a performance of neutrality to help students "measure their own assumptions" using "the very values and history they claimed to cherish" referring to the school's ethos and its "Methodist-affiliation" (249). He claims that such a stance "did not stifle politics, difference, or diversity, but [facilitated] the emergence of these things by encouraging the exchange of ideas" (250).

Jennifer Thomas and Allison L. Rowland's penultimate chapter, "Moving from Transparent to Translucent Pedagogy" resonates with earlier chapters in framing the resistance less as a political challenge than a pedagogical one. They posit the idea of *teacher transparency* as a corollary concept to *teacher neutrality* with a pivot towards a *"translucent pedagogy"* (252, emphasis original). They offer an argument to "highlight the conflation of competing transparency rhetorics in higher education [... and provide] a set of criteria in which to tell them apart, and suggest ways of adopting learning-centered transparency to the contemporary neoliberal moment" (253). Learning-centered transparent teaching is more about "the *how* and *why* of their learning" (257). Their approach accounts for how student learning habits and ways of being develop and sometimes need spaces that invite conflict to promote growth (259). They encourage teachers to ask students to join them in hard conversations about privilege and difference, but in a more intentional way and at a slower pace, which they name a "translucent pedagogy," that "gesture[s] to the possibilities inherent in strategically withholding learning purposes, goals, or other information [...] in the initial phases" of an activity or lesson and with a "'debriefing' discussion activity" afterwards (261). Teaching practices such as these are an option for potentially making use of potential student resistance.

Daniel Richards closes out the collection with a reflective essay that attempts to bring all the various threads into harmony through a narrative from one of his own teaching experiences that was a fraught site of non-neutrality. In responding to a student critique about a class where students had various responses to the outcome of the 2016 US Presidential election, he finds himself disclosing to a student his disappointment with the results. This reaction (versus what he would have preferred as a considered response) seems to trouble him as not something he would normally do, but felt in this moment that he was trying "to genuinely forge a personal connection with a student" (275). What he thinks is a better option is to have conversations "*with* students and guide and co-explore more educationally the language of teaching performance and politics" (277).

This collection does what it is meant to do in that it complicates our understanding of teacher neutrality and how it operates ecologically within educational contexts. Readers will find much to agree with and contest throughout the essays as they consider the merits and drawbacks of performing teacher neutrality. It is important to note that Karen Kopelson published a follow up to her essay from 2003 just as this collection was coalescing. Her frank reframing of her former assertions highlights a few of the important themes from other contributors here; for example, the need to consider teacher and student development as factors related to neutrality and that teaching as an action should always be rhetorically and reflectively informed. Ultimately, for Richards, this action requires a willingness to be "fair, considerate, self-aware, and critical of all standpoints" (277). I hope that most teachers strive for that positionality.

Mobility Work in Composition

Edited by Bruce Horner, Megan Faver Hartline, Ashanka Kumari, and Laura Sceniak Matravers
University Press of Colorado, 2021, pp.242

Reviewed by Meng-Hsien (Neal) Liu
University of Illinois at Urbana-Champaign

Our world is no stranger to mobilities, ranging from molecular movement in ecological systems to quotidian economic transactions and social interactions to transnational voyages across continents. Thus, readers of the *Community Literacy Journal* (*CLJ*) are sure to be engaged by this eclectic addition to the current scholarship on mobilities work, with the construct of mobility emerging as a central theoretical idea that underpins the epistemological and methodological premises of many disciplines, including that of cultural geography, feminist studies, critical race theory, queer studies, and composition and rhetoric. With a universalizing and broad focus on composition-in-mobility, this edited collection—organized in two sections across which all the contributing authors unpack and articulate the *mobile* nature of mobility and composition—answers the central question of what constitutes and sustains mobility in our divergent, diverse, literate activities and practices. The volume editors—Horner, Hartline, Kumari, and Matravers—advance a *mobilities paradigm* to further unpack the dynamic constitution of mobility in composition and rhetoric and to cast a norm-based light on mobility-in-composition work (3). In particular, rather than treat mobility as a matter "requiring adjustment or accommodation", Horner et al. argue that the proposition of mobility as a commonplace or even as a fact is long overdue (4-6). One hallmark that characterizes this paradigm is that mobilities are poly-faceted forms, whose social value is mercurial, relational, and provisional (4-6). This critical premise holds the potential to shift our perspective of viewing language, composition, writing-curriculum administration, writing pedagogy, or writing research as impermeable to perceiving them as fruitfully unsteady and potentially subject to transformation.

As the volume addresses the nature of mobility in composition, the organization of the twenty chapters—divided into Part I where case studies in mobility-in-composing-practices (e.g., community literacy, translingual composition, or digital and professional writing) are reported and Part II where critical responses to Part I are articulated—also attempts to reflect on the nature of mobility, with each chapter conversing with another chapter for a never-ceasing *reworking* of the mobility work through mobilized disciplinary expertise (11). This edited volume offers an outstanding balance between theoretical interventions and pragmatic uptakes of *a mobilities-paradigm* to reveal a kaleidoscopic tapestry of how mobility characterizes and can be mobilized in our everyday literate lives, writing research practices, composition pedagogies, or WPA work.

In "Mobile Knowledge for a Mobile Era: Studying Linguistic and Rhetorical Flexibility in Composition," Christiane Donahue yokes the mobilities paradigm to writing knowledge transfer and adaptation, which leads to a view of communicative competence in a mobile world that involves a dialogic co-construction of meaning- and knowledge-making. According to Donahue, knowledge mobility—in tandem with knowledge transfer—is not marked by a static movement from one point to another; rather, it is always transformed through interrelated, yet not-so-neatly-nested, processes (22–23). With a specific focus on language-in-use or composing practices, Donahue further adopts a translingual disposition to highlight the problematics of mobilizing discrete linguistic systems as extractable units of analysis. Thus, terms such as *code* and *competence*—which are often abstracted as stable and interaction-void—must be reworked. For instance, based on Bakhtin's formulation, codes only become meaningful when uttered and turned into (unstable) bits of signs that are in constant contact with one another and "that combine and recombine in an unending transformative mobile activity of production of *utterances*" (27). Through the lens of codes-beyond-fixity, Donahue observes that we could further reconceptualize our approach to (translingual) knowledge competence in terms of mobility; specifically, Donahue articulates that terms such as 'communicative competence' or 'situated competence' all similarly point to the socially situated and discursive nature of knowledge making, adaptation, and transfer. Mobile competence enabled by transfer is thus characterized as flexible, relationally oriented, and partial (28–30).

As Ann Shivers-McNair argues in "Marking Mobility: Accounting for Bodies and Rhetoric in the Making," (im)mobility—in the sense of boundary demarcation—is marked such that the politics of mobility entangles many facets of our bodily and linguistic performance (37). Extending the concept of 'diffraction' (Barad 2007) in theorizing differences, Shivers-McNair delineates that 'diffraction' compels us to understand (im)mobility as both markedly relational and experiential in our knowledge-making practices. More important to the politics of mobility—through the lens of diffraction—are questions of inclusion and exclusion in our research methodologies, apparatuses, and spaces; thus, what matters and figures into our methodological approaches informs the ways in which our epistemologies are formulated (40). Shivers-McNair's illustration of one mobility-marking moment is a multi-year ethnographic case study of a makerspace in Seattle—where she interacted briefly with the founder of the makerspace who was engaging in laser cutting—sheds light on how her role as a participant, interviewer, and observer (which she calls 3-D interviewing) was marked by the (im)mobilities of bodies, machines, materials, networks, ideas, and exchanges in that particular space and moment. Specifically, Shivers-McNair describes that this fleeting moment of interaction, documented through a camera worn on her head, propels her to 'diffract' this seemingly banal and linear experience with movements and mobilities that precede and ensue the interaction (45–46). In chapter 16, Kumari integrates Shivers-McNair's 3-D interviewing and diffraction practices with Scenters-Zapico's "Small m to Big M-Mobilities" model. Kumari also discusses the critical implications of the 3-D interviewing and "Small m- to Big M-Mobilities" model to consider how we could explicate and attune to unaccounted-for dimensions or alternative perspectives in our space-making and how such a process may inform our research roles vis-à-vis participants, objects, materials, and times and spaces (199–200).

In "Small m- to Big M-Mobilities: A Model," John Scenters-Zapico advances the paradigm of small m-mobility and Big M-Mobilities to describe complex professional movements. Specifically, Scenters-Zapico had spent more than a decade working as a writing program administrator (WPA) at the University Texas, El Paso (UTEP) and performing responsibilities in the program prior to quitting the job and undertaking another WPA role at California State University, Long Beach. Drawing on the key hallmark of mobility that is posited as active emplacement, Scenters-Zapico investigates how composition classrooms and programs are often rendered static by institutions. Scenters-Zapico lists three stages that culminate a small m-mobility paradigm as follows: 1) the envisioning of mobility stages, where professional advancement is planned and chronicled; 2) the positioning of contingent and emergent events that serve as anchors to understand the flow and immobility of professional experiences; 3) the consideration of inertia (57). Utilizing the three components of small m-mobility, Scenters-Zapico narrates his dissatisfaction at UTEP, accounting for how some contingent and emergent events of and encounters with institutional leaders dampened his vision for the writing program. Moreover, UTEP was further plagued by a lack of sufficient funding and other institutional hardships. The friction at UTEP was complicated by institutionally imposed delays by administrative superiors who, according to Scenters-Zapico, demonstrated indifference to or strategic avoidance of Scenters-Zapico's requests for more funding, hiring of more writing center tutors, and other programmatic assistance. Scenters-Zapico describes that he was kept "in a state of professional statis or inertia" by the UTEP administration (62). In short, Scenters-Zapico's invocation of a paradigm of small m-mobility—to account for his professional experiences with UTEP's administration—showcases the complicated, socially endowed, and constructed meanings of mobilities.

In "Managing Writing on the Move," Rebecca Lorimer Leonard traces the literacy practices of a multilingual immigrant, Nimet, and unpacks the movement of Nimet's literacy practices pre- and post-immigration in relation to institutions. Specifically, Lorimer Leonard attempts to understand how a lived literacy, when it is defined through mobility and the (in)equalities that accompany it, is *paced* by differing social institutions which attempt to expedite or stall literacy practices and developments. By contrasting Nimet's literacy experiences in the pre-immigration time with those in her post-immigration time, Lorimer Leonard discovers divergent attitudes showcased by institutions toward literacy movement of a multilingual speaker/writer and strategies for this multilingual speaker/writer to maneuver around the roadblocks. Nimet, according to Lorimer Leonard, had been teaching English to local students and teachers in Azerbaijan prior to her movement to the United States (69). During her teaching career in Azerbaijan, she had managed to circumvent the government-mandated language-and-literacy curriculum that focused solely on reading and writing and diminished the importance of speaking and listening (70). Thus, Nimet founded an Azerbaija English Teachers Association to integrate a more well-rounded language curriculum that permitted more teacher collaborations and more diverse pedagogical practices and materials, such as visual aids. Nimet also organized several initiatives and projects to garner funds for the Association, moving towards a more self-controlled and self-paced literacy development for herself, her students, and her fellow teachers. After her immigration to the U.S., Nimet registered in a nursing program that demanded quick "English-based writing skills," which Nimet had never experienced before (74). Lorimer Leonard attributed Nimet's experiences of feeling stalled in writing in English, in the U.S., to not only a linguistic factor but to an institutional one. Lorimer Leonard reports that Nimet's multilingual capacity was deemed to be a detriment to her progress in the nursing program, which, according to another participant of the study—Paj—used Nimet's multilingualism as an excuse to sideline her and other international nursing students. For Nimet, the stalling of her literacy development included not only extra costs and an extended timeframe, but misguidance. She was required to take additional ESL courses that did not fruitfully improve her English ability (79). Lorimer Leonard concludes that literacy agency can be "slippery and highly contingent on the conditions that greet mobile literacy upon arrival" (77). Lorimer Leonard's research on Nimet's transnational literacy experiences illuminates that literacy is controlled and negotiated by different agents, entities, and material constraints.

Carmen Kynard in "'Pretty for a Black Girl': AfroDigital Black Feminisms and the Critical Context of 'Mobile Black Security,'" lends critical insight into how colorism works and is subverted. Specifically, Kynard describes the practice of 'cultural-spatial contouring' to spotlight how one of her students—Andrene (who had had little web design experience prior to taking Kynard's course)—used linguistic resources, narratives, images, video clips, and artifacts to build a website ("Pretty for a Black Girl") to express her skill as a rhetorician and to critically depart from white academic conventions (86–87). Andrene's multimedia 'blackscape' highlights her "full range" of "rhetorical savvy" (164).

Scott Wible in "Composing to Mobilize Knowledge: Lessons from a Design-Thinking-Based Writing Course" examines how textual practices—in the design thinking process—get re-articulated into problem (re)definitions, solution ideation, and knowledge transformation in professional writing courses. Mobilizing design thinking as a recursive and iterative knowledge-in-mobilization process, Wible showcases the steps his professional writing students took to help new faculty members better adapt to a new professional environment. Wible had his students engage in diverse textual genres (e.g., empathy maps, Post-it brainstorming notes, interview transcripts, and research field notes) to craft point-of-view (POV) statements to not only acquaint themselves with the empirical research process but also to work iteratively through the five phases of design thinking: "empathetically researching, defining, ideating, prototyping, and testing" (99). Through the use of POV statements and a knowledge-mobilization paradigm, Wible grounds his pedagogical interventions in the politics of mobility (109).

These interventions are inclusive of, but not limited to, questions such as how to incorporate more humanistic and ethnographic research processes that can be better aligned with (local) community needs, as evidenced through Wible's observation of how his students interacted with the local campus environment and the community members therein. Wible concludes that "[b]y critically engaging with design thinking methods as knowledge mobilization work," writing studies scholars, teachers, and students can further their understandings of and approaches to the ways in which mobile writing and knowledge making can positively support local community needs (110).

In "Rethinking Past, Present, Presence: On the Process of Mobilizing Other People's Lives," Jody Shipka articulates that agencies and collaborations in composition are not the province of humans; rather, they are distributed across both humans and nonhumans. Shipka focuses on the mobility of a deceased couple's (Dorothy and Fred's) collection. Shipka, whose increasing familiarity with Dorothy and Fred's collection had stabilized and sedimented her perceptions of the collection, initiated the "Inhabiting Dorothy" project to "remobilize the potentials of this collection" and to see how interpretations of this collection could be expanded (115). The "Inhabiting Dorothy" project asked participants to engage in collaboration to articulate the relationship between materials, bodies, affects, and most importantly, the past, the present, and the future. Through this project, Shipka argues that it is necessary to view mobility as both distributed and variegated, with the composing process being conceptualized not only as pertinent to the production of the present moment but also as relevant to the past and the future.

In "Imagine a School Year," Eli Goldblatt draws on the notion of networked literacy sponsorship to trace and understand the movement of the Cecil B. Moore School schoolyard redevelopment plan, which was initially devised as an afterschool literacy center for children and their parents to engage "both academic and imaginative reading and writing" (130). Rather than glorify the emancipatory capacity of literacies as taken-for-granted, Goldblatt forwards the argument that literacies can be constrained, encouraged, or qualified by sponsors whose collective power, which Goldblatt remains cautiously optimistic about, provides a hopeful and promising picture, or even a necessary social-justice orientation towards community literacy development (143). Although Goldblatt's articulation of a networked sense of literacy sponsorship serves as a critical entry point for community literacy scholars to draw upon, several questions remain unanswered. For example, Hartline states that Goldblatt's explication of the process—from problem identification to solution design—remains somewhat occluded (186).

This edited volume is by no means comprehensive, and some chapters are more descriptive than applied; however, as Horner et al. cogently describe, the aim of the editors is to offer differing perspectives and engagements through which a *mobilities paradigm* may be useful to composition researchers and teachers, especially given that the paradigm is still relatively new (11). This edited volume provides multiple entry points for *CLJ* readers to explore what mobility could mean in our research, teaching, activist work, and everyday encounters.

Works Cited

Barad, Karen. *Meeting the Universe Halfway: Quantum Physics and the Entanglement of Matter and Meaning*. Duke UP, 2007.

Mapping Racial Literacies: College Students Write About Race and Segregation

Sophie Bell
Logan: Utah State UP, 2021. 215 pp.

Reviewed by Angela F. Jacobs
North Carolina Agricultural and
    Technical State University

As a multitude of writing scholars have noted, first-year writing courses (often referred to as FYC or FYW) cannot be taught without content, merely focusing on general writing skills. In Bell's text, *Mapping Racial Literacies: College Students Write About Race and Segregation*, she aptly carries on this ideology by noting how an FYW course can be used to help students grapple with important aspects of their daily lives. In her particular case, she utilizes her FYW course to help students grapple with racial literacies and the racial geographies that govern their identities. In a mixed methods study spanning thousands of student texts from 2014 to 2018, Bell's text not only demonstrates the importance of lower division courses aiming for greater importance in students' lives, but also the idea that lower division courses, such as FYW, can better assist students in understanding their place in the world and the university itself.

In her initial analysis, Bell first seeks to position herself as a white woman teaching at a predominantly white school with a troubled history of conforming to calls, and legislation, for integration. Although Bell does not appear to have been instructed or required to teach or address race in her classroom, she saw a need for it, especially when students started demanding more racial equity on campus, in particular when students started protesting after the killing of Michael Brown in Ferguson, Missouri in 2014. To answer this demand, Bell structured her FYW course to address racial identity, focusing primarily on racial geography and language, to help her students grapple with their own ideas and attitudes regarding race.

In order to accomplish her goal, she used a variety of scholars specializing in aspects of race, society, and higher education to not only ground her endeavor, but also to guide her understanding of how her students were tackling the issues of race and racial identities she was asking for them to discuss in their writings. Throughout her teaching, she continued to learn more about the scholars engaging in racial identities in order to improve her courses and her understanding of her students. Each academic term brought with it a new challenge that Bell eagerly sought to address to better serve the needs of her students. While Larry Blum's "racial literacy" (19) research may have been a major curricular guide, the work of Beverly Daniel Tatum, an antiracist psychologist, and Lani Guinier, a Critical Race Theorist, served as the racial literacy sponsors for Bell's own racial identity development. In other words, rather than simply design a course on racial literacy, Bell did the work she expected of her students.

Each section of her text explores a different aspect of her FYW course that she seeks to disclose with her readers. Throughout, she uses a mapping metaphor for each section (Mapping Racial Geographies, Mapping Linguistic Geographies, Mapping Futures) to highlight how much racial identity and attitudes are grounded in real-world places, such as the various New York City boroughs from which some of her students hail. Although much of the discussion regarding race centers on the struggle between black and white America, Bell prominently features many Latinx and Asian American students (to include those from South Asia, as well) to demonstrate how their attitudes regarding race are just as important to consider, including the unique nature of their racial identities against the American backdrop.

In the introduction, Bell first explores the idea behind her class and how she started this journey. She includes student work and explores her methodology in order for her readers to understand how she went about her research, to include the scholarly underpinnings of her research and the importance of her findings. Bell notes several scholars who she credits with not only inspiring the impetus of her course, but also the scholarship she credits with being instrumental in her own racial identity journey as a white female teacher, a profession she states has often been "a relatively secure source of employment for white women" (7). The particular emphasis on this point denotes Bell's ethos in writing this particular text, especially considering her own experiences within the K–12 educational system. She feels it is important for white female instructors to be active in the recruitment and support of faculty of color, stating,

> . . . we must do our own racial identity work in order to stay cognizant of [Sara] Ahmed's point that our whiteness protects us—as she puts it, our "residency is assumed"—and obscures from us the harmful practices in which we participate in educational institutions. (8)

To further assist in her own "racial identity work," especially in the classroom and higher education broadly, Bell reflects upon her own upbringing in a hypersegregated environment and how her desire to teach diverse students meant having to confront her own racial upbringing. For this particular course, Bell drew upon Tatum and Guinier, but also Ahmed's work on diversity work within the university, Laura Wexler's "sentimental imperialism" (7), Carmen Kynard's observations of the racial hypocrisy within American schools, Larry Blum's "racial literacy" (19), and Yolanda Sealey-Ruiz's work on racial literacy for education preservice teachers (19–20).

Bell closes this section by providing explicit details regarding her textual ethnography and digital archives, to include extensive note-taking techniques that not only took into account student texts, but also reflections on her pedagogy and institutional and national context that may have impacted a particular semester. Throughout her study, Bell is careful to note the backdrop of St. John's University, where she is full-time faculty. Despite it being named one of the most diverse universities in the nation, St. John's was a Catholic institution bent on avoiding the push towards the integration and more inclusive admissions practice of CUNY, to include relocating from its original location of Bedford-Stuyvesant to Brooklyn to further maintain de facto segregation. She notes the peculiar nature of this institution's eventual integration despite federal mandates which ultimately led to the institution integrating just as schools across the nation faced the resegregation efforts of the 1980s. It is through the lens of school resegregation that Bell ties her students' racial identities to their geographic locations, thus grounding her course with her students' lived experiences.

Beginning in the first chapter, Bell foremost lays out the context underlying the initial form of her first-year writing course, starting in 2014. Drawing upon the work of Nikole Hannah-Jones, Eduardo Bonilla-Silva, and Aja Martinez, this chapter lays the groundwork for the guiding principles for her course. With the backdrop of the Michael Brown murder and subsequent national racial strife, Bell aptly links school resegregation and hypersegregated white communities as tools for understanding racial vision and dismantling the notion of colorblindness.

In chapter two, Bell explores how various students understood their neighborhoods and how peer review groups helped students to unlock their ideas. She focuses on a specific peer review group of three female students to illustrate how students through the years interpreted their racial identities by their environments. Within her analysis of student writings and peer review exchanges, Bell is able to explore the difficulties of subverting colorblind racism. Using Krista Radcliffe's "rhetorical listening" (71), Bell is able to develop the notion of the "emotional imperative," which she defines as the "call for telling stories with emotional impact on peer reviewers" (93) in order to increase the level of empathy she hoped students would develop as they read about another's racial experience. Although she noticed some resistance to moving beyond a certain level of empathy amongst her students as they grappled with racial literacy, this notion prompted her to overtly link racial geographies to colorblind racism in future assignments.

Within chapter three, which the author herself notes as being a seeming detour from addressing racial geographies, Bell explores how linguistic geographies can govern how a student may see their racial identity and understand race itself as she examines students who were, at one time, placed within the ESL program before attending college. In her exploration of student responses to their own linguistic resources, Bell utilizes scholars such as Suresh Canagarajah and his examination of Geneva Smitherman's work regarding Black language and code meshing. As she appropriately notes, the trope of using Black language "to mark the limits of acceptable academic discourse" not only promotes anti-Blackness, but also completely ignores the multiple dialects intrinsic across the English speaking world, setting the stage for multilingual speakers to disregard their language resources (108).

Chapter four explores how past experiences assisting students in understanding racism on a broader scale led to Bell creating a special research assignment into institutional racism, which had students linking institutional racism to their program of study. Bell also highlights the racial literacy journey of a white female student who, much like herself, sought a career in education and was raised in a hypersegregated environment, but who also had a law enforcement connection. Bell used this particular analysis as a reflection of the lack of racial literacy on St. John's campus, while also using this journey to better understand the circuitous nature of developing racial literacies. Bell comments on the general sense that people of color are seen as being obvious racial literacy sponsors, but she also describes the tenuous journey towards racial vision that she notices in her white students, especially the one highlighted in this chapter. Bell offers that these white students can make solid racial literacy sponsors, especially in her subsequent FYW classes.

Within the book's epilogue, Bell recognizes that she likely receives less resistance in teaching this subject matter because of her whiteness, noting that her colleagues of color were often met with resistance that stems beyond a student's difficulty in writing. This section also sees the author continuing to revise the course, learning from her students and their experiences with racial literacy development. Ultimately, it is her goal to be an active participant in aiding the university in being antiracist.

There are several aspects that readers should grasp upon completing Bell's interesting text. First, Bell is open regarding her own racial literacy development and the work she still continues to do, not only in terms of curriculum, but also in terms of grappling with her own racial identity. She also notes how important it was for her to not only learn how to properly ground and frame the course, but that it was also important for her to research the appropriate means by which to read student work. This distinction is important to note in that she asks students to tackle a sensitive subject matter that requires a certain amount of tact and sensitivity so that students understand she is not assessing their experiences but how they tackle the assignment requirements. This concept is important for all FYW teachers to keep in mind. Bell also guides the reader through her journey as she makes constant revisions to her course, keeping the overall goal of lifelong learning in mind, a common goal of FYW. While the chapters are long and can feel winding, Bell sufficiently guides the reader as she transitions from one aspect of her subtopic to another, insistent upon being with her reader every step of the way, thus making the text accessible. The subject she selected for her FYW course is not for the faint of heart or for those who simply wish to virtue signal. Additionally, the sheer number of scholars she draws upon can seem daunting, but what Bell shows is the importance of staying current in our scholarship in order to make a course that some believe is irrelevant into something worthwhile. Bell provides a way for the FYW course to matter in the 21st century, providing not only a blueprint for teaching a composition course on racial literacies and geographies, but she also provides copies of her assignments for those interested in following in her footsteps to support students in developing a deeper level of racial and social consciousness.

Turn This World Inside Out: The Emergence of Nurturance Culture

Nora Samaran
AK Press, 2019, pp. 140

Reviewed by Erin Schaefer
Indiana University Northwest

In *Turn this World Inside Out: The Emergence of Nurturance Culture*, Nora Samaran asks us to reconsider western views of violence, justice, and healing. She suggests that by looking at these things through a holistic, compassionate lens, we could bring about radical changes which would allow for the birth of cultural norms that enhance the welfare of everyone. The book grew out of the author's essay, "The Opposite of Rape Culture is Nurturance Culture," which went viral in 2016 and came from a desire "to make sense out of several bewildering forms of harm that [she] observed in [her] life and in the lives of people around [her]" (11). This essay examines violence through the lens of attachment theory, arguing that violence arises from early conditioning that teaches us to feel ashamed of our desires to connect. This shame manifests as self-hate and violence towards others. Samaran argues that ". . . we need . . . a model for slow self-love that brings shame into the light and finds reality checks with those who accept you unconditionally, hold you accountable, and aren't going anywhere" (35). In turn, she offers a holistic exploration of self- and community care, allowing the book's dialogue chapters to offer diverse and nuanced examples of its practice.

The book is organized into three nurturance chapters and six dialogue chapters. The dialogue chapters "hold together, expand upon, and connect [the] ... nurturance culture essays: 'The Opposite of Rape Culture is Nurturance Culture,' 'On Gaslighting,' and 'Own, Apologize, Repair: Coming Back to Integrity'" (13). The dialogues not only create a space for individuals to describe their individual lived experiences from their own viewpoint, but also a space for us to "learn from and listen to directly affected people who know most about these systems of harm, who are producing theory and analysis as they organize" (10). This book, then, allows readers to take part (to the extent that written words allow) in these conversations, while also providing a model for readers to do the same in their own local communities. Chapter one, "The Opposite of Rape Culture is Nurturance Culture," argues that "Violence is nurturance turned backward" (18). This chapter joins those scholars who argue that care of society and care of self are inseparable, as stated in the book's core thesis: "Compassion for self and compassion for others grow together and are connected" (18). She argues further that,

> This means that men finding and recuperating the lost parts of themselves will heal everyone. If a lot of men grow up learning not to love their true selves, learning that their own healthy attachment needs (emotional safety, nurturance, connection, love, trust) are weak and wrong—that anyone's attachment or emotional safety needs are weak and wrong—this can lead to two things: 1) They may be less able to experience women as whole people with intelligible needs and feelings. . . . 2) They may be less able to make sense of their own needs for connection, transmuting them instead into distorted but more socially mirrored forms. (18)

In order for men[1] to stop being violent, then, they need to learn how to love both themselves and others (18). She calls for a holistic approach to transform misogynist rape culture, one that moves beyond a simple call for men to 'not assault,' and instead works through fostering men's nurturance skills (19). The problem, however, is that men have few if any models from which to learn these skills. Cultural norms make men afraid to express nurturance because it is believed to be antithetical to masculinity, and thus spaces where men can teach one another how to develop these skills are very rare (21). As a result, men are unaware that they have the capacity—the "deep gift"—to care for and even heal others (19).

Samaran emphasizes the importance of having role models that can model and embody care, and she uses attachment theory to advance this point. Chapter one continues with an introduction to attachment theory, drawing from Sue Johnson's *Hold Me Tight: Seven Conversations for a Lifetime of Love* and Thomas Lewis, Fari Amini, and Richard Lannon's *A General Theory of Love*. Attachment theory holds that humans develop one of several attachment styles formed during the first several years of life that are influenced by whether they have a consistent source of nurturance from an "attuned" parental or guardian figure (22). The ideal attachment style, secure attachment, is what allows individuals to connect and care for others while also giving them space and autonomy (27–28).

Samaran then introduces three insecure attachment styles that, without understanding or awareness, can ultimately contribute to violent interpersonal dynamics: 1) the *anxious* attachment style, in which people "actively seek closeness and are afraid of losing it, and have a harder time knowing and trusting that their partner will be there for them" (24); 2) the *preoccupied-avoidant* style, in which people "crave closeness but are afraid to show it, and will show it instead through sulking or silence, hoping their partner will guess" (25); and 3) the *dismissive-avoidant* attachment style, in which people "have a need for intimacy. . . but at a very early age they complete a transition to a belief that they are autonomous and do not feel their need for intimacy" (25). Importantly, Samaran notes that attachment science estimates that "about 50 percent of the population has an insecure attachment style;" in other words, these styles—and the difficulties often associated with them—largely influence how humans communicate with one another (24). Readers will likely recognize these styles in those they interact with daily and have interacted with in the past.

Though these attachment styles are formed at a young age, they are not set in stone; over time, and with deliberate effort, individuals can develop an "earned secure attachment" (26). What makes this so difficult, however, is the power of shame, a key dynamic that Samaran continually interrogates. Essentially, people learn to be ashamed of those parts of themselves that they have never known to be accepted by others. Furthermore, they often project this shame of self onto others: "Whatever is in us that does not get mirrored or held in a larger container of acceptance by others becomes a source of shame simply for not being accepted. And if you have shamed something in yourself . . . so early and so completely that you don't even notice you are doing it, you will interpret that same need as shameful when you see it in others . . . ." (28). She then applies this theory to misogynistic culture, explaining, for instance, that "in a culture that does not expect men to show up for their emotions, *women get blamed for unaddressed male shame*" (29).

In this important core chapter Samaran claims that assault is mediated by both embodied/psychological and cultural dimensions. She notes that, "This is all happening in the body, below the conscious level, not in a vague 'unconscious' but in a recognizable region of the brain: the limbic brain, which does not have language" (29). Some, however, might fault this chapter for focusing too much on the embodied/psychological dimensions and not enough on the cultural ones. The author acknowledges this issue in a footnote in which she explains that she has come to a more complex understanding of assault after reading Lundy Bancroft's *Why Does He Do That*. Her new understanding "includes questions of acculturated entitlement, which are explored more fully in the dialogue pieces in this book" (30). Samaran indeed provides a rich understanding of both the embodied and cultural dimensions of violent and nurturance cultures throughout the book, aided by the diverse positionalities of her dialogue participants.

Samaran ends chapter one by calling for readers to create a culture that understands and absorbs shame. Self-love and compassion are necessary because they account for people's typical relating patterns when shame arises, helping us "respond to the needs of others rather than freeze and become defensive, invasive, or paralyzed" (35). This process is necessarily social. Samaran explains that "This is men's work to do, and yet it is needed by people of all genders who have men in their lives" (37). She emphasizes the importance of men pulling their weight in this work because women should not have to take primary responsibility for it "while also protecting themselves from male violence and neglect, which is still endemic and thus a daily part of women's lives" (37-38). She ends by asking men how they might create the kinds of social spaces described in this chapter, as well as encouraging readers to share the book with men and then inviting them for dialogue (38).

Chapter two, "How Masculine-Identified People Might Use This Book," provides a dialogue with "John Snow," an amalgam of conversations with "several readers who have male privilege or experiences of masculine socialization, and who are using 'The

Opposite of Rape Culture is Nurturance Culture' in their efforts to reclaim lost parts of themselves and grow their capacity to nurture others" (39). Here, she acknowledges that this John Snow dialogue will not and cannot represent a "'finished' position;" it is meant to help those wishing to begin the journey to feel part of a community as well as "shed light on the path . . ." (39). This chapter explores the often difficult, but ultimately rewarding, process of reconnecting the parts of themselves that they were conditioned to be ashamed of, while also "growing their capacity to nurture and show up emotionally in an ethical way with integrity and accountability" (40). The chapter also highlights the pain of coming to terms with the ways in which they have distanced and harmed others (43), as well as the grief of recognizing what is lost when we practice shame (44), including losing "the most beautiful and most powerful aspects of the self. . ." (47). This chapter also helps those wishing to engage in this process recognize that it is a layered process; they may discover parts of themselves that they had desired to connect with for some time.

Chapter three, "Turning Gender Inside Out," is a second dialogue chapter with Serena Bhander, a Punjabi Sikh/Welsh/Irish gender fluid woman, Community Relations Coordinator with the Anti-Violence Project, "writer, activist, and educator" (49). This chapter "articulat[es] the ways in which any understanding of masculinity, or of gender, will be most effective when it positions transness at the center of the analysis" (13). Here Bhander notes those parts of "The Opposite of Rape Culture is Nurturance Culture" that resonated with her and offers some criticisms. For example, she feels that it is targeted at a cis audience and re-inscribes a gender binary that assumes one can be either wholly male or wholly female. It also, she thinks, assumes that trans readers can/cannot understand what it is like to be either male or female (e.g., the false assumption that a trans woman can know what it's like to be male, or that a trans woman cannot know what it's like to be a woman) (52-53). Bhander draws attention to the ways systems of harm affect trans individuals, and notes the importance of integrating these harms into the core argument. To her credit, Samaran listens and validates these concerns, echoing and building upon Bhander's ideas.

In chapter four, "On Gaslighting," Samaran explains that gaslighting occurs when a person "undermines your trust in your perceptions and you feel crazy because your instincts and intuitions and sometimes even plain old perceptions are telling you one thing, and the words from someone you trust are telling you something different" (59). Here, the author challenges the notion that gaslighting is always an intentional tactic of abusers. She provides numerous reasons why people might unintentionally gaslight, including a lack of emotional intelligence/self-awareness, an overwhelming physiological response to the rise of difficult emotions, and poor role models from their past (61–63). Expanding this definition is helpful because it allows us to see the pervasiveness of gaslighting. She also provides a useful personal example of when she was gaslighted to demonstrate its insidiousness and pervasiveness. Framing gaslighting as either intentional or unintentional is also valuable because she insists that, regardless of intentionality, the effects of gaslighting are the same (63).

This chapter is also useful in that it provides practical advice for those experiencing gaslighting. Samaran explains that since gaslighting is structurally part of misogynistic culture (60, 67–69), it is easy for those experiencing it to ignore, overlook, or dismiss what their intuitions and perceptions of reality are telling them (65). While acknowledging that their perceptions of others and their feelings are not always accurate (i.e., we might read that someone is having an underlying emotion when they may genuinely not be), Samaran encourages those experiencing gaslighting to respect their own intuition, and lay it side by side with what the other person says (66–67).

Samaran directly validates how harmful gaslighting is—for individuals and our society as a whole—while also providing a compelling argument for others to practice listening, believing, and empathizing with those harmed by it. She explains that while men experience it as well, gaslighting of women or femmes "picks up the larger cultural gaslighting of people socially positioned as feminine, as well as the cultural training to center men" (71). To address this dynamic, Samaran encourages us to prioritize and center the experiences of female-identified people (72–73), which is a move supporters of the #MeToo movement should appreciate. Importantly, doing so does not negate space for those who engage in gaslighting to grow (73).

Chapter five, "Building Strength through Movement and Afrofuturism," is a dialogue with Ruby Smith Díaz, an "arts-based anti-oppression facilitator, a multidisciplinary artist, and a personal trainer supporting marginalized communities in feeling powerful and grounded in their bodies" (75). Díaz defines Afrofuturism as a communal and creative practice of Black people imagining their lives in a peaceful future. Díaz explains that Afrofuturism allows Black people to "create a reality that isn't solely created in resistance to an oppositional force, but is created in a noncoercive way, on our own terms" (75). The conversation then turns to the many creative ways Díaz has found to practice self-love in spaces centered on care. Building from her own journey of coming to love her body for what it is and what it is capable of, Díaz works to create space for people with marginalized identities to do the same (78–79). They discuss the need for such accessible spaces given current western gym culture and health disparities among these populations (78–81). This dialogue reminds readers that care of the body is a critical aspect of both self-love and community care, and that "Nurturance is one of the ways that we reclaim our agency" (83).

Chapter six, "Cultivating Empathy and Shame Resilience," is a dialogue with Aravinda Ananda, a social ecologist whose "life's work is supporting a shift in dominant human relationships from linear extractivism. . . to regenerative relationships of mutuality and healing" (85). Building on Ananda's experiences facilitating white people's "unlearning white supremacy conditioning" (85), they discuss how they understand and navigate shame. This dialogue helps the reader understand the difference between ego- and performance-based self-love—a common cultural narrative of white people—and love of a core, authentic self (88). Ananda explains that understanding that there is a core, authentic self allows white people to move beyond white fragility[2] responses (89). This chapter provides useful insights for community leaders and/or educators who wish to facilitate discussions about white supremacy. Ananda cautions that even though a facilitator may have carefully created a safe space for growth, white people can quickly resort to "shame-evasion behavior" (94). "Samaran and Ananda end by reiterating the importance of creating "clear structures in our community for handling harm" (94).

Chapter seven, "Own, Apologize, Repair: Coming Back to Integrity," is the final cultural nurturance essay. This chapter notes that, when asked to be accountable, men (and white people) often respond with an angry attack and become stuck in a vicious cycle of guilt and anger (100–102). Samaran explains how she practices self-care when she discusses misogyny and racism with her students and others. She does this by creating boundaries and respecting the limits of her engagement with her audience, boundaries she learned to create from her relationship with an abusive father (103–104). She then turns to speak directly to men[3] with a series of questions and steps designed to help them understand how harmful their sense of entitlement is and move towards accountability and listening. Samaran prompts her audience to "own, apologize, and repair," as well as to "Imagine replacing guilt with curiosity" (111).

Chapter eight, "Free, Prior, and Informed Consent," is a dialogue chapter with Natalie Knight, a Diné (Navajo) organizer with the Alliance Against Displacement, whose "writing and organizing focuses on urban Indigenous people and Indigenous people who are removed from both [their] territories and our nations" (113). Partly drawing on her own journey as a doubly dispossessed Indigenous woman, Knight discusses the importance of Indigenous people connecting with their cultures and cultural stories to heal the internalized shame caused by Colonial violence (116–120). She describes the complexities of coming to understand the ways that Colonialism causes harm while denying it has done so, including her experiences of both anger and empathy towards those who caused this harm (118–119). They then discuss the importance of the role of "free, prior, and informed consent" for both the body and the land, explaining that "colonialism. . . simultaneously assault[s] our bodies and our lands" (120). For Knight, becoming whole requires decolonization, which necessitates rejecting capitalistic anthropocentrism and "relearn[ing] . . . diverse cultural knowledges that are rooted in land relationships" (121).

The final chapter, "Moving into Action, Mapping Terrains of Struggle," highlights the difficult realities of working to repair harm and create nurturing spaces and cultures. This dialogue is with Alix Johnson. Johnson, a "mixed race (Chinese and White) survivor of sexual violence, she was a core and founding member of the Bay Area Transformative Justice Collective" and past "crisis counselor, first responder, and advocate for survivors of sexual violence. . ." (123). Samaran and Johnson describe how their own familial cultures both did and did not support their work and the hard work, successes, and disappointments involved in creating spaces that nurture care (123–126). This chapter should inspire those wishing to create such spaces in their own communities, as they encourage readers to think small-scale, beginning with just "two people who are going to show up for you," then two more, etc. (126). The chapter reiterates a recurring theme in the book: a need for boundaries and a recognition of when people are truly ready to collaboratively take part in this kind of radical cultural change (127–131). It closes by reminding readers to prioritize listening to and validating survivors, regardless of how well we know them (130–131).

Once one reads *Turn this World Inside* Out, it is not difficult apply its many ideas and perspectives to real life. I have found myself looking at people in public spaces, and marveling with both sadness and hope at the power of shame and systems of harm, as well speculating on what it would mean for us to learn and practice a culture of nurturance. The book also offers an incentive for those who have engaged in harmful behaviors to practice nurturance. For instance, chapter three, "How Masculine-Identified People Might Use This Book," understanding men's conditioned shame about their inner desire to connect is presented as an enticing "doorway to reconnecting in a more whole way with the self and with others" (45). Those who have experienced harm and/or internalized shame should relate to the remaining dialogue chapters. As I read these chapters, I found myself reflecting on my own internalized shame and desire to connect as I grew up in a largely homophobic culture with lesbian parents. I also recognized the protective mechanisms that arise when one does not feel safe, accepted, and cared for. In this way, I found the book to be both validating and encouraging.

As an emerging scholar of mindfulness and the rhetorics of emotion and the body, I appreciated Samaran's stress on how quickly shame-evasion and other harmful responses to shame become habitual. However, while she mentions that the limbic part of the brain works much faster than the more conscious parts, she does not offer much instruction on how to calm these emotions and physiological triggers. The dialogue chapters often do a better job of acknowledging the power of emotional dimensions than the cultural nurturance essays. For instance, chapter two emphasizes that the process of (men's) healing requires an emotional and cognitive connection (41), chapter five describes how toxic behaviors are encoded in the body (83–84), and chapter six discusses the need for an individual's sense of emotional safety prompted by "unconditional positive regard" in order to practice it (88).

In particular, I wished that chapter seven—"Own, Apologize, Repair"—had incorporated and synthesized the emotion-oriented instruction from the aforementioned dialogue chapters. Samaran describes what an empathetic person might say in terms of emotion, such as, "I'm grateful you took that risk, and I'm taking it to heart," and describes empathy as a "physiological relating with other human beings" (112). Yet, she seems to address this dynamic from a mostly cognitive stance. For example, she asks men to manage their shame-aversion and shame-attack responses with rational questions such as, "If your focus is more on the fact that harm got named than it is on the harm itself, does that strike you as peculiar?" While chapter one and the chapter six dialogue, especially, argue that accountability necessitates the person knowing that they are loved unconditionally so they can own harmful actions, chapter seven does not directly address how to do this during the reparation process. My concern is that those wishing to be accountable and repair harm might go through the motions on a cognitive level, without being able to empathize on an emotional one because they are still in a physiologically stressed mind/body state. Many scholars on listening have emphasized that empathy requires self-awareness, and while Samaran prompts men to not be self-*conscious*, I wish that she had stressed the necessity of being self-*aware* of one's emotions and/or psychological lens as a component of empathy[4] in this important chapter.

Interdisciplinary mindfulness scholarship and literature (provided it presents non-neoliberal versions of mindfulness[5]) on emotional regulation (e.g., Gunnlaugson et al.; Nhat Hanh; Winans), mindful listening (e.g., Rakel), and other methods of enhancing emotional literacy and emotional self-regulation (e.g., Stevenson) might complement Samaran's approach to dealing with people's defensive, stress-driven responses to self-awareness and/or automatic shame-responses. In addition, guided mindfulness exercises that focus on self-compassion could provide more direct instruction for people practicing this work individually, particularly when men might have not yet developed an ability to listen empathetically without centering their ego-driven needs. In turn, those who practice mindfulness, particularly as a part of a social justice practice (e.g., Berila; Sajjad and Shahbaz) should connect with Samaran's holistic understanding of compassion, listening, and social justice.

Indeed, *Turn this World Inside Out* offers a holistic way of understanding misogyny, racism, and other forms of harm, as well as a rich offering of tools, tips, and guidance on how to create nurturance culture. It joins conversations that stress the need to account for and productively respond to shame and guilt in ways that do not result in self-absorption (e.g., Stevenson; Swiencicki; Trainor; Winans), self-absorption that de-centers those who have been harmed by systems of racism, sexism, homophobia, and other systems of hate. The dialogue chapters also show readers the many different ways that we can practice listening and care, from simple, small acts of self-care (77) to forming communities for this work to happen (123–131).

This book should certainly be of interest to educators. The author, an English professor, draws on her experiences teaching, for instance, about Colonialism, illustrating how concepts and theories presented in this book help her navigate students' unequal power dynamics, defensiveness, and vulnerability (102–103). With the book's focus on attachment theory, scholars in the behavioral and social sciences as well as interdisciplinary scholars in the humanities interested in understanding the embodied dimensions of social phenomena, should also find this book helpful.

Ideally, the book should be read more than once. As the amalgam dialogue with 'John Snow' (39–48) stresses, the process of shifting one's orientation towards the shamed parts of one's self, as well as coming to terms with and changing one's habits of disconnecting from and/or harming others, is long and difficult. Samaran's book is designed to promote ongoing dialogue, and asks big and often challenging questions. It is also intended as a starting point for people from a variety of positionalities to create nurturance culture, and I believe it is successful in doing this.

In sum, *Turn This World Inside Out* should be of interest to people in multiple disciplines, sectors, and contexts. It speaks directly to those who—whether intentionally or inadvertently—perpetuate violence, as well as those most harmed by that violence. In addition, it suggests ways of building a culture centered on nurturance and compassion, with emphasis on transforming systems of power built on racism, sexism, homophobia, transphobia, xenophobia, and other forms of prejudice and discrimination. While acknowledging how difficult it will be to transform our culture, this looking forward—as well as acknowledging how various community organizers and leaders are already making meaningful changes—makes this book inspiring and productive.

Notes

1. The author provides a footnote in chapter one: "The Opposite of Rape Culture is Nurturance Culture," the original essay that inspired the book, that explains her use of the word "men" is "intended to signify all masculine-identified people, including trans men, and nonbinary people who may only partially identify with the term" (17). In the following chapter, she uses dialogue to interrogate and complicate her use of the word, as I will touch on shortly in my summary of chapter two.

2. White fragility refers to the defensive and sometimes violent responses to being confronted with their own racism, or even the idea that racism exists (90–91).

3. I was uncertain, as I read this chapter, who the intended audience was. It seemed at times that it was geared towards men/masculine-identified individuals, and at other times towards white people. In general, however, her advice seemed applicable to anyone who has caused harm and wants to make reparations.

4, Ivor Goodson and Scherto Gill, for instance, argue that true listening requires both people to practice self-awareness. Chapter seven encourages self-awareness of one's thoughts/lenses (certainly an important task) but less so of their emotions during the dialogue process. Similarly, Howard C. Stevenson argues, "listening is impossible if fright, flight, and flight reactions are ignited" (141).

5. For more discussion on neoliberalism and mindfulness, see James Reveley's "Neoliberal Meditations."

Works Cited

Bancroft, Lundy. *Why Does He Do That?: Inside the Minds of Angry and Controlling Men*. Penguin, 2003.

Berila, Beth. *Integrating Mindfulness into Anti-Oppression Pedagogy: Social Justice in Higher Education*. Routledge, 2015.

Lewis, Thomas, Fari Amini, and Richard Lannon. *A General Theory of Love*. Vintage, 2001.

Hanh, Thich Nhat. *At Home in the World: Lessons from a Remarkable Life*. Random House, 2016.

Goodson, Ivor, and Scherto R. Gill. *Narrative Pedagogy: Life History and Learning*. Vol. 386. Peter Lang, 2011.

Gunnlaugson, Olen, et al., eds. *Contemplative Learning and Inquiry across Disciplines*. SUNY Press, 2014.

Johnson, Sue. *Hold Me Tight: Seven Conversations for a Lifetime of Love*. Little, Brown Spark, 2008.

Rakel, David. *The Compassionate Connection: The Healing Power of Empathy and Mindful Listening*. WW Norton & Company, 2018.

Reveley, James. "Neoliberal Meditations: How Mindfulness Training Medicalizes Education and Responsibilizes Young People." *Faculty of Business Papers*, 2016. *EBSCOhost*, https://search.ebscohost.com/login.aspx?direct=true&db=edsoai&AN=edsoai.on1086601594&site=eds-live.

Sajjad, Aymen, and Wahab Shahbaz. "Mindfulness and Social Sustainability: An Integrative Review." *Social Indicators Research* 150.1 (2020): 73–94.

Samaran, Nora. "The Opposite of Rape Culture Is Nurturance Culture." *NoraSamaran.com, February* 11 (2016).

Stevenson, Howard. *Promoting Racial Literacy in Schools: Differences That Make a Difference*. Teachers College Press, 2014

Swiencicki, Jill. "The Rhetoric of Awareness Narratives." *College English* 68.4 (2006): 337–355.

Trainor, Jennifer S. *Rethinking Racism: Emotion, Persuasion, and Literacy Education in An All-White High School*. SIU Press, 2008.

Uusberg, Helen, et al. "Mechanisms of Mindfulness: The Dynamics of Affective Adaptation During Open Monitoring." *Biological Psychology* 118 (2016): 94–106.

Winans, Amy E. "Cultivating critical emotional literacy: Cognitive and Contemplative Approaches to Engaging Difference." *College English* 75.2 (2012): 150–170.

Coda

Editors' Introduction

Kefaya Diab, Leah Falk, Chad Seader, Alison Turner, Kate Vieira, and Stephanie Wade

Welcome to the second edition of Coda: a new section of the *Community Literacy Journal* devoted to the creative work that ensues from community writing! While our name evokes aural imagery and calls into question the idea of endings, in our second issue we turn our attention to visibility, the power of its presence and the pain of its absence. The diversity of the writing we are privileged to publish in this issue is a testament to writing's unique affordances to make metaphorically visible our lived realities, in all their desires and complexities, as well as our intimately imagined worlds, in all their carefully constructed plot twists and details. *We exist*, our stories, essays, and poems say. *And we have something, with love, to share.*

The writers in this issue ask us to reckon with the ways being seen differs from being heard. At a moment of state-sponsored censorship that regulates language, stories, and bodies, these writers raise questions about what it means to be seen in a world where power structures seek to erase difference. They draw attention to the vexed, dangerous, and sometimes deadly paradoxes of hypervisibility and invisibility. As poet Vivian Lorena Carmona writes elsewhere: *Para algunos soy invisible / para otros completamente visible. For some I am invisible / for others completely visible.*

Some of the pieces grew out of partnerships with community writing organizations whose missions connect visibility to action and who create spaces for writers to respond to institutional failures, particularly those of the state. For example, the poet quoted above participates in Poetry for Peace workshops run by EncantaPalabras, a Colombian educational NGO devoted to, in the words of co-founder Juana María Echeverri, writing a new page of Colombia's history after decades of armed conflict. We also have work from several participants in Exchange for Change, an organization in Florida that sponsors writing for incarcerated people so that, in their words, "students can become agents of social change across different communities in ways they may otherwise have never encountered." According to the National Institute of Corrections, the United States has the second largest incarceration rate in the world; and globally, over ten million people are incarcerated. Those of us who engage in literacy work have a special responsibility to examine our complicity in the school-to-prison pipeline and to do better. Because the writers in this issue are finding new ways of being seen, they document these imperatives.

As these writers explore visibility, they offer readers new ways to think about community–what it means to be isolated from community, what it means to act in concert with others, and indeed to write together. Gustavo Guerra cultivates empathy to counter the erasure that results from stigma. In "Bad Habits," he mourns the possibility of being in love and in a relationship. With that he resists invisibility. As an incarcerated person, he is denied that possibility, yet he continues to have hope. In "Frozen Margaritas," Guerra's memories of a past love are crushed under the reality of incarceration. Yet, the taste of the margaritas' salt and lime remain with him as if to say that memories of love would always remain visible, free, and would never be incarcerated like him. "In a community, you don't need everyone to love you, but you need people to see you," writes Don Unger in his narrative about the disintegration of a queer, xennial community. For Unger, community is a place where people can be seen, which sometimes provides protection and other times makes him the target of violence. Meanwhile, Ryan Moser recasts images of incarceration: Moser's sangha becomes a visible agent of peace amidst violent surroundings. The excerpt we've printed of Devin O'Keefe and Justin Slavinski's collaboratively written story, "The Missing Briefcase," shows the two Exchange For Change participants' long-running writing partnership. The story conveys the authors' love for the hard-boiled noir genre, from the dialogue to the wardrobe details, and it is a testament to the potential of writing collaboratively.

Some writers explore visibility and understanding on a more individual basis. In "I Remember," Frank Morse shows how it is possible to see new life and possibility in the rubble of trauma and tragedy. He writes that "My second chance began in a burning car, in a ditch, upside down, smashed, broken, and dying." While sharing the story of how a need for OxyContin resulted in a deadly car accident, Morse invites us to think about what we might be able to find buried in our own tragedies. "What second chance have you received?" he asks. "Who paid the price for it?" Vivian Lorena Carmona and Fresban Alexis Bueno both write poems from their perspective as members of the embera chamí community, an indigenous community that for decades was caught in the crossfires of warring factions in Colombia's armed conflict. In both writers' poems, set in what Carmona tells us are the mountains of Colombia, writing becomes a vehicle for both inner peace and political peace, resembling the music of the many varieties of birds that they call attention to as populating their land. "Drought" by H.L. Smith recognizes the space a community writing project created for her to reckon with the toll the pandemic had on her as a teacher. Continuing this theme, in the poem "Notes," Parisa Mosavi (Pavie) describes the chronic fatigue that so many activists encounter in oppressive and violent environments. As a description of the author's own forms of resilience against this fatigue, "Notes" challenges us to do more than see what is around us: now is the time, the speaker beckons, "To observe and react/To hear and answer back."

As you observe and react to the work on the following pages, we urge you to answer back in your own ways and to share your answers with us.

Gustavo Guerra

Reflection

Writing was one of the last things I ever thought I would have had a passion for. In spite of my life sentence and contrary to reasonable expectations, I discovered I really love writing. But even more, I love writing with my friends. We all met through a program called Exchange for Change (E4C) that brings writing classes inside prisons. Currently, I'm taking a Poetry Workshop (an E4C class) taught by Georgia Franklin, a poet of some renown. We write to a prompt and then workshop the poems the following week. The poems l am now submitting are a result of this class. Overall, I've realized that my best work is those pieces that I have worked on with my friends, other writers who themselves use the written word, not only to communicate, but to create art of our inane existence.

Bad Habits

You are not for me.

There I said it. It is released into the ether, into the repository of hard facts rarely spoken. It was supposed to empower me. Almost like the articulated sound waves would somehow mystically remove the sting of your voice echoing similar words.

You are not for me.

But here I sit, fingers hovering over keys with no thoughts to type. Words fluttering in my mind like half-seen shadows, like waking up hungover and grasping for a fading dream.

You are not for me.

How did you even penetrate my defenses? I like to believe that I am competent, able to protect myself. Knowing the cancer of my sentence, I am always hesitant, aware of the deterrent that it serves. That no one wants to love a blue-clad prisoner, a hard-faced murderer, a saboteur of all that is good. No one wants a future with someone with my past. No one wants me, at least not in that way.

You are not for me.

Still, I can't wait to sit across from you and talk for hours. To make you laugh. To watch your eyes squint when you're deep in thought.

Hope seems to be embedded in the DNA of a lifer. Hope that the laws will one day change. Hope that society will realize the cruelty of natural life sentences. I guess that's what makes it easy to hope you will one day change your mind.

Frozen Margaritas

The taste of tequila on your lips,
on your neck, excites me. Salt and lime
adding passion as I drink you in.
It started with a smile, a shy
hello, your eyes alight with mischief.
Your hair ablaze as you danced for hours,
as you twirled strands of fire atop my
unkempt bed. A sheen of contentment
glistened your brow as you spoke with
half-lidded eyes, of how you'd die
for some flan.

But then, the light shined in my face
and for a moment, I was lost.
Tangled in a charcoal gray blanket
the truth sank in. There was no fire
haired vixen, no tequila,
only the fading memory
of salt and of limes.

Author Bio

Gustavo Guerra discovered a passion for writing as a result of the nonprofit Exchange for Change which brings creative writing classes behind the wire. He battles daily to maintain a positive mindset and occasionally battles ogres in various D&D campaigns. He has been published in *Don't Shake the Spoon*, Vol. 2; *Hear Us*; *Scalawag Magazine*; and most recently in *ReSentencing Journal* from Tufts University. He is serving a natural life sentence in the State of Florida.

Don Unger

Reflection

"Free Pride Hugs" grapples with aging and the ephemeral, or maybe more accurately, the shifting nature of community, by reflecting on some of my experiences with the LGBTQ+ community in Albany, New York, in the late 1990s and early 2000s. For me, these issues coalesced during my participation in the World Pride and Reclaim Pride marches held in New York City in June 2019. The events commemorated the 50th anniversary of the Stonewall Riots.

Free Pride Hugs

It had been 17 years since I last spoke with Steve. In life, moving forward had always meant leaving people behind. Before social media, it seemed natural, though lamentable, that when someone moved to another city, their life simply changed. You lost touch. Steve and I lost touch.

Steve and I were close friends when I lived in Albany, New York. I moved there when I was 18 to attend the State University of New York at Albany, but dropped out after becoming disenchanted with college and getting deeply involved in activism. Over the nine years that I lived there, I worked in about a dozen service industry jobs. I also promoted a couple different weekly parties at clubs, but that didn't go anywhere. In 2002, I left Albany to go back to college.

Once I left, I didn't return. Getting my bachelor's degree led to more school, more degrees, and eventually a job in academia. It meant moving around the country for almost twenty years. Since leaving Albany, I've lived in Marathon, New York; Anchorage, Alaska; Lafayette, Indiana; Austin, Texas; Oxford, Mississippi; and now, Memphis, Tennessee. While I've had to leave folks that I love behind in each instance, I have done a better job maintaining some of those relationships than I did when I left Albany. Technology has helped. But every time I move, it feels more difficult to keep up with friends and to grow roots in a new place. Moving so often has also made me susceptible to nostalgia. Social media does not alleviate the psychological weight of lost connections and fading memories. It won't let us go back. Still, it prompts us to *look* back, and it provides opportunities to reconnect with some of the people from our pasts.

* * *

In the late 1990s and early 2000s, Steve and I shared a couple different apartments in Albany. For a while, we worked together at a trendy wine bar and art gallery called Cafe Lulu on Lark Street. Lark Street sits in the middle of Albany's Center Square neighborhood. When we lived and worked in Center Square, it had dance clubs, music venues, record stores, bookstores, a "Gay and Lesbian Community Center," a few quirky gift shops, and a slew of well-reputed bars and restaurants. Albany in general, and Center Square in particular, shaped my expectations for what a community should feel like.

In a community, you don't need everyone to love you, but you need people to *see* you. It provides you with the sense that you belong there. Also, you need people who trust that you see them. Steve and I were part of this community. We could walk down Lark Street any time of the day and run into friends and acquaintances, and we'd share anecdotes about what we were doing, how work was going, and if we had seen so-and-so. The conversations weren't always deep, but they pointed to the many connections we shared.

Both Steve and I are gay. In our 20s, queer bars played important roles in developing this sense of community. In the late 1990s, Center Square queers had a few choices for going out. If you were a gay guy and you wanted to hook up, you went to Water Works on Saturday nights, which we referred to as Wally World. You could dance there, but it had a tiny dance floor that was often overcrowded. In addition to Center Square residents, Wally World attracted older white men from the suburbs and rural areas outside of Albany. I never saw many women at Wally World, and the crowd was often very, very white. If you just wanted to hang out with a small group of friends, shoot pool, and listen to Mariah on the jukebox, then you went to Oh Bar, also known as Slow Bar. Oh Bar had regulars who held up the bar and dropped quarter after quarter into the tabletop game console at the far end of it, but I never went there unless I was meeting friends. If you went out during the week that meant going to Power Company, or PoCo, on Wednesdays. It was their 18+ night, so it drew the biggest crowds of any queer venue all week. It was also the most integrated night of the week in terms of race and gender identity; it had the best dancefloor; and the two-for-one drink special meant that a lot of straight folks would come out to drink with their queer friends.

Steve and I rarely missed a Wednesday night at PoCo. In fact, we elevated getting ready into a ritual. Sometimes, we'd go clothes shopping that afternoon. More often than not, Steve wanted a new shirt. He always chose something plaid or something shiny. That evening, we'd pregame with 40-ouncers and house music, often Junior Vasquez or Armand van Helden remixes of some pop diva. We'd bop around the apartment waiting for a Freeman's mud or clay mask to dry. We'd talk about who we did or didn't want to see or about something we'd heard recently about someone who would undoubtedly be at the club. We'd compete for space in front of the bathroom mirror where we plucked our eyebrows. (It's beyond me how anyone's eyebrows survived the '90s.) Once we got ourselves together, we'd make the rounds, dropping into Lulu's or Café Hollywood to have a drink and catch up with friends who worked or hung out there. In Albany, bars stayed open until 4 a.m. so we didn't have to rush to get to the club. At around 12:30 a.m. we'd head to PoCo. The crowd peaked around that time.

At times, we'd try to be one another's wingman, but more often than not, we mingled separately, crossing paths and checking in with one another periodically. At the end of the night, we'd either make plans to get food before heading home, or Steve would let me know that he was hanging out with someone. While I made out with folks at the club, I almost never hooked up. AIDS made each of us determine where we drew the line.

In the '90s, Center Square might have been a queer mecca, but it wasn't exactly a playground. The threat of anti-queer violence also loomed in the back of our minds. I had been gay bashed in Center Square a couple times. Once a couple guys called me faggot, sucker punched me, and ran off while I waited for a couple slices of pizza at the joint down the street from PoCo. Another time, I was harassed in front of Lulu's. Some friends and I were standing out front smoking cigarettes when three white guys passing by tried to pick a fight with us. They started in on my friend Nina, but when they saw me, their focus turned.

"He. She. It. I don't know what the fuck you are." One of the men shouted at me, gesturing at my clothes. I wore a flowy skirt, a lace top, a leather jacket, and make up. It wasn't drag so much as androgynous, and it really pissed him off. I loved that and leaned into it, which just pissed him off more.

The noise prompted Susan, a middle-aged, butch lesbian who washed dishes at Lulu's, to come outside. She hurried my group of friends into the café and shut the door. The homophobes promptly smashed it. While we couldn't completely escape the threat of violence, the fact that someone stepped in meant that people in the community had seen us. A community can't always protect you, but it can defend you.

* * *

Over the years, memories of life in Albany cohered into a sort of personal mythos. Periodically, I dug around social media platforms for profiles of folks who lived there back then. I needed to reminisce with someone about those times and add dimension to my memories. Finally, I found Steve's profile on Facebook in 2018. I looked for him a few other times over the years, but I didn't have any luck. After we friended one another, we messaged occasionally. At one point, Steve said, "If you are ever in NYC, we should meet and catch up." In June 2019, I traveled to NYC for the festivities honoring the Stonewall Riots' 50th anniversary. I also reconnected with Steve.

By the time I made it to NYC, Steve had moved to Hackensack, New Jersey, having been priced out of the city. He took the train into the city on the day of the Pride Parade, and I met him outside Penn Station. We grabbed lunch at the West Bank Cafe in Midtown where we talked about where we lived and worked now. Then, we made our way to the Village.

As we wandered down 7th Avenue, Steve asked, "Are you doing what you imagined you'd be doing?" I wasn't sure what he meant. He continued, "I always thought we would be dead by now. When I look back on things, I never expected us to reach our 40s."

I didn't say anything. I thought about his question. We partied quite a bit and there were sporadic acts of violence, but I never thought of life in Albany as particularly dangerous.

Steve mentioned Jimmy. He co-owned PoCo with his partner Al. "Remember, Jimmy was really sick. Then he started AZT, and he got better. But he looked so terrible afterward. It wrecked his body," Steve said. "He didn't come to the club much after that."

Steve was talking about AIDS. He didn't think we'd survive to reach our 40s, but he didn't mean just us. He meant himself, our friends, and all gay men of a particular vintage.

"I don't remember Jimmy. I only knew Al, but we weren't close," I said. "If you mean did I ever think I'd be a professor, then no. I didn't know what I would be doing when I left Albany. I just needed something."

The conversation shifted. Steve and I talked about how we never imagined marriage or having kids. "They weren't anything I have ever thought much about. They weren't something we did," I said. What you see shapes your possibilities. I didn't know any gay men who had kids. No one talked about marriage.

"No, they weren't."

The parade ended. Throngs of people milled about the streets trying to figure out what to do next. We walked single-file through the crowds, veering away from 7th Avenue below Christopher Street.

"Jell-O shots? You want to buy Jell-O shots?" A young, Black, female-presenting person carrying a small cooler walked up to us. They wore rainbow socks.

Steve shook his head. He had just taken a drag on a cigarette. He pushed the smoke out quickly and said, "No, thanks."

The young person kept walking, "Jell-O shots?"

We kept walking. Steve steered the conversation from how we saw ourselves then to how young people see themselves nowadays, "What do you think about the fact that so many of them don't identify as gay or straight or whatever? They just go with it. They don't question it or worry about it."

"Think about how much bullshit we went through for being gay. I still go through it in the South. We don't have any rights there. I can't relate to these kids at all," I replied as I weaved around people blocking the sidewalk.

"Yeah, they don't really care about all that." Steve continued, "I'm jealous of them."

As we made our way down 8th Avenue toward Washington Square Park, we began talking about old friends and acquaintances. Steve had family in Albany; even after he left, he kept connections to people there. He had stories, sometimes detailed and sometimes impressionistic, about what happened to them. We worked our way through a list of people we knew from past jobs, from going out, from the neighborhood. One of us would offer a name and brief description of the person. At times, we couldn't remember last names. We'd spend a moment or two describing our connection to the person.

"He worked at Justin's."

"Remember, he used to come into Margarita's all the time."

Occasionally, one or the other of us wouldn't remember who the person was, so we dropped any conversation about them. These folks disappeared in the kind of rapid conversation that collapses 19 years into a few hours. Some died from drug overdoses or suicides. Some went to jail. Others developed serious illnesses. Some left Center Square or Albany altogether: they got married, moved to more remote areas of upstate New York, and had kids. Many of the gay men disappeared without a trace. We hadn't heard what happened to them. We used to see them all the time. We were connected to them, but we weren't necessarily close with all of them.

While we recounted these stories, I pictured the community that we had been a part of disintegrating. I have never recaptured that sense of community in the many places I've lived. I've come close, but then I had to move again for school and work. It's difficult to understand when people disappear, whether through death, prison, or family. Where do they go? It's part of growing older. I imagine how, for other people, I might be one of those old acquaintances who simply disappeared—the connection severed. Without that sense of community, I barely exist nowadays. Who *sees* me now?

The older I get, the more I become the old guy standing in the corner in a room full of young people watching the band but not interacting with anyone. I eat dinner alone at the bar. I show up alone to the concert. I am not sure if it's just me or if there's a whole generation of gay men who spend most of their leisure time alone. We didn't die; we didn't go to prison; we didn't partner off, adopt some kids, or move to the suburbs. We weren't the generation ravaged by AIDS—though we certainly experienced or witnessed some of that. We are the remnants of the next generation: a generation that learned how to be gay from one another and from the few films and books that broke through into public consciousness in the late '80s and early '90s. In the Albany bar scene in the '90s, we didn't have many elders around to tell us about what things used to be like or how they might be different. There were a few older queens. They stuck together or sat alone, often at the bar. I suppose we didn't try to unearth their histories. At least, I didn't. Why didn't I see them?

"I don't think most people understand our generation. They call us xennials—born at the tail end of generation x and the beginning of the millennials. We're the smallest generation and the one most likely to die from a drug overdose," Steve continued.

Steve and I were part of a much smaller group within that generation. We came out when we were teenagers in the early '90s: long after Stonewall; but long before LGBTQ+ folks had many legal protections outside so-called queer meccas like Albany; long after folks established Albany's Gay & Lesbian Community Center and Pride Parade, but before the highly publicized murders of Brandon Teena, Ali Forney, and Matthew Sheppard. We came out after *And the Band Played On* but before *Queer as Folk*. The LGBTQ+ rights movement shifted among struggles for basic rights and representation and struggles for liberation. Later, those struggles turned toward survival. But by the '90s, part of this movement became the "gay community" as I knew it, marked by death but focused on living openly and without apology. My sense of this community disintegrated when I left Albany. In the years that followed, a segment of the movement regrouped around "gays in the military" and marriage equality—two issues I never thought about in my day-to-day life.

As we entered Washington Square Park, we passed throngs of young people enjoying Pride, ostensibly celebrating the 50th anniversary of the Stonewall Riots. Our conversation separated us from the revelry. I continued, "We're sort of our own thing, xennial gay men but queers in general. How many older gay men did you know when you were their age? How many went out to the bars? Too many young people take for granted that LGBTQ+ people are ubiquitous—that there are generations before them and that there will be generations after them. I didn't feel like that when I was in my twenties. I didn't feel like we were everywhere or always. I didn't feel like I could do whatever I wanted."

"You did whatever you wanted, for the most part," Steve countered.

"I guess so. It's just different now." I looked around the park, staring at two masculine-presenting youths sitting on a park bench. One of them was holding up a hastily painted sign that read "Free Pride Hugs."

Steve lit a new cigarette off his previous one. "It is."

Author Bio

Don Unger is an assistant professor in the Department of Writing & Rhetoric and affiliate faculty in Women and Gender Studies and in the Community Engaged Leadership program at the University of Mississippi. Additionally, he serves as part of the *Spark* Editorial Collective. He lives in Memphis, Tennessee.

Ryan Moser

Reflection

Being part of a community of meditators, a sangha, is important in Buddhist culture. When I first came to prison and with introduced to meditation and yoga over fifteen years ago, I did not understand the importance of community–not just in Buddhist circle, but also with writing workshops, educational projects, neighborhoods, etc. After practicing now for many years, the sangha has become an important piece of my learning path, and being able to find a community at Everglades (in the before times, our class has been cancelled) allowed me to grow as a person.

Finding the Buddha: Seeking Solace in Prison

> *"No matter what part of the world we come from, we are all basically the same human beings.*
>
> *We all seek happiness and try to avoid suffering."*
>
> –His Holiness the 14th Dalai Lama
> Acceptance of the Nobel Peace Prize, Stockholm, Sweden

Ringgggg….

　Ringgggg….

　　Ringgggg….

I breathe deeply, inhaling air through my nostrils and exhaling from my belly. The final chime of the bronze Tibetan singing bowl reverberates through our confined space. Sounds of arguing echo from outside the classroom as I adjust my zafu cushion under the base of my spine, aware of the noise but letting it go. My lanky six-foot frame is folded and I look at my tattoo of a purple lotus flower on the inside of my forearm. Long ago, I refused to slow down, to open up, to try new things–my mind wasn't teachable. But now I have an Om stamped on my flesh and spirit. Now I sit still.

I smell cheap *Fresh Scent* deodorant. The blood flows to my legs as I am erect and at attention, eyes slightly closed and tongue pressed against the roof of my mouth, hands circled in a mudra, monkey-mind racing, anxiety slowing.

　I breathe in….
　I breathe out….

This isn't my first time in a prison meditation class; I'm leading this morning's zazen with our outside sponsor Ta-o, a kind soul from Miami who's hip and wears beaded jewelry. We sit at the head of the class, facing six students and easing into thirty minutes of silent contemplation, insight, and painful body aches. As a long-time Zen practitioner, I'm considered a mentor and a dharma teacher in my *sangha*, or community, and after two years facilitating the group I've grown to like the men in the room: Ed and Ramirez, Leon, Papa Zoe. We run into each other on the rec yard and bow respectfully, as if we share a secret. Our meditation group meets every Thursday morning in a space the size of a large walk-in closet, avoiding the extra desks stacked in storage and sweeping before we set up our blankets and cushions, eager to start our weekly moment of peaceful silence.

My sangha is a community of like-minded men studying our minds through meditation, and the origin of this convergence dates back to the Buddha himself. During a time in India when people were shunned for being born in a lower class, Buddha invited one person from all four caste systems to him as disciples. The irony is not lost on me that I now sit in a modern day sangha as an outcast from society; the ethics of my sangha is to include anyone, anytime into the community of seekers.

I never imagined that I would meditate inside the violent walls of prison: after all, living as a conscious being of peace while surrounded by brutality is a true dichotomy. The duality of the two worlds is comprehensive and stark. But after I was introduced to the ancient art of quietude during my first year of incarceration, I knew that it would remain a part of my lifestyle forever–thanks to a bald-headed ex-Green Beret with a bamboo stick.

Coming to prison is traumatic—a crisis similar to going to war, being abused, or living with a grave disease. The reason for the suffering is self-imposed in my case, as I chose to break the law, but the pain it inflicts remains the same. Regret, fear, misery, and loss are all universal sorrows experienced by people in these situations, and just as someone who faces personal turmoil in their life must learn to cope, prisoners like me must look deep inside to find a way to get through it.

When I first entered the penal system, when all was bleak and life seemed over, as my family accepted my sentence and I lost everything I'd ever owned, while fighting and searching for some way to make the years bearable, I couldn't find hope. I wasn't even close to centered, and I wanted to fight at the slightest provocation. Worry consumed me, and I didn't know how to let go. I wouldn't try. Growing up I was filled with constant worry, and as I aged from an anxious boy to a neurotic adult, it seemed that I would never find inner peace. My brain wouldn't tune out or turn down. This nonstop firing of circuitry caused many meltdowns, and when faced with the chaos of prison, it felt like I was destined to lose my mind.

Then a small ray of light came into view in the form of a simple Buddhist monk.

He was an imposing, stern-looking Polish man wearing traditional robes and twisting his mala bead necklace, a scowl on his rosy face and sweat glistening atop his clean-shaven head. I'd never met a monk before (let alone a large white one) and was unsure of the etiquette as he reached out his large paw and gripped my hand like a vice.

Casey was friendly, with the relaxed confidence of an ex-boxer. I stepped into the prison chapel and looked around; a group of four inmates were gathered by a table of free books by Alan Watts, Thich Nhat Hahn, an other Zen masters. I picked up a copy of *No Mud, No Lotus* as we were ushered into an empty space behind a partition with several cushions lined up in an orderly row.

Casey lifted his robes above his knee as he squatted onto his cushion and waited for us to join him. The room was silent of the usual chatter you hear in every space within the walls of a penitentiary. The teacher stared at us for a moment before bowing with his palms pressed together at his chest.

"When I was in Nam' I killed people for a living, and I was good at it." A long bamboo stick was lying on the ground next to his cushion, alongside a bronze bell and a flower. His abrupt confession threw us off. "After the war I spent some time in Cambodia studying Buddhism at a monastery, then traveled to South Korea for a three-month silent meditation retreat in the mountains."

I raised my hand. "You mean you didn't talk for three months?"

"That's correct."

I didn't understand why someone would *choose* not to speak for so long, and was skeptical of the motivation. But looking over the hardened warrior, I respected him enough to keep listening. Our group spent the next hour discussing the human mind and science, breathing techniques, and how meditating can help calm our fears and worries. I was intrigued but not convinced; furthermore, I'd read new age-y things for years, and Casey wasn't solving any of my current problems with his stoic whimsy.

I was living in a faith-based prison in Florida and had volunteered to check out the meditation class solely out of curiosity. I'd read the book *Zen Mind, Beginner's Mind* a couple of months prior, and the philosophy of studying one's own mind had appealed to my nonreligious beliefs. But now that we were lighting incense and hearing a monologue on loving-kindness, I had some reservations.

I was starting with a fifteen-minute sit. "Focus on your posture while breathing in and out through your nostrils. Now, let's begin."

The intimidating teacher stood and paced behind us while we sat in quiet concentration, occasionally stopping to adjust our position gently with his hand and thrice hitting one of us sharply on the trapezoid with the bamboo stick, startling me back into the moment. When we were beckoned to end our session by the ring of the bell, Casey edified the benefits of being aware of every second and letting go of our worries.

"The past is gone and tomorrow is not guaranteed, men–focus on the now."

That first meeting was auspicious, as I was searching the narrows of my mind for a reprieve from the pain of prison, and mining my heart for inner peace. Meditation–Zen in particular–called to me. I'd shunned the dogmas and ceremony of other religions, but here was a practical guide to living: right thoughts, right speech, right action.

Our meditation classes got incrementally longer until our small group was doing zazen for thirty minutes straight–a feat I'd never imagined possible. When Casey lectured before and after our sit (dharma talks), I was enthralled, but I was still testing things out myself. He became a sage guide for the prison world we lived in, one of cruelty and manipulation.

"The Dalai Lama teaches that only the enemy can truly teach us to practice the virtues of compassion and tolerance. See the obstacles around you in prison as a test."

I began to transform the way I looked at my environment and the incarcerated residents around me, observing their intrinsic worth instead of their flaws. I understood that happiness was only a state of mind. My racing, irritating thoughts started to slow down. In time, I became more centered and dealt with problems differently: I was less on the edge and more balanced; I practiced equanimity amidst distractions; I attempted to lose my ego and felt more empathy.

Each night in my noisy dorm, with cigarette smoke hovering in the air and commotion all around, a heavy pall of misery weighed down the mood. I would sit on my bed bunk, contemplating my mistakes, while sitting in silent meditation on top of my pillow. I'd try to still my mind by counting slowly with each breath, using the tips I'd learned, but thoughts would sprint laps around my mind like a greyhound.

I forgot to buy coffee at the canteen...The nurse looked really good today...She smiled at me again...Man, I haven't had sex in two years...Don't forget to watch American Idol tonight...

Inhale . . . exhale . . . one . . .

Inhale . . . exhale . . . two . . .

How the fuck did I end up in prison...? Why can't I stop using drugs and go back to living a normal life . . . ? Will anyone remember me when I get out...?"

Inhale . . . exhale . . . one...

Harnessing my mind was like corralling a wild mustang, so I always came back to the breath. Casey, Thick Nhat Hahn, Watts, all the teachers in my nascent meditative life preached the same thing:

Still your mind. Follow the breath.

In the mornings I would read about the Four Noble Truths and it made sense to me–all of my suffering in life was avoidable! I was attached to every single thing that I felt made me happy, and when those comforts were stripped away, or change came, I was dissatisfied. This aversion to change and attachment to people, places, things, and ideas caused me such great misery, so I adopted a lifestyle in prison that I could continue when I got out.

Several months after my first meditation class with the decorated soldier, I attended a three-day silent meditation retreat with Casey and 10 other inmates in the education building–only returning to our dorms to sleep. We ate peanut butter in quiet and practiced yoga and *kinhin* (walking meditation) in between our grueling 30-minute sits. My back hurt. My legs were numb. I had anxiety over the silence and got hit by the bamboo stick a lot. But above all, I found insight and calmness in the eye of the storm.

During the retreat, the deep sense of existential crisis I'd fought since coming to prison was laid bare before me, and I had no choice but to confront it–fighting for your life is not unlike facing down death. I needed to find my true nature and stop living so superficially. After days of being honest with myself, I admitted that prison was the only place that could force me to examine my past so introspectively, and I never would've taken the time to immerse myself in self-betterment and meditation if it wasn't for being isolated for a long period of time. I had hit rock bottom as an addict on the streets, and it would've gotten worse if I weren't arrested. Against all reason, after much emotional struggle, I acquiesced to one hard truth: prison may have saved my life.

Years later and long after Casey had retired, I sit at the head of a meditation class with Ta-o, watching over the Blue Lotus Sangha like an inquisitive guardian. Having a community of friends brings me a sense of connection. I wonder if these men are asking the same question or finding the same answers that I am while contemplating a better life.

Ringgggg....
    Ringgggg....
        Ringgggg....

I breathe deeply, inhaling air through my nostrils and exhaling from my belly. The final chime of the bronze Tibetan singing bowl reverberates through our confined space. I am finally at peace–at least for a moment.

Author Bio

Ryan Moser's work has been published in *Evening Street Press, Progressive, Muse Journal, Santa Fe Literary Journal, december, Iconclast, The Marshall Project, Wild World*, and more. In 2020, he received an award by PEN America, including publication in the *Pen America Literary Journal*.

Devin O'Keefe and Justin Slavinski

Reflection

The following excerpt from "The Missing Briefcase" comes from the first chapter of a much larger work by Devin O'Keefe and Justin Slavinski, incarcerated writers who met in an Introduction to Creative Writing class taught by an Exchange for Change (E4C) volunteer at Everglades C.I. in Miami. E4C is a volunteer-led organization founded by Kathie Klarreich which teaches writing classes in South Florida prisons. The cohort of writers who have taken any E4C classes at Everglades C.I. is at least 200 strong—about 10% of the population. Both Devin and Justin had written small pieces independently prior to and while in prison, but truly began writing in earnest within the past three years. After both gained employment in the Education department, they developed several short, co-written stories which were traded from computer to computer on 3 ½" floppy disks. Quickly, they discovered their offbeat sensibilities meshed and began the creation of two larger works: an urban fantasy set in the Atlanta area, and a quirky detective story set in Milwaukee.

Devin and Justin alternate who writes what every 300-600 words, rarely leaving notes for each other, and letting their stories develop organically. They fly by the seat of their pants and hope for the best. Only after a chapter or series of chapters is finished do they sit down and harmonize—though, having worked together as writing partners for three years, they are most often on the same page. They hope to see Woody Tukker, of Woody Investigations, recover Jean D'Eau's briefcase—and for the world to read about it.

From The Missing Briefcase, Chapter 1

Beep . . . beep . . . beep blared the insistent alarm, waking Woody to another Monday. He stifled a moan and threw off the sweaty covers. Sitting up in bed, he grabbed his head as the hangover from another long night out on the city punished him. He had to return to his office early to check for new cases, but the hangover and his gut told him that today would be three more strikes. Again. He had been down on his luck and hadn't seen a case in far too long. An unnecessary check of the fridge was a testament to his dire circumstances: half a bottle of Heinz mustard and a half loaf of moldy Wonder bread lay within.

A cold shower was a sensible decision for someone with a hangover, yet he took one this morning because he hadn't paid his gas bill in over a month and couldn't shower in hot water if he got down on both knees and prayed. Besides, most of his prayers last night were spent at the toilet. Woody cranked the handle in the shower and dunked his head under the cold, refreshing water. He hoped for refreshing, but in reality he hopped in and out of the water stream just soaping his crotch and armpits and then quickly toweling off before heading out into the warm, summer air.

If he didn't get a case this week he was not sure what he would do; a man can only go so long on nothing. That his receptionist even dared to stay on with no pay so long surprised him. Rachael was far too loyal, but she had a hipster boyfriend, and they went out every night during the week. She was the only fortune he had had in this long dry spell. Everything else had turned to shit. Checking the fridge for the same two sad items, he went off to his office to roll the dice again. Would today be his lucky day?

A quick check of his wallet revealed no walking around money for today. He had spent it all on last night's drinking, which in hindsight was not his best decision. Ascending the steps to his office, he crossed his fingers that today would be the day. The lights were already on; Rachael had arrived in the office before him. He opened the door like the past mornings, his hopes full. A smile shone on her face: Rachael seemed unusually chipper this morning. Her copper blonde hair flashed in the overly bright fluorescent lights, waving an envelope in the air.

"Good morning, Rach. I sure hope that's a job," Woody said.

"Another late bill, Woody. Another goddamn late bill. How the hell am I supposed to pay my bills, boss?" Rachael asked as her smile inverted to a frown. She'd set him up, but at least she had still come to the office.

Woody shook his head and slammed the door shut behind him. He shrugged off his stained, rumpled raincoat and hung it on the coat rack just inside the door. In three short shuffling steps, he arrived at the only chair in the waiting area just in front of Rachael's desk and slumped into it. He wore his guilt like a dog caught shitting on the couch. Shame and self-loathing battled within him for supremacy, and despair launched itself off the ropes for a match-ending body slam.

"Rachael, you know I've tried. I've really tried. I...I'm at a real loss for what to do here. It's been what, six..."

"Eight."

"Fine, eight weeks since we've had a job. And what, five..."

"Six." Rachel knew this routine all too well from the past two months.

"Yeah, six since I paid you. Rachael, I know a big case is just around the corner. I can feel it. You know that feeling you get when you're at the plate, and the pitcher is winding up, and you dig into the clay with your cleats and you feel the grain of the bat through your batting gloves, and you just *know* you're going to hit a double over the head of the second baseman? It's like that. I know there's a big case. I promise you Rachael; all our troubles are about to be all fixed up. I promise."

"I don't play soccer. But I think I follow your metaphor."

"I can't tell if you're fucking with me right now, Rachael," Woody said.

Rachael crumpled the letter into a loose ball and threw it at him. He made no effort to stop it from smacking his bulbous nose. He simply looked down at the threadbare, mauve carpet under the chair's rollers. A defeated sigh escaped his lips before he could control himself.

"Hey, what's that?" Rachael asked.

"What's what?"

"That, in your raincoat pocket? Looks like a letter." Rachael gestured at his raincoat on the coat rack. "You getting mail at home again? I thought last time you did that someone mailed you, like, a rotting mango or something. That's the whole reason we got a P.O. box."

"I don't get mail at home. And it was a papaya. And it stained my carpet."

Suspicious letters in his pocket when he knew he didn't get mail? And no one had bumped past him on the street? Suspicious. He may have been getting up there in the years, but he still had a few years' more skill than most of the lowlifes in this town. This could be the break he felt. This could be the chance to make things right. This could be that frozen rope over the second baseman.

Rising from the chair, he took three steps back to the coat rack. Plucking the letter out of the pocket, Woody withdrew a seven-inch folding blade out of his front pocket and sliced it open. "You are hereby served by the Milwaukee County Court that you are to appear in court for a divorce hearing…" Woody said, his grin suddenly turned to a frown like a nice summer day erupting into a potent thunderstorm without warning. He had *felt* it deep in his bones that this was the big break.

Like any good batter, he thought he could easily take another fastball to the body and walk to first, but he was not so certain anymore. He slumped back into the chair, and his head starting the regular pounding which had tortured him over the past few weeks. Rachael picked up the letter, crumpled it, and tossed it into the waste bucket with the growing mound of late bills. Compassion must have overcome her, for she reached out a hand for his shoulder. "Wood, I . . ."

Woody stood with a grunt, brushing her hand away. "I'm heading out for the day; it was a long night and I can't handle this shit right now."

Woody abruptly headed for the door when Rachael called out, "I'll call your cell if we get a client."

He scoffed at her enthusiasm. "Rach, my service went two months overdue three days ago. No service. My phone is a paper weight." The door slammed behind him.

He descended the stairs two at a time with his hands in his pockets, mind elsewhere, when he slammed into a solid form. He lost his balance and fell on top of the person who was ascending the stairs. Limbs entangled trying to stop their fall, they both landed on their sides. Woody saw a gruff man with puffy red eyes pushing himself off the floor, offering his hand to Woody.

"I didn't zee you, messieur, hope your suit is alright," the man said.

Woody took his hand. "Don't worry about the suit, it's seen worse days."

"Would you happen to know where ze office of the Woody Tukker is located? I am in desperate need of his services and his number keeps saying it is out of service." Woody could hardly believe his luck, he had run face first into the pitch!

"Uh, right this way. Sorry, I had a, uh…big case on my mind," Woody half-mumbled. He gestured back up the stairs they had just fallen down.

Disappointment flashed across the man's face. "I don't want to burden you with more than you can handle. I've heard you're the best, and we—er, I can't afford to have a distracted detective on this. I guess I'll have to…"

"NO! I mean, no, it's alright. Nothing that can't be assigned to my, uh, associate. I'm Woody of Woody Investigations, and you are?" Pressing a hand to the potential client's elbow, he began easing him up the stairs.

"D'Eau, Jean D'Eau. I'm afraid I must insist on the privacy of your office to discuss more . . ."

"Of course, of course," Woody smiled and urged D'Eau back up the stairs.

On the third landing, he jingled the keys in the lock to let Rachael know he was back. "Hey, Rach, I think we've got a—Jesus!" Rachael was sprawled across her desk, twitching. A strobe effect from the computer monitor illuminated her stricken face.

"Goddammit! D'Eau, call an ambulance! I don't think she's conscious!" Woody shouted as he ran a hand through his thinning hair. The scene just didn't make sense. D'Eau stuttered through the situation to the 911 operator. His French accent complicated the matter, and he had to double back.

A quick look at Rachel's monitor revealed a flashing, swirling image of random colors and patterns. Suddenly, everything clicked into place like an epic game of Connect Four. Rachael's epilepsy had struck her again. It was the very ailment that had sunk her chances of becoming a cop: the flashing lights on the cruisers set her off. There was no way she'd have done this purposely. Woody examined the computer and noted she had been in the office's email inbox. Someone must've sent the email targeting her. An old case? An angsty exboyfriend? Woody closed the window and the flashing ceased. Pulling out his notepad, he wrote a reminder to have an IT guy check the email's origin. He'd have to investigate this later.

Woody stopped his examination and hurried over to his potential client. He hoped he wouldn't lose the case due to the unusual circumstances. D'Eau took the phone from his ear and said, "Paramedics cinq minutes. Should I do anything?"

"No, no," Woody said absently while righting the lone visitor's chair mechanically, and gestured for D'Eau to sit.

"No, sir, I couldn't possibly while this mademoiselle is in distress." Regardless, he pulled out a silver cigarette case from his back pocket, deftly removed a hand-rolled cigarette, and lit it. He puffed away, holding the cigarette backwards. Woody resisted rolling his eyes and leaned down beside Rachael. For the briefest moment, it looked as if her eyes were about to flutter open to tell him what had happened.

Sirens dopplered up the avenue and screeched to a halt before his building. Without a knock, two paramedics burst into the office and immediately set to work on Rachael after gently moving Woody out of their way. He stood off to the side with D'Eau as the paramedics worked. They manhandled his loyal secretary, quickly divining the cause and extent of her injury. Soon, the burly paramedic held down her arm and injected something that reduced her shaking. After strapping her to a backboard, they lifted her onto the stretcher. He turned back, "Look, we'll be taking her to Memorial. You know the number?"

"Yeah, yeah. I got it," Woody mumbled.

The paramedics banged the edge of the stretcher against his doorframe—there goes the security deposit, Woody winced—and, more delicately this time, descended the narrow staircase.

Bewildered, Woody looked around the room and at the supremely calm, smoking D'Eau. Clapping his hands once, he righted the chair behind Rachael's desk and sat down. Drawing a deep breath, he opened, "Alright, well...uh...that's...Have a seat Mr. D'Eau. Let's talk about your case."

Author Bios

Devin O'Keefe is an incarcerated writer who has helped develop curricula for multiple writing courses inside the wire. He is previously unpublished. He is known as much for his wacky ideas as his calm under pressure. Mr. O'Keefe loves playing video games and creating fantasy worlds.

Justin Slavinski is a former textbook editor who unwillingly lives in Miami, Florida. His previous publications include Don't Shake the Spoon, volume 2; Hear Us: Writing from the Inside During the Time of Covid; Iconoclast, issue 121; Resentencing; Coda; and the Iowa Prison Writing Project. Mr. Slavinski enjoys teaching classes with Exchange for Change, running Dungeons and Dragons games, and eating Nutella.

Frank Morse

Reflection

This is the product of working several months with about a dozen people as we prepared to hold a TEDx event at Everglades Correctional Institution. Each of the nine speakers were asked to share their personal journey, and this is mine. The event never happened because of COVID-19 shutting everything down, but the experience of working with a group of men to write, rehearse, and perform this piece is one I will never forget.

I Remember

Lights illuminate the darkness. Trees appear clothed in strobes of red and blue. Wind rushes around me through the open windows. I am a passenger on a hopeless journey. Opioids had taken me down many roads, none of them good. When the spike strips appear, followed by her desperate cry, "I can't steer!", I know this road will be the same.

The streets are littered with the broken dreams of people like me: people caught in the rip currents of addiction. The waters of our world are rewarding and unforgiving. The opportunities in the land of the free are beyond compare, but second chances are hard to come by.

Unimaginable pain floods my senses. I can't move, it's dark, I feel encased, trapped. Time seems to stop. Am I awake? There are no sounds. Why do I feel so cold? "Stop moving, stop moving!" I hear banging, glass shattering, "Can you hear me? Who's with you? Who's with you!" I'm awake now, crying out in pain. "Jessie! Jessie's with me! Help!"

My second chance began in a burning car, in a ditch, upside down, smashed, broken, and dying. From a hospital bed in 2003 until today, I have faced many obstacles. The things in my life that fueled my actions didn't disappear like magic. I was still an addict who feared rejection. An addict; a broken person. It would be some time before I could grasp it, but eventually, I had a realization. This realization would become the spark that ignited a passion that transformed my life.

I remember experiencing a little pill that has changed our world and completely altered my life forever. At the age of 19, I had two rules: no heroin, no needles. Living in a small Florida retirement community, I would never see these things. That stuff was in the big cities where the grimy TV addicts lurked in alleyways with their dirty needles. My knowledge of pills consisted of, if it's a pain killer, take it, so I took it. Soon my life became consumed by an unquenchable thirst for these little pills. In time I would discover what they truly were. These little OxyContin pills were nothing less than heroin sold in pharmacies instead of alleyways.

For an hour, I was going in and out of consciousness. I begged them to give me something for the pain, but they said I had to wait until we got to the hospital. Strapped to a board, the distinctive sound of whirling helicopter blades, the cold air made me want to shiver. Where's Jessie? Where are they taking Jessie?

When I grabbed a needle and shot up OxyContin, it wasn't because I wanted to have fun. Growing up, I knew I would never shoot up drugs because I was just a regular kid having a good time. I went to youth group, attended Boy Scouts; I even won a Most Outstanding award at the Sheriff Department's Explorer summer camp. Never considering it could go from just having fun to just having to use. Never imagining that I could think a life without heroin wasn't worth living.

My story is a success story, thanks to a second chance. That may be hard to understand from the outside looking in or from the perspective of someone who isn't an addict. After all, I'm living inside a prison today with a natural life sentence. That doesn't sound very successful! At least not until you consider the life of an addict is a perilous one. A second chance is never a sure thing. The other side of the coin is death; Jessie and I were both heroin addicts. On the morning of July 31, 2003, we decided to get help. I would turn myself in, and Jessie would go to the methadone clinic; I would go to jail and get my life in order, and one day it would be happily ever after. Before that though, we decided to get high one last time for old time's sake.

Waking up in the hospital after my first surgery, my mom and dad were at my bedside. In my heart, I knew the answer before I asked the question. I looked at my mom and asked where they had taken Jessie. She didn't answer me. I looked at my dad then and asked him. I think you already know, was all he said. One last time for old time's sake. Three weeks after her 21st birthday, no more chances, Jessie was gone.

After the accident, I struggled with the question of "Why me?" Why not let Jessie live instead of me! Why not let the man in the truck she hit live instead of me! Why, why, why. Lots of questions, no good answers. Who deserves a second chance anyways? Some people say everyone does. After the accident though, I didn't feel like I should be the one miraculously surviving to tell the story.

Unfortunately, Jessie's story is not an uncommon story. Hundreds of people die every day in America from opioids, heroin. The rip currents of addiction stealing their last breath. A second chance is a gift of mercy, and it was hard for me to grasp. I realized Jessie's story could help someone, and I was alive to tell it.

A second chance isn't promised. I received one to tell Jessie's story. My journey started in a ditch, but it isn't ending there. What second chance have you received? Who paid the price for it? Many have paid the price for mine, and I'm living each day honoring the sacrifices made for my opportunity. Will you join me? Will you step into the realm of the unknown and make beauty from ashes? It won't be easy, but telling this story wasn't easy either.

Author Bio

Frank Morse is a self-taught portrait artist, writer and public speaker who has been incarcerated since he was 23 years old. He is the president of the Draft Pick's Gavel Club, an affiliate of Toastmasters International, staff writer for The Endeavor newsletter, a prison publication at Everglades Correctional Institution, a peer facilitator in the Horizon Faith and Character Program dorm, and facilitator of the Art Expressions Program. He is incarcerated in Florida.

Vivian Lorena Carmona

Reflection

Me siento orgullosa de mi etnia embera chamí. Me destaqué en los procesos de escritura que realiza el Colectivo Pedagógico y Cultural EncantaPalabras, procesos que son apoyados por la Secretaría de Educación del departamento de Caldas, la Universidad de Manizales y la empresa Chec. Participé activamente en el semillero de comunicaciones, en la emisora estudiantil. Además, publiqué mis poemas y textos en la cartilla del Proyecto "Poesía para la Paz" y en la Revista "Relieves y Torrentes" del Proyecto Comunicación Intercultural. Creo que los temas de mis poemas son identitarios e intimistas, creándolos fui descubriendo los beneficios de escribir para mi formación integral como joven, mujer e indígena. Mi sueño es seguir adelante con mi educación, graduarme como licenciada y seguir escribiendo.

Solía ser...

Solía ser muy tímida, no me gustaba hablar
ni expresar lo que sentía
pero ahora mediante la escritura
me voy liberando y sin miedo
muestro quién soy y esa es mi salida…
Me siento tranquila después de escribir,
descubrí un mundo lleno de magia
a través de las palabras…
Ahora ya no temo decir lo que siento,
me siento en paz,
en una profunda tranquilidad
después de escribir un verso
donde deje claros mis sentimientos.
Irme lejos y observar mi entorno,
disfrutar de lo que me rodea, me ayuda a pensar
para un nuevo poema relatar.
Es hora de cambiar la historia,
a través de la escritura se encuentra paz.
 Y ahora les dejo este verso para que al igual que yo
puedan encontrar paz en las palabras.

Author Bio

Nací el 22 de agosto de 2004 en Manizales porque a mi madre la remitieron para atender su parto prematuro en la ciudad. He vivido siempre en San Lorenzo. Cursé mis estudios de básica secundaria en la Institución Educativa San Lorenzo ubicada en el Territorio Ancestral Indígena, municipio de Riosucio, departamento de Caldas, en las montañas del centro de Colombia. Me reconozco como mujer de la etnia embera chamí. Sobresalí como líder durante la secundaria y fui mejor bachiller en el año 2021, año en el que terminé mis estudios y me gradué. Actualmente estudio mi primer semestre universitario en el pregrado de Educación Física, Universidad de Caldas.

Fresban Alexis Bueno

Reflection

Me reconozco como joven de la etnia embera chamí, siento gran admiración por mi cultura y el paisaje donde nací. Me gusta mucho la música y escribir. Sobresalí durante cuatro años en los procesos de escritura que realiza el Colectivo Pedagógico y Cultural EncantaPalabras con el apoyo de la Secretaría de Educación del departamento de Caldas, la Universidad de Manizales y la empresa Chec. Participé activamente en el semillero de comunicaciones. La escritura de poesía y el rap me han ayudado a superar momentos muy difíciles de mi vida.

Soy quien soy ahora, cada uno es quien es por todo lo que ha sucedido

por las cosas que ha vivido, por todo lo que ha pasado.
Hemos luchado mucho en contra de nosotros mismos;
es primordial trabajar para construir la paz.
He pasado cada segundo de mi vida luchando por conseguirla,
muchas veces he fracasado; luego entendí que es una lucha constante,
que la paz se consigue, pero así mismo se pierde…
La paz la añoramos todos, pero está en uno mismo, igual que la felicidad.
Mi aporte es este: la paz no es fácil de conseguir
pero cuando escribo y explico mi sentir,
mi alma vuela de alegría porque sabe que escribir la hace libre,
porque sabe que, aunque sea a pocas personas,
mis escritos cambian formas de ver y entender la vida.
He luchado mucho por mi propia paz, conmigo mismo he batallado
incontables veces, pero esta lucha no la he realizado solo,
hay quienes han luchado por lo mismo y entienden el sentir;
en mi caso afortunado, hay una persona muy especial
que me ha ayudado demasiado por este arduo camino.
Mi camino a la paz, es mi dulce escritura
escuchando el ritmo de la naturaleza y al son del cantar de las aves;
así consigo mi paz, así espero brindarla a muchas otras personas.
Y…es el anhelo de todo escritor, dar paz contando sus experiencias
por la vida, para que quienes aún la buscan, al fin las puedan conseguir.
Nada es fácil, todo es una batalla y si nos rendimos
nunca podremos conseguir lo que por toda la vida anhelamos.

Author Bio

Nací el 17 de abril de 2003 en la vereda el Rodeo, zona rural, que está en nuestro Territorio Ancestral Indígena San Lorenzo, municipio de Riosucio, departamento de Caldas, Colombia. Estudié mi secundaria en la Institución Educativa San Lorenzo y me gradué en el año 2021. Estuve encargado de la emisora de radio estudiantil del Colegio. Publiqué mis escritos, poemas y raps en la cartilla del Proyecto "Poesía para la Paz," también fui publicado en la revista "Relieves y Torrentes" del Proyecto Comunicación Intercultural. Actualmente estoy trabajando para luego poder estudiar.

H.L. Smith

Reflection

Last year, I had the opportunity to take a group of students from a middle-school GSA to a poetry workshop hosted by SAY Poetry DSM at a local high school. It was an unreal experience. The space fostered such vulnerability and open-mindedness that allowed me, as well as my students, to access and accept our creativity in a way that we had not anticipated. After being given a simple prompt, we were all given time to see where our creativity took us, and this poem is the product of that time. Not only was I given space to reflect on how the past year had impacted my mental health, but I also felt more than supported to share that insight with my students. The works they created in this space also absolutely blew me away, and this small group that came into community with one another really made something magical happen. We came together and saw one another as humans.

Drought

I know they say
"You can't pour from an empty cup."
But, trust me when I say
"I am thirsty."
Parched.
Gasping after work weeks.
Spending 9-5 in the sunlight's relentless beams.
No clouds for a moment of shade.

But…
I know I want to give.

If only tears could nourish seeds
Because I know I want water to pour
Freely and effortlessly from me like
The tears I have spilt throughout this year.

I want to be the sustenance those around me need.
That brings their already brilliant, sewn seeds
To vibrant flowers.
I want to be a part of their path towards flourishing,
When all I can do is wilt.

I know that's who they need me to be.
But…
I also know that isn't who I am right now.

I know I show up with…
A smile.
A positive attitude.
And dressed up clothes
Like I have my life together.
But, it's…
A smile that drops when my mask comes back on.
An attitude that shuts down at 3:03 PM.
And clothes I lay out the night before
So I can get
Just two more minutes of sleep in the morning.

I know they say
"You can't pour from an empty cup,"
And they mean well and good.

As long as it doesn't break your contract hours.

Author Bio

H.L. Smith is a queer writer who is currently a 6th grade Language Arts teacher. She has been teaching for five years, as well as advising her school's Gay/Straight Alliance. H.L. Smith is also well known for her passion for horror movies, exploring local businesses, and her two cats, Toast and Franklin. This will be her first official publication.

Parisa Mosavi (Pavie)

Reflection

Everything started when I met Daphne Morgen from Youth UnMuted back in Greece for the first time, while she facilitated a storytelling workshop that I participated in. Even after she left, we stayed in touch and started talking about our passions. We became friends and found out later we share a lot of beliefs and agree on how to make ourselves and the world better in every aspect. Daphne later asked me to be one of the four founding members of the Youth Advisory Board for Youth UnMuted, an international NGO amplifying the voices of displaced youth. We the four Youth Advisory Board members are all refugees, all women, all young, all activists in our own ways, and all chose to take on this role because we wanted to be louder. We started talking to each other about how we can grow to be better and how frustrated we are with repeating history as the young generation, and we formed friendships and felt seen and heard by each other. We decided to start the Now You Hear Us (NYHU) video podcast, in which we shared our opinions about current world events.

Through this work with Youth UnMuted, I later on started working with great people from Amplifying Sanctuary Voices in California. Amplifying Sanctuary Voices is "a community-based oral history project centering the stories of Bay Area residents who have come to the U.S. seeking sanctuary," and in this work, they supported the NYHU podcast. I actually wrote this poem, "Notes," for Amplifying Sanctuary Voices' annual gala, speaking as a young woman about my journey fleeing from my country to Germany. This whole journey, meeting new people and learning from them, talking out loud about the events that take place around us, makes me hopeful for having better communication with each other as human beings, and that is what we do as a small community in Amplifying Sanctuary Voices and Youth UnMuted.

Notes

These days there is just pain in our hearts
This pain is locking us in a room with these crazy thoughts

And how hard it is to make ourselves believe
What is going on in front of our eyes
Is real, and it takes life

And it is even harder
When you realize
That you can't stop right now, at this time

It is hard to leave your land, but it is even harder

When you watch those who did not survive
Die again, every day and there's no last time

It is hunger, fear, war
It is politics, power, pride
But who is really paying the price?

The people who vote for good, but we find out what our chosen ones are telling us is all lies

I am tired of knowing the truth and not being able to admit it, not even at my school, not even at my house

I'm tired of watching kids in blood
I'm tired of seeing the crying faces of the moms, daughters, women
That won't survive this time

These days are full of pain, knowledge, wishes
That have not come true
These days I see myself drowning in thoughts
That will never leave me to live
Until I die

These days I feel powerless, but I can't pause
These days I feel weak and strong at the same time
I feel weak because I can't stop those broken glasses from hurting broken hearts
I feel strong because I have a voice that might change the future of all of us

I am nothing more than a voice
But I'm alive
I am nothing more than a human being
But I will never be shut down for the sake of each one of us

And it makes me hopeful when I realize
I am not alone until you hear us

I am alive and heard by people
Who cared and will care about every one of us
Out here, doing what makes us feel good
Doing what makes sense to us

Life and all its goodness and ugliness
Has brought us to this time
To observe and react

To hear and answer back
To the event that should have never happened
To the wrong that will never be right
To the day I die
I swear to live and not just be alive

Author Bio

I am Pavie. A tree that has roots from Afghanistan but has grown to blossom in Germany. I am 18 years old, and I enjoy photography, painting, and writing poetry. I'm currently a high school student and want to study political strategy after graduating.

PARLOR PRESS
EQUIPMENT FOR LIVING

Now with Parlor Press!

Studies in Rhetorics and Feminism
Series Editors: Cheryl Glenn and Shirley Wilson Logan

Emerging Conversations in the Global Humanities
Series Editor: Victor E. Taylor

The X-Series
Series Editor: Jordan Frith

New Releases

Global Rhetorical Traditions, edited by Hui Wu and Tarez Samra Graban

Rhetorical Listening in Action: A Concept-Tacticc Approach by Krista Ratcliffe and Kyle Jensen

A Rhetoric of Becoming: USAmerican Women in Qatar by Nancy Small

Emotions and Affect in Writing Centers edited by Janine Morris and Kelly Concannon

MLA Mina Shaughnessy Prize and CCCC Best Book Award 2021!

Creole Composition: Academic Writing and Rhetoric in the Anglophone Caribbean, edited by Vivette Milson-Whyte, Raymond Oenbring, and Brianne Jaquette

Check Out Our New Website!

Discounts, blog, open access titles, instant downloads, and more.

www.parlorpress.com

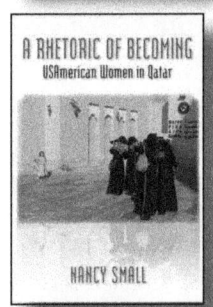

CLJ **Discount:** Use CLJ20 at checkout to receive a 20% discount on all titles not on sale through September 1, 2022.

www.ingramcontent.com/pod-product-compliance
Lightning Source LLC
Chambersburg PA
CBHW031317160426
43196CB00007B/570